W9-CSU-828

TOWPATH GUIDE

to the

CHESAPEAKE & OHIO CANAL

Georgetown Tidelock to Cumberland

By THOMAS F. HAHN

Published by the American Canal and Transportation Center

Copyright, 1985, Thomas F. Hahn

ISBN 0-933788-64-9

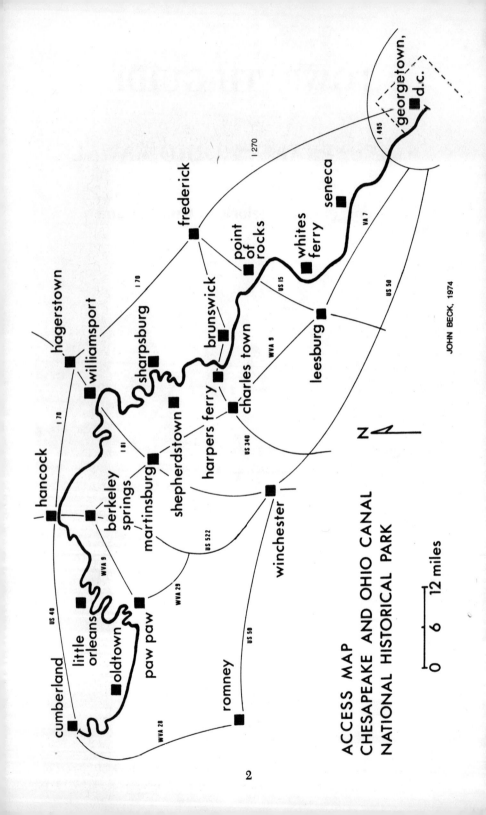

ACCESS MAP
CHESAPEAKE AND OHIO CANAL
NATIONAL HISTORICAL PARK

JOHN BECK, 1974

0   6   12 miles

N

georgetown, d.c.
seneca
whites ferry
point of rocks
frederick
brunswick
charles town
leesburg
harpers ferry
sharpsburg
shepherdstown
williamsport
hagerstown
martinsburg
berkeley springs
hancock
winchester
romney
paw paw
oldtown
little orleans
cumberland

I 495
VA 7
US 50
I 270
US 15
WVA 9
I 70
I 81
US 340
US 522
WVA 29
WVA 9
US 40
US 50
WVA 28

2

Two long-time canal enthusiasts — Justice William O. Douglas (right), and the author, Capt. Tom Hahn, take a "breather" during a 1973 hike along the C & O Canal.

The *Towpath Guide to the Chesapeake and Ohio Canal* provides towpath users with step-by-step descriptions of the canal; physical descriptions of canal structures; historical events which took place along the canal; and the presence of nature as seen and heard from the towpath. The guide is based on first-hand observations and on historical documents.

The Guide was originally published in four sections. At the suggestion of many readers, the Guide has been combined into one book. Corrections and additions to the Guide are welcome. Send them to me at the address below.

For those who would like to know more about the history and descriptions of the canals of the Americas (and elsewhere) and what is being done to restore them, see the inside back cover for information on the American Canal Society. For those particularly interested in the preservation and use of the C & O Canal, write to the C & O Canal Association, Box 66, Glen Echo, MD 20812.

I'll see you on the towpath!

Dr. Tom Hahn, Industrial Archaeologist
Captain USN (Ret.)
Founding President
American Canal
Society and Editor,
American Canals
P.O. Box 310
Shepherdstown, WV 25443

Washington City Canal, looking east toward the unfinished Capitol Building, at the start of the Civil War. The canal turned south at this point and divided into two branches. (See map below.)

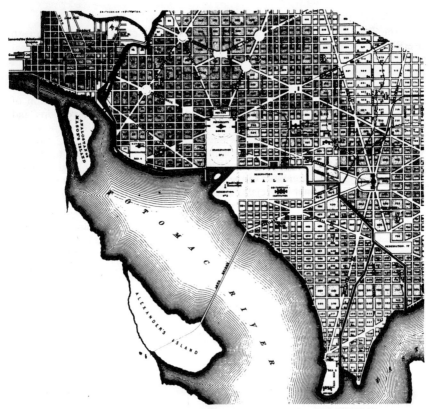

This 1855 map of Washington and Georgetown clearly shows the old Washington City Canal and its branches.

TOWPATH GUIDE

(Mileage figures from tide-lock indicated in bold face type.)

A set of detailed maps makes hiking and biking even more interesting. Recommended are the US Geological Survey 7½" quads, scale 1:24,000 (1" = ⅜ m.): Washington West, Falls Church, Rockville, Seneca. Available by sending $2.50 check or money order for each map to: Distribution Section, Geological Survey, 1200 S. Eads St., Arlington, VA 22202 or pick up at USGS distribution desk on main floor of GSA building on F between 18th & 19th in Washington. Washington.

Call 301-739-4206 in case of emergency when on the canal.

WASHINGTON BRANCH OF C & O CANAL

The Washington Branch of the C & O Canal was a 1-mi, 373-yard tidal canal from Rock Creek Basin, generally along line of Potomac River, to Tiber Creek at 17th St. and Constitution Ave., connecting with Washington City Canal in 1833. Its purpose was to provide low cost transportation at a time when roads and streets were few and real mudholes in Washington. It was used until about 1855, after which it fell into decay and gradually filled up. Lock house at 17th and Constitution still stands, now a public toilet! It is ironic that with demolition of temporary office buildings, it now stands as the only building from Washington Monument to Lincoln Memorial. Bronze tablet has inscription: "Lockkeeper's house, formerly eastern terminus of the Chesapeake and Ohio Canal, erected about 1835. The canal passed along the present line of B Street in front of the house, emptying into Tiber Creek and Potomac River."

WASHINGTON CITY CANAL

Though quite a bit has been written about this canal, most accounts are vague in detail or in conflict, so that a complete, clear picture does not exist today. A city canal was included in L'Enfant's plans for Washington, with a canal from tidewater in Tiber Creek to tidewater in James Creek. Tho proposals for cutting a canal were received as early as 1 Sept. 1791, 1st sod of Washington City Canal (Washington Canal/Municipal Canal) was turned by President Madison 2 May 1810; L. H. Latrobe, Engineer and Elias B. Caldwell, President of Canal Co. in attendance. Canal began at 17th & Constitution connection with lock of Washington Branch of C & O Canal and went to vicinity of Capitol where it went S. to near Canal St. where it divided, a branch going to Anacostia W. of Army War College, another to Anacostia near Old Navy Yard. Principal products carried were coal, flour, firewood and bldg. material. Canal fell into disuse after Civil War and portions turned into sewer beginning 1871. Today there are no visible remains of either the Washington Branch of C & O Canal or the Washington City Canal.

5

Georgetown Tide Lock, "Mile Zero" of the C & O Canal. Note dam across Rock Creek. Circa 1900.

Same spot in 1973 looking east toward Kennedy Center (right) and Watergate (left). Washington Branch of C & O Canal began on opposite bank of Rock Creek near center left of photo. (Photo by Tom Hahn)

GEORGETOWN TIDE-LOCK

0.00 Access: From Thompson Boat Center parking lot on W. side of intersection of Virginia Ave. and Rock Creek and Potomac Parkway, take service road & sidewalk around the boat center to tide-lock on left at Potomac River. Boat center open 7-5, tel. 333-4861; canoe and bike rentals. **Tide-lock (also known as Tidal, Tidewater & Outlet Lock) is the communication between Rock Creek Basin & Potomac River.** Lock rests on wooden piles and built of Aquia Creek freestone with backing of walls of granite rubble; work laid in hydraulic cement. Lock badly silted in and damaged by floods. Almost all of upriver side lock wall missing. Lock raised 4'2" in historic period at upper end so it could function as guard lock to hold back flood water from Rock Creek. Lock measures 91' 4½" between gate pockets (recesses in lock walls for holding gates in open position). At some time after close of canal in 1924, 12" x 12" creosoted timbers were installed vertically against lock walls to stabilize them. Tide-lock here may have been referred to as Tide-lock 'A' to differentiate it from Tide-lock 'B' at 17th & Constitution. **Indications are that towing path (towpath) was on Potomac River side of Rock Creek from tide-lock up to Green St. (29th St.), where it crossed to land side of the canal.**

Tide-lock is 'zero milestone' from which measurements on canal are calculated; those used in this guide were made by Orville Crowder who pushed a measuring wheel 184½ m. to Cumberland! Name Chesapeake and Ohio Canal (rejected were names Potomac Canal & Union Canal) was chosen from intent to connect Baltimore on Chesapeake Bay with Ohio River at Pittsburgh. Here at tide-lock is the spot from which the canal departed from tidewater and headed upstream into a 100-year struggle with topography and the flooding river, with the frailties of man and the complexities of finance — never to reach the prize of Ohio River navigation. Its towpath passes through a mighty river valley, past rock cliffs and bottomland woods, through wild gorges and peaceful valleys, through virtual wilderness and the mountains and past man's boldest engineering efforts — 184.5 m. to Cumberland, end of the trail for the hiker and biker and for the canal's dream of greatness.

Lockhouse "B"
on the Washington
Branch of the C & O
Canal, circa 1860.
Presently located
at intersection of
17th Street and
Constitution Avenue.
(Library of Congress
photo)

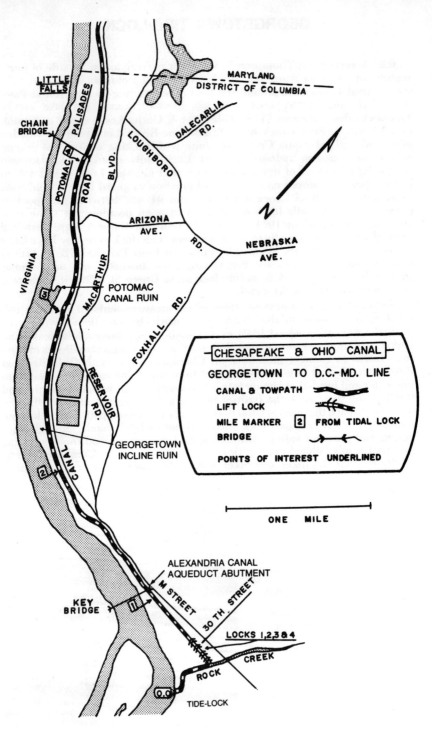

LITTLE FALLS

MARYLAND
DISTRICT OF COLUMBIA

CHAIN BRIDGE

PALISADES

POTOMAC

DALECARLIA RD.

LOUGHBORO

BLVD.

ROAD

ARIZONA AVE.

RD.

NEBRASKA AVE.

VIRGINIA

MACARTHUR

POTOMAC CANAL RUIN

FOXHALL RD.

RESERVOIR RD.

GEORGETOWN INCLINE RUIN

CANAL

CHESAPEAKE & OHIO CANAL

GEORGETOWN TO D.C.-MD. LINE

CANAL & TOWPATH

LIFT LOCK

MILE MARKER [2] FROM TIDAL LOCK

BRIDGE

POINTS OF INTEREST UNDERLINED

ONE MILE

ALEXANDRIA CANAL AQUEDUCT ABUTMENT

M STREET

30 TH STREET

KEY BRIDGE

LOCKS 1, 2, 3 & 4

CREEK

ROCK

0.0 TIDE-LOCK

JOHN BECK

8

ROCK CREEK BASIN

0.01 E. terminus of C & O Canal was tide-lock and end of Rock Creek Basin where Rock Creek flows into the Potomac River. Basin originally formed by dam built across mouth of Rock Creek which impounded water 3' above mean high tide, forming part of extensive quay or landing place, one of its faces being on Rock Creek and the other on the Potomac River. Length of quay on Potomac face was 1080'; 200' of which occupied a tumbling dam for delivering surplus water of creek into the Potomac River and 38' occupied by tide-lock, leaving 840' (or so) front on the Potomac. Width of quay was 160' except at Washington City end where it narrowed to 80'. Space in center of quay was set aside for warehouses and stores; rest of space left open for streets and landing places. Here goods were taken from canal boats and stored or transferred to coastal ships. Bridge was constructed over head of tumbling dam, connecting Georgetown part with Washington part of quay. Inside of quay forming Rock Creek face was protected by a well laid dry wall. Walled face of creek extended up on both sides for ½ m.

Original dam seems to have been repaired and rebuilt on several occasions, altering both appearance and location. A concrete wall now extends from mid tide-lock to a series of 6 wooden lift gates in the dam. These gates controlled the water level in Rock Creek Basin. Adjoining end of gates is what is left of the wooden-faced, stone-filled tumbling dam which extended 200' across the creek and tied into the Washington side of the creek.

There is no longer a towpath to follow from tide-lock to the 1st lift lock (Lock No. 1) in Georgetown .3 m. upstream. **To reach Lock 1 take bikeway along Rock Creek and Potomac Parkway,** but first walk a short distance along bikeway toward river to get a good view across Rock Creek of dam remains and tide-lock. Tho most think the Watergate Complex across parkway takes its name from the gates of the dam across Rock Creek or tide-lock, this is probably not so. The more likely source is the ceremonial watergate near Memorial Bridge.

For towpath conditions or other questions concerning the canal between Georgetown and Seneca call NPS Palisades District Office at 301-299-3613.

0.31 Godey Lime Kiln Ruins. In the last century, lime manufacturing was an important local industry in Washington. The 2 stone structures across the parkway are remains of lime kilns operated by Godey family between 1864 and 1897 and by others until 1908. Limestone for kiln came down canal from Knotts Quarry near Antietam and from quarries above Seneca.

0.35 Canal enters Rock Creek Basin. Before canal was built, navigation extended up Rock Creek to P St. Bridge, ½ m. above. Good view of tier of 4 Georgetown Locks from Rock Creek Bridge. Turn left after bridge and go up asphalt "towpath," next to which is historical tablet: "One of the best preserved and least altered of old American Canals, the Chesapeake and Ohio grew with Washington's vision of linking the valleys of the early west with the east by ties of communication. The Potomac Company fostered by Washington to improve navigation of the Potomac, transferred its rights in 1828 to the Chesapeake and Ohio Canal Company organized to connect the Ohio at Pittsburgh with Georgetown by a continuous canal. Today it is a memorial to national progress and the canal era."

Lift Lock No. 1 Georgetown. Rock Creek can be seen below the lock.
Note chimneys of Godey Lime Kiln on opposite bank of Rock Creek. Circa 1900.

LOCK No. 1, GEORGETOWN

0.38 Access: At 29th St. 1 block S. of M St. Bus service to Georgetown and Subway Station Foggy Bottom. Lock 1 is 1st of picturesque series of 4 closely-spaced Georgetown locks separated by boat basins. It lies .38 m. above tidelock and .04 m. below Lock 2. Compass orientation N 86° W.

There are 74 lift locks between Georgetown and Cumberland with lifts of between 6′ and 10′ (avg. 8.2′) for total lift of 609.693′. Lift of this lock 8′. There are 24 lift locks between Georgetown and Seneca (22.8 m), highest concentration on canal. Locks are 90′ long (between mitre sill of upper gate and mitre sill of lower gate), 15′ wide and 16′ deep. Turning basin adjoins upper end of lock on one end and Rock Creek on other. Modern cut stone wall S. of lock hides any trace of original towpath which was on W. side of Rock Creek from tide-lock to Lock 1. Apparently tow animals (both horses and mules were used) were unhitched from towline, taken up to Green St. (present 29th St.) bridge where they crossed canal to N. bank and taken down to foot of turning basin and rehitched to towline. Mule rise of about 8′ (like a gradual ramp) goes from just above Rock Creek bridge to lock. Towpath was on N. (land) side of canal from Lock 1 to Frederick (34th St.) until 1856 and after than from Lock 1 to point above Alexandria Aqueduct (above Key Bridge) where bridge was built to carry animals and towpath back to river side of canal. Except for 2 stretches of slackwater operation in river behind Dams 4 and 5, towpath stays on river side of canal to Cumberland.

Lock is faced with Aquia Creek freestone, much rebuilt with granite, limestone, concrete and brick. Note graffiti on lock coping (top layer) stones. Only N. lock wall coping stones show evidence of tow rope grooves. Lock measures 90'3" between gate pockets. **Side pond** on S. side was used to turn unloaded boats around. As entrance to pond allows only 3' water depth, pond could not have been used for loaded boats, tho entrance is 15'3" wide. On N. side of lock above upper end is an 8' recess (allowing a 3' water depth) which could have led to another side or holding pond. One on S. bank is shown on old maps; other is not. Towpath bridge would have been necessary at either site. Most locks have by pass flumes (ditches of one sort or another) to keep water at right operating level and to get rid of excess water. There is no trace of such flumes around the locks at Georgetown. Alternative use may have been to allow water to overflow tops of closed gates, as is done now. Above lock is **boat basin** (called 'pool' historically) 100' long by 46' wide. Though there is no present evidence of lock houses in Georgetown, records and historical numbering systems indicate there were 2, perhaps acquired or leased, as records do not show money expended for construction of lock houses here. As were all but one of locks thru Lock #27, Georgetown Locks were built with chambers in lock walls, fed by openings in upper gate pockets and water let out thru openings in lock walls below. **Green (29th St.) bridge**, originally (1830-31) a low arched stone bridge, was raised and replaced with an iron span in 1867. Present bridge is concrete span with steel handrails. Four Seasons Hotel is adjacent to the lock.

LOCK No. 2, GEORGETOWN

0.42 Access: From 29th or 30th Sts. Bike rentals and bike repairs at Big Wheel Bikes at 1034 33rd St., NW, tel. 202-337-0254.**Lift locks such as this one operate as follows:** Boats moving downstream enter a full lock, upper wooden lock gates are closed and water is released thru small wicket gates located near bottom of lower wooden lock gates. When water level in lock is same as that of canal below, lower lock gates are opened and boat passes out. Reverse happens for boats moving upstream. Lock tenders normally opened gates on berm (side opposite towpath) and mule drivers gates on towpath side. To balance weight of gates in historic operating period, usual method was to fasten rock-filled box on free end of balance beam (the large timber on top of and protruding from lock gate). Lock gates on restored portion of canal between Georgetown and Violette's Lock are modern replacements, but perhaps replicas of historic ones.

Lock 2 is 2nd of 4 closely spaced Georgetown locks, .04 m. above Lock 1 and .07 m. below Lock 3. Compass orientation N. 86°W. Lock originally built of Aquia Creek freestone but much rebuilt with brick, concrete, limestone and granite. Lock shows 1939-42 Park Service practice of using concrete rather than replacing original stones in upper parts of lock, except for upper 2 courses of stone; concrete substitution was below water line and did not show, thus preserving appearance of watered lock at greatly reduced restoration price. Lock built with masonry bypass culverts to carry water around upper gates, thru and out openings in lower portion of lock walls. This watering system was abandoned during historic operating period. Length of lock between gate pockets 90'. Lock lift 8'. Basins between locks in Georgetown were 46' wide, allowing 15½' clearance on each side, plus the 15' lock width in middle. Tho boats could tie up on each side and have sufficient space for other boats to pass thru, towpath side was probably kept clear for traffic and river side of canal used for mooring. This basin 120' long. Lower extension walls of lock span 29th St. (Green St.) and are abutments for bridge carrying traffic over lock. Bridges were placed below lower gate pockets where possible to take advantage of additional 8' of clearance.

LOCK No. 3, GEORGETOWN

0.49 Access: At 30th (Washington) St. Historical tablet in park-like patio notes Georgetown Historic District designated a National Historic Landmark in 1967. Ancient name of site of Georgetown is Tohoga, signifying an entrance or gate. Call 202-472-4376 for information on the boat, The Georgetown operating mid-April to mid-October. Charters available. This is a favorite spot in Georgetown with someone sunning, reading, or eating lunch on clear days in all seasons. Gray building on S was **Duval Foundry c1856.** Georgetown Inland Steel carefully preserved this building during their construction here 1973-74.

Lower extension walls of Lock 3 lying under 30th St. bridge carry original stone bridge abutments. Lock has 8' lift. It was built originally with masonry bypass culverts; inflows (now stoned up) were openings about center of lowest portion of upper gate pockets; flow of water was controlled by cast iron wicket gates in openings. The 3 outflows (openings) of the masonry bypass culverts are in lower courses (rows of stones) of the lock walls, about 9', 25' and 49' below the upper lock pockets on the berm side (side opposite towpath) and 13', 21' and 45½' below on the towpath side; culvert outflows are still open. Original transverse foundation timbers of the lock flooring (which appear to be hewn, and scraps of sheet pine planking) can be seen mid-lock when canal is dewatered. The original timber floor of the upper lock pocket has been replaced with concrete. Lock made of Aquia Creek freestone, rebuilt at least once, with granite substitutions. All gate straps (curved metal bars anchored to stones — part of mechanism which holds lock gate in place) are slotted loop type and appear old though refitted with late period nuts and bolts. Basin above lock is 120' long and 46' wide.

0.53 **Old Masonic Lodge** on N.W. corner of **Thos. Jefferson St. bridge** was used by the Potomac Lodge beginning c1810. When Jefferson first arrived in capital to be Secy. of State, he lived at 1047, S. of canal, in a block since razed of houses.

LOCK No. 4, GEORGETOWN

0.54 Access: Thos. Jefferson St. Lock is .05 m. above Lock 3 and 4.48 m. below Lock 5. Uppermost of 4 Georgetown locks, Orientation N. 86° W. Thos. Jefferson St. Bridge crosses over lock extension walls; original stone arch of bridge did not have sufficient width to allow towpath to pass under it. Tow rope was unhitched from animal and passed under bridge while animal went over N. bridge approaches to be rehitched on other side. Lock is 89'10" between gate pockets and originally built of Aquia Creek freestone. Lock originally built with stone culverts in both side walls around upper lock gate. Lock walls in relatively good alignment and there are fewer stone substitutions than in lock below. A low dam of rubble stone (a unique feature) was laid just below the mitre sill (timbers upon which lock gate rests). Towpath has rounded cobblestones to 31st St., tying houses and old lock into a composition which has made this spot one of most photographed, sketched and painted

Duvall Foundry (at time of photo, a veterinary hospital) and Lock No. 3, Georgetown. Circa 1914.

on canal. Canal prism 6' deep, 46' wide to Frederick St. Lunch n' Boy, near the lock, is a handy place to pick up breakfast or lunch.

0.59 31st St. (Congress St. & Fishing Lane) Bridge. Bridge originally (1830) low arch stone, 40' span. **1st of 5 stone bridges to span canal in Georgetown.** Towpath probably went under bridge. All original stone bridges have been described as ". . . very neat and substantial structures, faced with Aquia Creek freestone, well laid with hammered faces." Iron spans replaced stone bridge in 1867; present bridge built 1924. **Next towpath access at 34th St.** Suters Tavern (Fountain Inn) built c1760 (perhaps earlier), occupied 1783-1795 by John Suter, razed c1896. Geo. Washington met neighboring landowners there to negotiate purchase of land for Federal City; House of Representatives met there to decide between Jefferson and Adams for President. At end of row of towpath residences at 31st St. are 'Tow Path Apartments,' built by Canal Co. in 1830 and used until demise of canal in 1924. **Canal Square bldg. on N.W. corner is interesting utilization of old canal-side warehouse.** Alternate hike for those desiring to see some of historic sites in Georgetown is a walk up M St. and dips up and down short blocks to left between M and canal, returning to towpath at 34th.

0.61 One of many water intakes on way to Key Bridge.

0.68 Wisconsin Ave. (High St.) bridge, built of Aquia freestone, 54' span, 17' rise, 5' towpath under bridge, last to remain of 5 stone bridges; no street access to towpath. Note faded plaques on downstream side of bridge which list C. H. Dibble as Builder, Charles Mercer President (of Canal Co.), Thomas Purcell Superintendent, Andrew Jackson President; keystone on upstream

13

High Street (Wisconsin Avenue) Bridge in the 1880's.

face has 1831 date and lists John Cox Mayor and James Dunlop Recorder. Other original low stone arch bridges were built to Erie Canal standards with 8' clearance; this one had 11½' clearance. As boats became larger, they could return empty easily only when canal water level below normal. Resulting traffic jams blocked access to Rock Creek Basin and made it necessary for most boats bound for tidewater to pass thru Alexandria Canal Aqueduct (mile 1.07). Georgetown bridges were finally rebuilt, abutments raised and (other than one here) replaced with iron spans in 1867. Modern bridges were added in 1924. Grace Protestant Episcopal Church, begun as mission for canal boatmen and workers in mid-1800's, stands on river side of canal to E. At N.W. corner of bridge is obelisk commemorating beginning of work on canal in 1828 and completion in 1850. Stone stands on site of 1st police station in Washington; part of bldg. used for debtors' prison in 1790's and slave pen.

0.79 Bridges passing overhead connected bldgs. of Capital Traction Co. Attractive high stone wall limiting width of towpath described in 1831 as "specimen of good work." Entrance to Georgetown Parking Center off the towpath.

0.80 Potomac St. bridge; no access to towpath. During early days of canal, Market House extended over canal. Adjacent to both sides of Market House were wooden bridges carrying traffic over canal from E. and W. Potomac Sts. Building formerly a tobacco warehouse, a corn broom factory, and omnibus stable.

0.81 Concrete intake on river side of canal admitted water to Wilkins-Rogers Milling Co. **From earliest days the one unfailing source of income to Canal Co. was water supplied to millers, founders and textile manufacturers on Georgetown Level.** Mill now converted to Flour Mill Apartments and Offices.

0.84 Steel footbridge (PEPCO) crosses canal from 33rd (Market) St; no access to towpath. Wooden bridge built here 1831. Street then known as 'Duck Lane' and bridge, of course, as 'Duck Lane Bridge.' Here was 1st culvert (means of carrying water under canal) (now non-existent) on line of canal, 8' span, for Market St. run.

0.93 Towpath crossover bridge at 34th St. (Frederick St.) carries towpath to river side of canal. Path directly ahead leads to M St./Canal Rd. This bridge is at site of 1st wooden towpath crossover bridge, built by Canal Co. in 1831 and used until 1856, at which time towpath continued on land side to upper end of Alexandria Aqueduct where another bridge carried towpath to river side. Present bridge built 1954. Width of canal from 34th St. originally 80', 6' depth to Lock 5.

0.98 Frame bldg. on towpath immediately below Key Bridge houses gate machinery for dual water intakes for Wilkins-Rogers Milling Co. (not now in use).

0.99 Francis Scott Key Bridge. Access: Crossover bridge at 34th St. Towpath passes under concrete branches of Key Bridge, which replaced Old Aqueduct Bridge in 1924. It is a 1450' long, concrete structure with 7 arches: central arch 208', arches on either side 204' and 187'; approach arches 152' and 85', latter over canal. Built on solid rock 23' below mean high water, using 65,000 cubic yards of concrete.

Key lived in house at E. end of bridge at 3516 M St. having moved there in 1805. House dismantled (and preserved) in 1949 to make room for Whitehurst Freeway. In that house Key is said to have first read The Star Spangled Banner before a meeting of his glee club. Key family left house in late 1830s because of turbulence along canal — construction of canal destroyed his hanging gardens and fruit trees on terraces leading to river. (Environmental problems existed even then!) Key, an attorney, was active in social causes and civic affairs and at one time or another involved in canal affairs — he was in charge of a case to bring injunction against Alexandria Canal Co. when clay and gravel were spilled outside cofferdams of aqueduct construction, impeding navigation. (He lost his case.) Canal walls extensively repaired in Georgetown 1982-83.

1.0x Cross under Whitehurst Freeway. Steps lead up to Canal Rd. and down to Water (Extension of K) St. giving access to Alexandria Aqueduct.

Civil War photo of Alexandria Aqueduct, taken from Analostan Island, today Theodore Roosevelt Island. (Library of Congress photo.)

Alexandria Aqueduct, Georgetown, in the 1800's. Note mule-crossover bridge in foreground. Towpath remained on north (land) side of canal to Lock 1.

ALEXANDRIA CANAL

Alexandria Canal Co. was chartered by Congress 26 May 1830 to construct an aqueduct across the Potomac River and to build a canal from C & O Canal in Georgetown (District of Columbia) to Alexandria. Construction began in 1833. The 7 m. 416 yd. canal formally opened to traffic on 2 Dec. 1843. It had canal prism 40' wide at water surface and 28' at bottom, with towpath "of sufficient breadth to apply the power of horses to the navigation thereof" and cost $500,000 to build. Excess or 'Waste Water' was rented to various mills and plants along the line. Route of canal nigh impossible to trace today. There were four lift locks at the Alexandria end of the canal. The outlet lock was excavated under the supervision of Industrial Archeologist Tom Hahn in 1982. Other structural remains are N. abutment of aqueduct on D.C. side above Key Bridge, S. pier (of 8) near the Virginia shore at Rosslyn and a bit of masonry on Virginia shore in line with the remaining pier (which is not original).

The outlet lock and part of the canal basin above were being restored in 1985 as part of the Trans Potomac Canal Center.

ALEXANDRIA CANAL AQUEDUCT

1.07 Access: From 34th St. .14 m. below or from stairway down from Whitehurst Freeway. Chief feature of Alexandria Canal was aqueduct across Potomac, formally opened 4 July 1843 and operated continuously until 23 May 1861, N. abutment of which can be seen on other side of fence on river side of C & O Canal towpath. It had 8 piers and 2 abutments carrying a 1100' wooden trunk 17' wide and 7' deep (heavily insured against fire) 29' above tidewater with wooden superstructure. Aqueduct itself 28' wide timber to timber. Width of towpath 5'. Stone for aqueduct from "a Quarry near Mason's

Foundry, ½ m. west." Aqueduct originally planned to have 12 stone arches supported by 11 piers and 2 abutments, but because of lack of funds a 350' causeway was substituted for 3 arches at S. extremity. Remaining 8 piers were 105' apart at high water mark: 2 of them were abutment piers, each 21' thick and 6 of them support piers 12' thick at high water mark with circular wing walls 13' avg. thickness at base, 66' in length. N. abutment built by C & O Canal Co., inland arch of which enlarged to accommodate B & O R.R. track. Each of support piers had ice breakers on upstream end in form of oblique conc sloping 45°, extending 5' below and 10' above high water mark, made of cut granite. Downstream end was circular and had slope same as sides, 1" to 1'. It cost $600,000. There was a towpath bridge across flume of aqueduct until 1856 when C & O towpath was moved to N. side of canal.

At beginning of Civil War, utility of continuing delivery of coal to Alexandria from Cumberland and service of distributing military supplies to Alexandria were considered insignificant against importance of a secure bridge connecting Washington with Va. shore. Accordingly, in early winter of 1861-62, water was shut off from aqueduct and its trunk converted into a double-track wagon rd. This curtailed activity on lower end of C & O Canal which had problems with low bridges, silt and accumulation of debris. A new aqueduct was built after 27 July 1868 out of N. Carolina timber and a highway bridge (toll) built over the water-filled trough. For many years the structure served both vehicular and canal traffic (tho usage diminished when Georgetown bridges were raised and Rock Creek Basin improved) until water was drained. Aqueduct was purchased by Fed. Govt. in 1886, at which time wooden structures were removed and iron truss bridge 24' wide with 3' sidewalks was built on old stone piers. In 1906, track of Great Falls and Old Dominion R.R. ran across bridge from terminal on Georgetown side. Old Aqueduct Bridge was replaced by Key Bridge in 1924, but it was not torn down until 1934. In Aug. 1962, 7 of 8 piers (all but one next to Va. shore) were removed. Adjacent to N. aqueduct abutment is oldest surviving boat club (Potomac 1869) along Potomac River.

1.10 At this point atmosphere of the canal changes from town to country in spite of rush of traffic on Canal Rd. There are fine views of the Potomac River, the towpath is pleasant and an entirely different mood takes over. The traveler mounting the Potomac Valley from the National Capital today passes thru 5 of the 6 great topographical sections of the eastern seaboard. From tidewater in the District of Columbia thru the Piedmont, the Blue Ridge and the great valley, to the massive Appalachian backbone, one may see every characteristic of the region; most species of nature's flora and fauna are still extant.

Here canal boats stopped and waited for orders as to where to unload. Once they started thru the locks in Georgetown, they had to keep going as Rock Creek Basin was too busy to pause long there. In 1870s, during heyday of canal, as many as 540 boats were operating. In peak year of 1875, about one million tons of cargo were transported. After 1900, scarcely 100 boats were in use. A typical boat of later yrs. was 92' long by 14'6" wide, draft of 4' and carried 110 to 130 tons of cargo. Team of 3-5 mules required generally for boating outfit; with 2 or 3 normally in actual use at any one time. Relief team was carried aboard in forward cabin. Boat capt. and family lived in small after cabin.

1.30 Street car trestle ruins, which served trolley line to Cabin John and Glen Echo, are visible in cleft in hillside above Canal Rd. This was surely

Georgetown Level, boats in port, circa 1900.

one of the most scenic rides ever to be taken, paralleling the canal and river for much of its distance; in winter, the views were incomparable.

1.35 Mission on the Towpath was established in 1894 by Mrs. S. E. Safford who lived across rd. from the canal, an area since cleared of buildings. A news story of 1905 describes mission as small brick house where children were taught to read and write and adults instructed in industrial arts and assisted in finding housing in winter, when very few lived in canal boats. News story of Dec. 1913 reports closing of mission, indicating that a different building on the old Foxhall Foundry site, was used. Across R.R. tracks was Terminal Ice Co., where ice was delivered in winter by sailing ships from New England.

1.48 Foundry Branch takes its name from **Foxhall Foundry** (1797-1849), which covered a 5-acre tract along the river and extended across present Canal Rd. The 4-story stone cannon boring mill and the shot tower, operated by Henry Foxhall (1801-15), were located above the canal and powered by an overshot wheel on Foundry Branch. Later, power was supplied by the canal under the foundry operation of Gen. John Mason of Analostan Is. Large numbers of cannon were bored here and during maximum production, 30,000 shot produced annually. Commodore Perry delayed the Battle of Lake Erie until his shop could be rigged with Foxhall-bored cannon hauled overland by 12-ox teams. British soldiers dispatched to destroy the ordinance plant in 1812 encountered a violent storm and turned back to Rock Creek. Site of the foundry has been used since 1849 as a flour mill, distillery, brewery, ice storage warehouse, summer resort and a boat yard. **There is a vestige** of a stone foundation remaining, but it will probably disappear if the construction of Three Sisters Bridge is resumed.

Foundry Branch culvert, 22' span, 10' rise. Main use was rd. culvert, now blocked to vehicles. Note buildings of Georgetown U.

1.51 Concrete spillway. This type spillway was also known as a 'mule drink,' as it was one of few places a mule could drink with ease.

1.52 Two closely spaced historic waste weirs. Lower one filled in. Upper one is late period construction with screw type lift gates, typical to most waste weirs on this canal. Waste weirs and spillway discharges are gathered together by concrete walls and carried under R.R. in a concrete culvert. **We are on the Georgetown level which runs for 4½ m. to Lock 5.** Canal was 80' wide, 6' deep in 'this area.

1.63 Three Sisters Islands in Potomac were bought in 1951 by Federal Govt. for $1200 from Stone family of Bethesda. Islands originally given to John Moore as part payment for work in building several locks on canal. Deed granting islands to Moore, a contractor, was signed by Pres. Pierce. At one time there was soil on the islands, but over the yrs. Potomac has changed its course many times and left little but barren rocks above water.

Interesting to note that a river crossing here is not a new idea as indicated by a report of L'Enfant delivered to Pres. Washington at Georgetown, 26 Mar. 1791, in which he recommended: ". . . Georgetown itself being situated at the head of grand navigation of the Potowmack should be favored with the same advantage of better Communication with the Southern **by having also a bridge erected over the Potowmack at the place of the two sisters where nature would effectively favour the undertaking.**"

2.18 Stop Gate remains; visible when water is low. The canal prism on the Georgetown level is generally 80' wide and 7-8' deep from Little Falls to Harpers Ferry and 60' wide and 6' deep above Harpers Ferry.

GEORGETOWN CANAL INCLINE (Inclined Plane)

2.26 Access: From 34th St. crossover bridge (0.93); or rd. culvert at Fletchers (3.21). Georgetown Canal Incline (also known as Old Boat Incline, Georgetown Inclined Plane and Outlet Lock) c1874 has a few remains next to towpath. near R.R. tracks and at river level. First boat to use incline (designed and engineered by Wm. R. Hutton) went from canal to river on 29 June 1876. In 1878, 1st yr. in which record was kept of boats passing over incline, 1918 boats used it. It was largest incline in world at time and a model was exhibited at World's Fair in Paris in 1878 as one of United States' best efforts in field

Mission on the Towpath, Georgetown, circa 1914.   (Hahn Collection)

of civil engineering. Hutton was also Chief Engineer of Canal Co. from 1869 to 1872 and consulting engineer to Canal Co. until 1881.

Boats went thru a lock gate at the upper level into a wooden caisson mounted on wheels. Caisson was 112' long, 16'9" wide and 7'10" high. It rested on 6, 6-wheeled trucks which were fitted to 4 iron rails 600' long on a 1:10 slope. Caisson was held tight by a clamping device which reduced leakage of water when canal gate and caisson gates were opened for boat to move thru, after which gates were closed and caisson prepared for lowering. Thru a pulley arrangement, counterweights traveled only half as far as caisson, which entered river at bottom. Incline originally built to operate on water power from a turbine, was later changed to steam power. Incline only really operated successfully for 2 yrs., 1877-78, tho sporadically thru 1889. It did not have a lock at the bottom, but did have stop planks for use in cleaning out silt. Area considerably torn up in construction of Wash. and Md. R.R. in 1906-07.

2.36 Floodplain broadens; from here onward it becomes, in spring especially, a fine, in-town wildflower display.

ABNER CLOUD HOUSE

3.13 Access: From Canal Rd. at intersection with Reservoir Rd. One of most outstanding structures along C & O Canal. Site of historical significance because it stands near beginning of former Little Falls Skirting Canal and because it is oldest existing structure on canal. Site of Abner Cloud House was included in original patent of land dating back to 1689. On 10 Dec. 1794 titled was owned by John Threlkeld, prominent landowner in Georgetown, who deeded the land to his brother-in-law Abner Cloud, Jr. on 19 Oct. 1795. Another source says Abner Cloud acquired 195 acres from Richard Arell in 1795. From 1801, when he built house with help of Italian stone masons (initials A. C. and date 1801 can be seen on stone in upper portion of chimney) and mill which bears his name, until his death in 1812, Abner Cloud lived in this house with his family. During this period he used basement

Abner Cloud House, built 1801, photo circa 1938. The porches were removed in 1962. (National Park Service photo)

20

Canal boat scene on the Georgetown Level, above Abner Cloud House. (Julius Fletcher)

which now fronts canal on S. elevation for storage of grain and flour he milled. His widow, Susan, continued to live here until 1852.

Mill built by Cloud was located near outlet of Potomac Co.'s Little Falls Skirting Canal toward river and ahead. Two other mills (one of which may have been named 'Old Locks Mill') and a distillery were located above this mill on Potomac Canal. Issac Peirce married a daughter of Abner Cloud & constructed Peirce Mill on Rock Creek in 1801. When property was sold to John B. (Bull) Frizzell in 1852, he lived at the site and operated the mill. Frizzell was a great grandfather of Julius Fletcher, owner of Fletchers Boat House. Sometime in 1860s, property was owned by Wm. A. Edes, Georgetown miller, who operated mill as Cloud-Edes Mill. In 1869, D. L. Shoemaker, member of a prominent Georgetown family, probably owned property and milled locally popular Evermay brand of flour. Ownership sketchy for 75 yrs. thereafter. James C. Copperthite probably resided here and was owner in 1939; in 1957 Mrs. Helen Redmon occupied house when it was condemned by govt., at which time it was badly run down. House described by architects as 'simple' random rubble stone house with stone gable E. and W. ends. House stands on a hillside sloping to canal to S. Wood frame interior with plaster walls and ceiling. Roof originally wood shingle. 'Ordinary' house of period. There have been several structural changes in the building but about 90% of original structure still exists. At some later period a porch was added, but was badly damaged and removed in 1962. House now used by Colonial Dames.

Area S. of canal between Fletchers Boathouse and Chain Bridge once had a fine mature stand of elms, sycamores and other river bottom trees with open understory, strong and fully capable of withstanding the ravages of flood. It was, 25 yrs. ago (and remains) an area of scraggly, vine-covered, debris-littered, fire-scarred thicket. Fires weakened and destroyed trees so that the top canopy was opened up, honeysuckle and other vines came in profusely, the trees became less capable of withstanding flood pressure and the mixture of vines and fallen trees formed an almost impenetrable thicket that caught more debris, increasing flood damage susceptibility so that it is now an almost impossible area to explore. Fires were quite numerous during the canal operating period; most of them were escaped campfires and smoker fires started by careless boatmen. So — the good old days were not always so good — to nature. Boats, canoes and bikes can be rented at Fletcher's Boat House reached from Canal Rd. Tel: 202-244-0461.

LITTLE FALLS SKIRTING CANAL

3.14 Fletchers Boat House, 202-244-0461. Rowboats for rental on river, canoes on canal and bikes on towpath. Picnic tables, refreshments, fishing supplies, toilets. River a favorite fishing location, especially during spring herring and shad runs.

Near this point to Lock 5 (mile 5.02) C & O Canal is in bed of old Little Falls Skirting Canal, a navigation of George Washington's Potomack Co. built to avoid Little Falls of Potomac. Canal was 3814 yds. long. Other canals of Potomack Co. were built at Great Falls, Seneca and Harpers Ferry. Entrance to canal around Little Falls obscured as is exact route from present C & O Canal to Potomac River. Original locks at Fletchers (Garrisons/Lock Cove/Lock Harbor) were built of wood; canal was completed 1795. They were replaced in 1817 by 3 stone locks with a lift of 37'. Upper portions of old locks and waste structures were destroyed in construction of B & O R.R. spur c1905. Capt. Edward Fleet sighted Little Falls 6 June 1633.

3.18 Battery Kemble culvert, 6' wide. Extended on outflow to permit passage under R.R.

3.21 Road Culvert at Fletchers has 14' (historically recorded as 15'3") span with 9½' rise at outflow. Extensively used to provide access to Fletchers Boat House area and towpath. **Surprising as it may seem, there are wild turkey and deer in this area. Doe and 3 fawn sighted on towpath at Fletchers June 1973. Potomac Co. lock remains on river side of culvert to right.**

3.23 3rd waste weir on level, believed to have served Edes Mill.

3.64 B & O R.R. bridge crosses canal at intersection of Canal Rd. and Arizona Ave.; 13.6' clearance over towpath, 10' clear width between abutment and canal side of towpath. Otter sighted 1975.

Civil War scene
at Chain Bridge.
(Library of Congress)

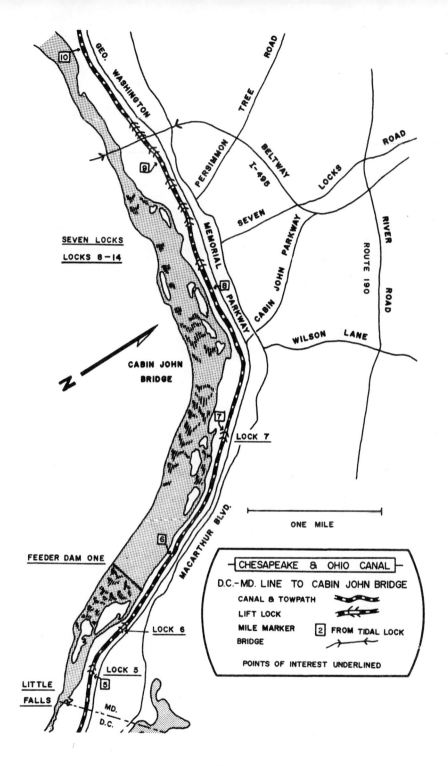

SEVEN LOCKS
LOCKS 8-14

CABIN JOHN
BRIDGE

LOCK 7

ONE MILE

FEEDER DAM ONE

LOCK 6

LOCK 5

LITTLE
FALLS

MD.
D.C.

GEO. WASHINGTON

TREE ROAD

PERSIMMON

BELTWAY I-495

SEVEN LOCKS

MEMORIAL PARKWAY

CABIN JOHN PARKWAY

ROUTE 190

RIVER ROAD

WILSON LANE

MACARTHUR BLVD.

CHESAPEAKE & OHIO CANAL

D.C.-MD. LINE TO CABIN JOHN BRIDGE

CANAL & TOWPATH

LIFT LOCK

MILE MARKER   2 FROM TIDAL LOCK

BRIDGE

POINTS OF INTEREST UNDERLINED

Canal boat approaching Lock No. 5. Brookmont, circa 1918. (Hahn Collection)

3.86 Spillway #2 is longest on canal — **354′ long** and 18″ below towpath level, built by Park Service in 1936 to relieve canal of surplus water. Was much undermined in June 1972 flood and rebuilt in 1973.

CHAIN BRIDGE

4.17 Access: GWM Parkway above bridge; extensive parking. Steps on far side lead up to bridge. Path across rd. goes to bus stop on MacArthur Blvd. A ferry operated here from c1737 to (probably) the building of the 1st bridge in 1797, which was a covered structure and collapsed in 1804. First 'chain' bridge was built in 1808, its roadway suspended from huge chains anchored from stone abutments; flood waters swept it away in 1810. It was probably rebuilt in 1811 and lasted until 1852, when it was severely damaged by a flood. The next bridge was built 1854, tho form of structure is not clear. There are Brady Civil War photos showing the bridge of timbered truss construction on the same masonry piers which exist today. The 1st Union Army sentinel to be court martialed for sleeping at his post in the Civil War had fallen asleep on the District end of the bridge. (Lincoln saved him from execution.) A Howe truss bridge (8 iron trusses) 1350′ long was built in 1874, with the timber floor laid on the old stone abutments, Bridge went out in 1936 flood and was replaced by the present steel cantilever girder structure.

The Chain Bridge area becomes a teeming mass of fishermen each spring during herring run. Our members of the herring family — American shad (*Alosa sapissima*), hickory shad and alewife — ascend Potomac to spawn in Mar. and Apr.; tho their numbers have decreased with pollution, the runs are still spectacular. Canoeists should avoid the section of the river between Chain Bridge and Great Falls.

4.54 Unused Dalecarlia **hydroelectric plant** and culvert under canal with deeply-cut outflow in a straight line to river 300 yds. away. This area of the river is being utilized by the Corps of Engineers for a supplemental source of water from the tidal estuary of the Potomac River (water coming up river by tidal action rather than down river by gravity). The concept is fine, but the location in a particularly scenic part of the river in view from Chain Bridge is poor.

4.72 Cross District of Columbia-Montgomery Co. line, upper limit of tidal water; Md. fishing licenses required above.

4.76 Large modern concrete culvert carries Little Falls Branch. Jack-in-the pulpits can be found in that valley in Apr., just before honeysuckle in bloom. An active beaver colony (unrelated to Corps of Engineer work cited above) between here and Lock 6.

LOCK No. 5, BROOKMONT AND INLET LOCK No. 1

5.02 Access: Via spiralling footbridge over GWM Parkway from outbound lane only; no access from parkway 7:00-9:30 a.m. Limited parking. Path up hill to Brookmont community, bus service. Toilets, drinking water. Two-story frame lock house torn down in 1957; last lockkeeper in operating period was Mr. Willard (lock known as 'Willards Lock' at that time). Last lockkeeper in post-operating period was Mrs. Walter King.

Just below Lock 5, C & O Canal turns inland about 15° and leaves original route of Little Falls Skirting Canal. Feeder canal angling toward river is remain of the Skirting Canal, bringing water from Historic Dam #1 .6 m. above Lock 5 at the head of Little Falls. It passes first thru the narrow channel between High Is. and the mainland and then thru the channel formed by the mainland on one side and by a long concrete spillway on the other, beginning at lower end of High Is. to the upper inlet gate, passing into the feeder canal proper thru the lower inlet gate and then to confluence with C & O Canal. Below Lock 5, construction of C & O Canal virtually eliminated all except minor traces of Little Falls Skirting Canal. Above the lock, robbing of stone, floods and elevation of dam have obliterated most of older, historic structures.

Raising Lock 5, 6' above its original level was probably an attempt to resist flood damage. A levee or guard dike is at this height and nearly perpendicular to run of lock, extends to the berm bank on one side and 100' to inlet gate of feeder on the other. Canal prism above was 60' wide and 6' deep. Lock 5 originally built of hammer-dressed stone in lower 6' from 'a quarry less than 1 m. distance' and remainder of freestone from Aquia Creek. Lock was rebuilt in 1878 of sandstone, local gneiss and Aquia Creek freestone. There are a number of stone masons' marks in the rebuilding. Guard dike and inlet gate abutments were done in concrete in 1939-42 restoration for flood resistance. Corner stone of Lock 5 laid by President Adams in 1829.

5.20 Service rd. leads to river to upper gate of feeder canal. River path goes to Dam 1. Swamp between C & O canal and feeder canal provides excellent bird habitat. High Is. (124' high) looms prominently between feeder channel and river. It is attractively wooded and has steep slopes with a level area on top. Possible sluices in the river on the far side for early batteaux.

Canoe locking through Lock 6, circa 1918. (Hahn Collection)

LOCK No. 6 (Magazine Lock), BROOKMONT

5.40 Access: From downstream (inbound) lane of GWM Parkway; parking lot. Valley Rd. across parkway leads thru Brookmont (and bus service) to MacArthur Blvd. Lock 6 is .38 m. above Lock 5 and 1.60 m. below Lock 7 with compass orientation of N. 10° W. Feeder canal (old Little Falls Skirting Canal) lies about 200 yds. W. of Lock 6. **Lock is called 'Magazine Lock' after US Powder Magazine .3 m. upstream where Pres. Adams inaugurated C & O Canal construction 4 July 1828.** Your author lived here 1972-75.

Lock originally a typical lock with swing (mitre) gates but was converted to one with a drop gate in the upper end. However, probably for reasons of economy, it was decided not to rebuild the entire upper end of the lock, which would have eliminated the original upper lock pockets. This was the method used in Locks 7, 9, 10 and 12. Rather, the breast wall was removed and the original lock pocket extended upward 16½'. Lock was later reconverted back to a swing gate. Lock measures 90'8" between lock pockets. Stones are much worn, showing many replacements or partial rebuilding with whatever material was handy. Lock originally built with Aquia Creek freestone with granite rubble backup stones common to area. Probably was built originally with wicket gates in the upper lock pockets to carry water around the upper gates and thru hollow chambers in the lock walls. Lower towpath wing wall shows many rope grooves as does upper 18" of exposed end of wall. Lower wing walls had vertical aligning timbers fastened to the turns of the lock wall to line up boats to minimize bumping into the lock. Traces of whitewash remain on lower portion of lock.

Lock seems to have suffered much of same type of damage it suffered in flood of June 1972. Towpath washout in 1972 uncovered a double row of wooden sheet piling at head of Lock 6. Between Locks 6 and 7 much of the embankment was exposed to river and for this reason a carefully laid and substantially built stone wall was originally built against slope to its top. Lock house (historically House #4) is a whitewashed stone structure of 1½ stories over a stone basement, 18' x 32'. Stone basement sidewalls were extended originally 6' on S. end to form a covered portion to basement entrance which supports a wooden porch for 1st floor. Original lock house built c1830-31 was destroyed in flood of 1847 and rebuilt 1848.

Forest cover along canal is of 2 distinct types, river bottom type S. of canal and in low flat sections N. of it and red-white-black oak mixture on slopes N. of canal and on high dry rocky area S. of Widewater. River bottom type is predominantly sycamore and American elm with considerable black locust, box elder and soft maple mixed in. Oak mixture is predominantly white oak with other oaks, hickories and Va. pine intermixed. Tulip poplar is common in both types. Land in the area was patented 16 May 1726 as Magruder's and Beall's Honesty. There was also a garrison built near Little Falls in 1695 under command of Cept. Richard Brightwell.

FEEDER DAM No. 1 (Little Falls Dam)

5.64 Access: From Lock 6. This point was scene of original ground-breaking ceremonies on 4 July 1828 at which Pres. Adams officiated. First completed section of canal from Little Falls to Seneca opened to navigation Nov, 1830. Path leads to end of old dam and end of feeder canal (Little Falls Skirting Canal). There were a number of cottages in area on plots leased from Canal Co., but all were destroyed in floods of 1936 and 1943. Growth of ivy in trees and old chimney remains testify to earlier habitation.

Remains of old 1750' loose rock dam originally 5' high, stretch in a curved line to lower end of **Snake** (or Woodchuck) **Is.**, thence in a straight line to Va. shore. Dam has concrete cap on portion between island and Va. Dam (built 1828) originally only went 855' to center of island. As with all C & O dams (there were 7 of them, tho 8 planned), Dam 1 suffered severely from periodic floods; ice freshet in spring of 1868 carried away half of dam. Today old dam is over-shadowed by new **Little Falls Diversion Dam**, which is about 1' higher, 100' upstream.

The Piedmont area commences at Little Falls, from which the Potomac Valley rises gently by a series of water-worn plateaus, principally of red sandstone, to the Blue Ridge W. of the Monocacy Valley. The surface of the valley is characterized first by gently rolling country of rich farm lands, broken at points much farther ahead near the river by stretches of majestic cliffs.

5.74 Historic Culvert #2 on sec. 2, 6' span.

5.78 Little Falls Diversion Dam and Little Falls Pumping Station, both constructed by Corps of Engineers in 1959. Dam is masonry structure reaching from Md. shore to Snake Is. and from island to Va. shore; latter distance 1500'. Tho dam is 14' high from river bed, it impounds water at a level only 1' above old dam. A 36" water main imbedded in upstream face of new dam carries water to Va. Pumping station, with capacity of 450 million gals. per day, is standby facility for pumping water directly from Potomac to Dalecarlua Filtration Plant on MacArthur Blvd. thru 4500' long tunnel, 10' dia.; used in low-water periods when natural flow at Great Falls, Md. is insufficient for Washington's water supply. Canoeists must pontage.

6.46 Sycamore Is. (Berry Island). Go across canal up path to GWM Parkway where it crosses before providing **access to MacArthur Blvd. at Walhonding Rd.** Parkway area on downstream side of parkway. Telephone and store on MacArthur Blvd. Just beyond bridge over canal is cable ferry to **Sycamore Island.** Montgomery **Sycamore Island Club** has owned **Sycamore Is. (3½ acres) and Little Ruppert Is. (4½ acres),** upstream, since 1885; both are near MD. shore. Sycamore Is. used for club activities, shore. Sycamore Is. used for club activities, while Ruppert Is. kept in natural state. Former is finishing point for annual canoe and kayak races run down Potomac from foot of Great Falls each spring. Beginning is at 13.83.

6.60 Upper end of Sycamore Is.; above are various small islands and Ruppert Is., **site of recent archeological excavations.** (Known as "Indian Island.")

6.98 **Old milestone;** legend reads "7 MILES TO W. C."

LOCK No. 7, GLEN ECHO

7.00 **Access:** From downstream (inbound) lane of GWM Parkway. Small parking lot. Footbridge at mid-lock to lock house, unoccupied. Parkway closely parallels canal to Cabin John Creek. Lock 7 lies 1.33 m. below Lock 8 and 1.60 m. above Lock 6. Compass orientation of Lock 7 is N. 48° W.

Lock made of granite obtained from quarry ⅛ m. away, except coping, which is Aquia Creek freestone. There are few replacements of stones in locks walls, testifying to quality of gray granite used. Original breast wall and all of lock walls above original swing gate quoins were removed and lock walls relaid to accommodate a drop gate in upper end. It is 101'11" between lock pockets which shows that drop gate pockets are some 10' forward of original swing gate pockets. On upper side of each gate is a projecting arm connected to an iron rod which extends over plank floor thru sleeves, to base of lock pocket wall where rod connects to a vertical iron rod thru a crank device. By turning lever from left to right, wicket gates opened to let water thru lock pocket floor where it flows into lower lock thru open end of cribbing. Reverse procedure closes them. Ease with which drop gates could be opened and closed and an 8' head of water above wicket gates (as opposed to equal-sized wicket gates in lower part of a normal swing gate) probably account for reduction of from 10 to 3 min. of time required to lock a boat thru. Upper end of drop gate pocket has no shoulders; lock is made up by tapered log cribs which lined up boats entering upper end of lock also prevented boat from touching (damaging) lock walls. Lock has 8' lift. Original lock had masonry bypass culverts.

Lockkeeper's house sits on an island formed by canal, lock and bypass flume. It is a whitewashed stone structure of 1½ stories over a full basement. Room was left on berm side of locks for a duplicate lock (to handle both upstream and downstream traffic simultaneously) should traffic warrant it. Lock house (House #5 historically) was completed sometime before 1 Aug. 1829, 1st to be completed on C & O Canal. An inspector on 2 Aug. 1829 said, "The Bearer James O'Brien (contractor) who has just finished Lock house No. 5 on Section 5 is an excellent stone mason, and has made one of the best if not the very best jobs of stone work on the line." In 1936, lock house was somewhat carelessly rebuilt after flood damage had torn away portions of the structure. Dormer windows and plumbing were added at that time. Last lock tender here was Shaeffer.

On bluffs above lock on opposite side of parkway was **site of the National Chataqua,** which finally failed (in part due to malaria outbreak along the canal.) The Glen Echo Amusement Park occupied site for many years, but closed after 1969 season. It was acquired by the National Park Service which removed some amusement structures and opened park to public in summer of 1970. Since that time an extensive cultural, educational and recreational program has been offered. 'Old Spanish Ballroom' held banquet of C & O Canal Association at termination of 16th Annual Reunion Justice Douglas

Hike from Seneca to Glen Echo, Apr. 1970. Large white frame house upstream from 'Glen Echo' was **home of Clara Barton, founder and long-time head of American Red Cross.** Reached from MacArthur Blvd., it is open to public 1-5 p.m. except Mondays. Toward river and thru woods is a side channel of river with Chataqua Is. beyond. Canal above Lock 7 is popular ice skating location, but due to many mild Washington winters, ice skating is but a fleeting form of outdoor recreation here.

7.10 Concrete waste weir. At least one weir is on all but the shortest levels. They carry off excess water. In canal operating period the weirs permitted draining of canal in winter to prevent ice damage and to carry out seasonal repair and cleanup of the canal. Ahead, flood plain supports many fine tall elms and sycamores. This typical bottomland woods is fine bird habitat. Ahead in river is **Cabin John Is.,** though changing river channels have destroyed its true island nature. Here in 1905 blue bells grew in wonderful profusion. Then boys in Glen Echo discovered they could be sold to visitors at the terminal of the Cabin John line. In a couple of yrs. the island was denuded and they never returned. Maybe this will explain to some (who ask why) flower picking is not allowed in a national park.

7.12 Modern concrete culvert carrying Glen Echo run (old 'Minnehaha' stream) replaces historic stone culvert #5; described in 1831 as a 'fine arched stone culvert,' which was 112' long, span of arch 22' and rise 5'.

7.50 Modern concrete box culvert carrying Cabin John Creek under canal replaced historic culvert #8 in the 1960's. Foot bridge across the canal provides access to Glen Echo Park .12 mi. downstream.

CABIN JOHN BRIDGE

7.50 Bridge is beautiful structure carrying MacArthur Blvd. and Corps of Engineers water conduit from Great Falls — readily seen 1000' up Cabin John Creek, spanning both creek and 4-lane Cabin John Parkway. Construction began in 1857 and water turned into conduit 5 Dec. 1863; bridge itself finished 1864. Bridge is 450' long, 57½' rise, with 220' span — at

Lock No. 7, in the early 1900's.

time of completion longest in the world, remaining today as longest stone arch in Western Hemisphere. Parapet walls built of red Seneca sandstone and cut stone arch granite from Quincy, Mass., carried here via ocean vessels to Georgetown thence C & O canal. Rubble arch and spandrels are of Seneca sandstone and abutments are of Port Deposit (Md.) granite. Bridge has 5 spandrels at W. end and 3 at E. end to relieve load. These are hidden inside walled facade. First engineer of bridge project, Montgomery C. Meigs, further utilized canal by building dam across Cabin John Run together with lock to pass canal boats from canal to pool under bridge. Meigs named bridge 'Union Arch' and it was called that for 10 years thereafter. Wm. R. Hutton (Washington Bridge in NYC, New Croton Aqueduct, Georgetown Incline and a chief engineer on C & O Canal) was chief engineer of Cabin John project when the water was turned on thru conduit inside bridge in 1863. Bridge designated a National Historic Civil War Landmark 30 Jan. 1973.

Valley of Cabin John Creek extending for 2 m. to N. used to be a beautiful, scenic, wooded area in which birds and plants abounded; in recent years, tho some of it is intact, much of valley has been seriously damaged with construction of highway connecting GWM Parkway with beltway and by various construction projects of Washington Suburban Sanitary Commission, part of which have (hopefully at least), reduced some of pollution which has entered Cabin John Creek and Potomac in this area. Two sewer lines parallel canal on berm between Brookmont and Cabin John. Smaller one, built many years ago, connects with sewer down Cabin John Creek Valley and carries sewage to Washington system in Georgetown. Larger one, built in 1960s, is Potomac Interceptor from Dulles International Airport to Washington Treatment Plant at Blue Plains; it is 7' dia. and laid in bed of canal in some places. Vertical iron pipes noticed occasionally are ventilators of old sewer; little masonry towers 2'-3' high ventilators of interceptor. Bridge to MacArthur Blvd. & Lock 7.

7.52 Cedar Is., but like Cabin John below, its island character ill-defined and varies with height of water in shallow river channels. River itself, brown at flood time or olive green at others is noisy among rock islands which stretch to Va. shore. Floodplain in spring a green blanket splashed with myriads of wildflowers: spring beauties, blue phlox, mint, Dutchman's-breeches, ragwort, violets and trout lilies all reach their blossoming peak at one time. Add a clear day with white arms of towering sycamores, the kaleidoscope of color is breathtaking.

8.12 Towpath comes directly on river bank, supported by laid masonry wall. **High wooded island is Minnie Is.**

LOCK No. 8, SEVEN LOCKS

8.33 Access: Inbound lane of GWM Parkway; parking lot. Steep path leads 200' down to lock. Alternate use for hikers and bikers only is from MacArthur Blvd. to 79th St. to Riverside Ave. where turn left to dead end, turn rt. on old road and then path which leads to Lock 8 to left. This lock 1st of series known as 'Seven Locks,' which raise canal 56' in distance of 1¼ m. Lock material is red sandstone boated down river 14½ m. from Seneca quarries. As an 1831 report put it, "It is the first with which we have met, which has the facing, or front range of its walls, made with the red sandstone of Seneca Creek . . . inferior, however, to granite."

Lock 8 is 1.33 m. above Lock 7 and 0.37 m. below Lock 9. Compass orientation N. 83° W. Lock had many repairs; many original stones replaced with concrete, brick and granite. Lock was once elevated 6" with wooden timbers bolted onto coping (top layer) stones of lock wall, probably to help overcome silting of Lock 8 level. Lock was built with masonry bypass culverts around upper gates, but abandoned early on. Lock has 8' lift. Note 4, 1" diameter blow holes which lead down into culvert openings to release air trapped in culvert when water let out of lower lock. Lock has a masonry breast wall, with the downstream face flush with the downstream face of the mitre sill of upper lock gates, as did most but not all locks thru lock 27. Lock measures 140'8" overall length and 90'6" between lock gate pockets. Each lock has a 'mule rise' at the lower end of the lock. This is the only place where the towpath goes up or down hill — the rest of the towpath is (or should be) perfectly level. This particular mule rise is 70' long and has a rise of 8' — same as lift of lock. Canal is 100' wide just above lock and could have been a turning basin. Canoe put-in/take-out for river.

Construction of lockkeepers' houses was undertaken within a few months after the official commencement of the canal on 4 July 1828. On 18 Mar. 1829 the Canal Co. received a proposal from James O'Brien for erecting houses 'Numbers 5 and 6,' (No. 6 is house at Lock 8) and house was completed and ready for occupancy a year later. First group of lock houses to be completed apparently were assigned for occupancy and use late in summer of 1830. A resolution adopted by the Canal Co. stated that compensation for lockkeepers "shall . . . in no case exceed $150 for a single lock; $200 where the same person keeps two locks, and $250 where three locks are kept by one keeper, per annum." One month later, Solomon Drew was appointed Keeper at Lock 8 at $100 per annum "and use of Lock house No. 6 on Section No. 7." House here is typical 18 x 30' stone structure, with 2 rooms on each floor and central fireplace on 1st floor. Walls plastered directed on masonry, ceilings lath and plaster. Exterior is random coursed stone painted white. House is attractively located 60' from lock wall.

8.40 Historic culvert #9, 4' span.

8.57 Wades Island.

8.67 Historic culvert #10, 6' span.

LOCK No. 9, SEVEN LOCKS

8.70 Access: See Locks 8 and 10. This lock and Locks 10 and 12 equipped with drop gates; attendant mechanisms (on berm side) in working condition. Lock .37 m. above Lock 8 and .09 m. below Lock 10. Lock built of granite brought 1¾ m. by land from quarry near Lock 7; except for coping, which is Aquia Creek freestone, and a few feet of ashlar (of red Seneca sandstone). Many of original lock stones replaced. Lock was laid entirely in cement mortar with no grouting. Drop gate was installed 10' above earlier swing gates so it is 101' 8" between lock pockets instead of 90'-92' of original. Overall length of lock 141' 5½". Lock has 8' lift. Hoisting gear is on top of upper berm lock pocket wall which has 4 lift levers operating 4 vertical rods which open 4 cast iron wicket gates in the wooden floor. Stone filled wooden cribs now in place probably approximate those used in operating period; apparently cribs had no standard dimensions, tho they were generally 12' in length, 3'-4' on upper end by 5'-7' wide on lower end. Cribs here are post-1939 construction as are all cribs on restored portion of canal. In addition to aligning boats and absorbing shock, they formed upper end of lock pocket. Vertical, heavy wooden timbers were commonly mounted at lower end of lock (on lower wings) to align boats and absorb shock to lock as with cribs; this lock had such timbers.

Lower towpath wing wall shows 3 periods of iron cramps (devices for holding stones together): oldest has ½" x 1½" iron stock with turned down ends which are fully let out in stone, measures 13" overall and was lead caulked; mid-period cramps ½" x 2" iron stock, 13"-14" overall length, ends shaped into round stock which are turned down and fully let into stone; and late period cramps 1" round iron with turned down ends, somewhat longer and ½ let into stone.

LOCK No. 10, SEVEN LOCKS

8.79 Access: From GWM Parkway; downstream (inbound) traffic only; parking, public telephone. Lock 10 is .09 m. above Lock 9 and .18 m. above Lock 11. Compass orientation N. 90° W. Lock originally built of granite, ½ from quarry near Lock 7, ½ from a quarry "four miles in the country. The transportation comes from land." Note several interesting stone masons' marks. Stones have stood up well with few exceptions. Lock house is about 100' below lock. Lockkeeper here served both Locks 9 and 10. House is 1½ story stone building over full basement and late dormer windows. House was historically House #7, erected c1830; contractor J. W. Maynard and first lockkeeper Thomas Burgess. Canoe put-in/take-out for Potomac River.

8.93 Rock Run Culvert has skewed arch; that is, it runs under canal in a diagonal with its outflow end downstream of its inflow. It is 152' long, span of arch 12' and rise 6'. **This culvert a fine example of one of outstanding structures under the canal which most do not see. Recommended for viewing; carefully work your way down to stream it carries to see if you don't agree.**

8.96 Entrance to **Plummer Island,** home of Washington Biologists' Field Club, a 15-acre site in Potomac River.

LOCK No. 11, SEVEN LOCKS

8.97 Access: At Lock 10. Footbridge leads across lock to berm path which goes to Lock 10 downstream and Lock 12 upstream. Lock is .18 m. above Lock 10 and .32 m. below Lock 12. Compass orientation N. 85° W. Lock

Rock Run Culvert below Lock No. 11 — one of many beautiful canal structures the average canal visitor never sees. Circa 1938. (National Park Service)

House at Lock
No. 11, circa 1938.
(National Park
Service)

built of Seneca red sandstone; interesting stone masons' marks. Lock has swing gates in both upper and lower pockets with no evidence of a drop gate. Lock house on towpath side of canal 42′ from towpath wall of lock a few feet below upper lock pocket. It is of stone, 1½ stories high. Last lock tender in post operating period was Charles S. Stewart, long associated with canal.

9.00 Old **historic milepost** marked "9 MILES TO W. C." (Washington City), probably gray sandstone.

LOCK No. 12, SEVEN LOCKS

9.29 Access: Lock 10. Lock 12 is 1st of 3 closely spaced locks of Seven Locks chain, .32 m. above Lock 11 and .08 m. before Lock 13. Compass orientation S 84° W. Lock in pretty setting, with pleasant grassy areas in spite of proximity of GWM Parkway and I-495 (Capital Beltway). Lock originally built of granite from quarry near Lock 7, transported by land 2 1/3 m. There is also evidence that original coping stones were dark red sandstone. Masons' marks few. As is common in locks below Seneca, mule rise of towpath begins shortly below lock and does not reach level of top of lock until about lower gate pockets; end of lower towpath wing was thus exposed in historic times and rope grooves in evidence on end of wall 32″ down from top. Later substitutions of granite copings do not show rope grooves, proof they were installed later than 1924. Lock 12 has swing gates in lower lock pockets and a drop gate in upper pocket. As with Locks 9 and 10, visible evidence indicates that these locks were built originally with all 4 gates of swing type. When drop gates were installed, it was necessary to remove breast walls and all walls upstream of breast walls. These walls were then rebuilt to full depth, original upper gate pockets obliterated and new lock pockets for drop gates constructed some 10′ forward of original lock pockets. This made lock 100 to 101′ between pockets (100′ 11″ in this lock) instead of 90′ to 91′. Lock measures 140′ 9½″ overall. Rock outcrops on berm side exposed above and below locks indicate this lock was built on bedrock rather than on wood cribbing. Canal prism 70′ wide from Lock 12 to Lock 14. Lock house (gone) stood on berm side.

9.30 Capital Beltway (I-495) bridges; upstream span goes directly over Lock 13.

LOCK No. 13, SEVEN LOCKS

9.37 Access: Lock 10. Lock 13 is .08 m. above Lock 12 and .10 m. below Lock 14, located directly under I-495 — a real No Man's Land! Lock orientation N82°W. Lock wall facing stones "Granite from the country . . . transported by land 4 1/3 m. with the exception of the coping and the hollow quoins, which are from Seneca." Canal is a straight line from head of Lock 12 to Lock 14. Tho there is evidence that this lock was converted from a swing gate to drop gate and back to swing, the evidence is not conclusive. Present evidence indicates Locks 4, 7, 9, 10 and 12 were once equipped with drop gates, but that only 5, 7, 9, 10 and 12 had drop gates during restoration in 1939. Of the canal locks below Seneca, this lock alone shows no evidence

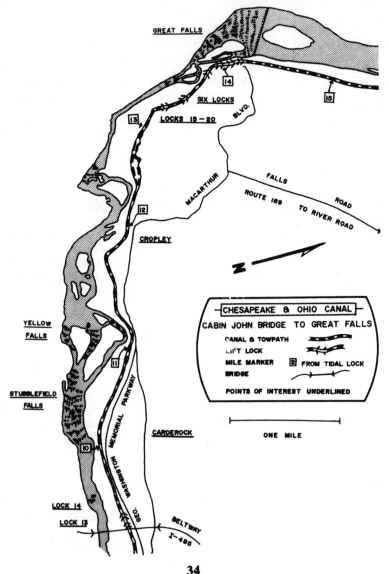

of having had masonry culverts around the upper lock pockets. It is also the shortest lock, being only 90' 3" between lock pockets. Note that both sets of lock gates are long gates, with the breast wall at the upper end of the upper lock pocket. Stones in this lock evenly spaced in height, with all 12 courses of stones exposed above the water line (when this level is drained) 12" in thickness. Note interesting inscriptions in upstream coping stone of lower berm lock pocket by one 'W. H. Davis'* with dates 14 Sept. 1923 thru 1932 (one per year); on the same stone is a stylized rose with leaves and initials 'S. D.' Lower walls of this lock (as with the others) were kept whitewashed to waterline and traces remain. There are no culverts or waste weirs on levels 12 and 13. An 1831 report states, "The engineer was constrained to these small pools (or ponds or levels between locks), from the peculiar character of the ground."

*W. H. Davis was the locktender here. 'S. D.' is his brother, Samuel Davis.

LOCK No. 14, SEVEN LOCKS

9.47 Access: Lock 10 or GWM Parkway (Exit 15 of Capital Beltway) to Carderock Recreational Area (1 m.) and thence downstream via towpath. There is a turn-around .2 m. beyond beltway for one needing to reverse direction and go back down-stream (inbound) on parkway. Lock 14 is uppermost of Seven Locks, .10 m. above Lock 13 and 3.98 m. below Lock 15. Lock built of granite,". . .½ from the quarry in the country referred to, Lock # 10, the other ½ from a quarry 5 miles distant." Locks 14 and 15 were completely rebuilt (according to historic records), Nov. 1871-Jan. 1872. Walls of all locks originally built to 15' width; width varied thru the years as locks aged. As boats were 14½' wide, lock had to be rebuilt when it tilted too far inward (approaching 14½"). Walls of this lock today measure 14' 8½" above upper pockets; 14' 5½" below upper pockets; 14' 8½" at midlock; 14' 11" above lower gate pockets; and 14' 9" below gate pockets. A standard C & O Canal boat could not pass thru many locks now. Even tho lock was supposed to have been rebuilt in 1871-72 period, masonry culverts around upper lock gates were retained; all 3 culvert openings in both lock walls are open and operative. It is 93' 4½" between lock pockets, an unusually long length; Lock 13 is but 90' 3". Locks 5 thru 23, excluding those with drop gates, vary from 90' 3" to 93' 4½", with only this lock and Lock 18 in excess of 91'. A typical lock was to have been 92' between lock pockets. Note USGS bench mark set in top of coping stamped "El.117." Wooden lock house on towpath side now gone.

9.63 Naval Ship Research and Development Center. Extensive installation includes **David Taylor Model Basin,** where Navy's ship and aircraft experts learn how ships and their machinery and aircraft are likely to behave in their honest-to-goodness element. **Deep water basin 2775' long.**

9.67 Concrete waste weir. Broad grassy area to left is **site of lower of 2 CCC camps whose workers restored canal in 1938-39.**

9.92 Carderock Pivot Bridge Remains a comparatively recent one of 9 Dec. 1941, built for better access to CCC camps, previous to which access was by rd. from MacArthur Blvd. and crossing under canal thru old Rock Run Culvert. Pivot type bridge was needed as NPS was operating barges in canal thru Carderock area.

10.02 Historic culvert #14, 4' span.

House at Lock No.12 (Hahn collection)   House at Lock No.13 circa 1942 (Hahn collection)

10.16 Stubblefield Falls, a succession of rapids in a narrow neck of river. Wide pool (turning basin) in canal ahead a favorite haunt of turtles which cover old logs protruding from water and quietly slide off when disturbed, accounting for name 'sliders' by which they are known.

10.41 Carderock Recreational Area. Access: Via GWM Parkway and marked access rd. passing thru modern **rd. culvert** under canal. Area extends to mile 10.95. Extensive picnicking facilities, toilets, drinking water.

10.42 Historic culvert #15, 11'-9' span, 6' rise. Field pussytoes, pale violet, wild ginger below road culvert.

House at
Lock No. 14,
circa 1938.
(National Park
Service)

10.76 Informal overflow helped control height of water before waste weirs were used.

11.10 Towpath directly on river escarpment atop high masonry wall. Towpath embankment on this level where it encroaches on the river is protected by a well built slope wall of dry laid masonry. Aside from strength it provided, it was described in 1831 as " . . . most convenient and economical way to dispose of stone." Sharp bend in river channel below turns end of **Vaso Is.** (formerly Herzog Is. — a name now applied to smaller triangular island upstream of Vaso). **Sheer rock walls and vistas up and down turbulent river channel make this an extremely spectacular viewpoint.** Known as "Highwalls."

11.44 Broad path to river is 2nd loop of Billy Goat Trail, leading 1.4 m. thru varied, beautiful terrain: past old farms, up and down river cliffs, skirting pools and a pond, thru open woods and thru magnificent patches of wild flowers. Loop ends after sharp ascent from S. end of Sherwin Is. to Cropley.

11.52 Footbridge across canal leads to MacArthur Blvd. Old rds. to left formerly led to farms on plateau between canal and river. One of these, just beyond footbridge, traverses old fields and past bits of former orchards and passes thru area called 'Marsden Tract' on way to river and joining Billy Goat Trail. Group camping and 'thru hiker' camping is allowed by permit, arranged by calling The Great Falls Tavern tel. 301-299-3613. Water, toilet.

11.75 Site of Potomac Granite Mill and wharf on berm in early 1900's.

11.76 Stone historic culvert #17, 10' span, 5' rise carries stream from flat wooded area, constructed 1828-1830 of granite gneiss.

12.26 Historic culvert #18, 8' span, constructed in 1830.

12.27 Path leads to **canoe launching site in river.** In area note blue phlox, buttercup, gill-over-the-ground, early saxifrage, Jack-in-the-pulpit, kidney-leafed buttercup, rue anemone, spring beauty, and star chickweed.

CROPLEY

12.28 Access: Service rd. bridge across canal leads to MacArthur Blvd. and 2 parking lots: upper lot (public telephone) is just across from Old Anglers Inn; lower lot 100 yds. below on either side of park maintenance rd., which is hikers access to towpath. Overflow parking lot just around bend up MacArthur Blvd. Lower parking lot is a good area from which to put canoes into canal or river. **Widewater (when repaired from floods) with its scenic coves and tiny rock islands offers excellent boating; downstream one travels 3 m. before coming to Lock 14.**

Path from towpath to river closes 2nd 'loop' of Billy Goat Trail and on out to Sherwin Is. Warning: Beginning/ending points of loops not clearly defined. Nice view up main channel of river of mouth of Difficult Run, a picturesque, rugged ravine on Va. side of river.

'Berma' Rd. is only practical way for cyclists to detour rocky path around upper end of Widewater and is useful detour for hikers as well when repairs necessitate it. In any event, it is a most pleasant alternative route. Rd. runs along top of conduit carrying water from the Potomac River at Great Falls to Washington, D. C. It is shaded and rock bluffs offer a variety of interesting rock formations. 'Berma' Rd. is also known as 'Burma' Rd. The former is probably a corruption of the word 'berm' — the side opposite the towpath — whereas the latter is probably a reference to the World War II high altitude rd. in Burma, as the rd. does give the appearance of having some elevation above the river and Widewater. Cross back to the towpath at Lock 16 if you use the road.

12.36 Concrete wall on berm side of canal; **remains of loading dock of Potomac Granite Co. Rock crusher was located near here.** In rock debris of quarry (or mine), above are iron rails which probably led to canal. Wall blocked off Culvert #18 at 12.38. Several gold mines were in operation after the Civil War. Maryland Mine operated until c1940.

12.47 Fine view of **Sherwin Island.** (Cupid's Bower).

12.51 Interesting **folded rocks** just ahead and at mile 12.60. Synclines and anticlines can be seen in rocks throughout Great Falls area where canal, roads, quarries and mining operations have exposed many hidden formations.

12.60 This section of towpath has been a trouble spot for yrs. Towpath here and at Widewater ahead is restored, having been one of major breaks resulting from Hurricane Agnes in June 1972.

WIDEWATER

12.62 Access: From Old Anglers Inn at mile 12.28. **Widewater (when restored) provides one of most attractive scenes along the canal,** its width about 400', its length ¾ m. and maximum depth about 65'. Old river channel was used here instead of constructing canal in cliffs. Stone wall sporadically supports towpath to concrete bridge at mile 13.00

13.00 Waste weir and concrete bridge, built 1939, over waste weir flume. Towpath in Widewater known as 'Log Wall' by old canallers because of log cribs **(washed out in 1924 flood). Path to waste weir leads on to river and Billy Goat Trail** which supported towpath (giving appearance of a wall from the water).

13.37 Towpath crosses old dammed-off channel of river on rock causeway. Note towpath ahead cut from bedrock. Moss and lichen, prickly pear cactus, Virginia pear, red cedar, white and green ash and stag sumac were abundant on lake shore only a few yrs. ago. Causeway and guard wall were built about 1850. The canal from Great Falls to Old Anglers Inn was closed during WWII as a security precaution to the Washington water supply system. Causeway and guard wall were built c.1850.

Lock No. 15, circa 1900.

LOCK No. 15, SIX LOCKS

13.45 Access: See Locks 16/20. End of Widewater. Lock 15 is 1st of a series known as 'Six Locks,' located in a 1 m. stretch). Lock 15 is 4.08 m. above Lock 14 and .18 m. below Lock 16. Compass orientation N. 6° E. Lock is located in old river channel which begins at foot of Lock 18 and continues down thru Widewater, an area much subjected to floods. Large, stone-filled, wooden cribs on the berm side of lock were replaced in 1939-42 by a concrete wall with 30' spillway, 1' below top of lock, normal operating level in historic operating period; cribs were simulated below dam on each side of spillway to preserve historic appearance. Historic records show lock was completely rebuilt Nov. 1871-Jan. 1872; appearance shows evidence of even more rebuilding. Note that much of upper extension wall, turns and wings were replaced with concrete in 1939-42 restoration and part plastered over with a special mixture of sand and cement to simulate red sandstone original stones.

Wooden floors of lock pockets were replaced with concrete during that period. All locks in the Six Locks area were built of red standstone boated down river from Seneca. This lock was badly damaged in the 1972 flood as was Lock 16. Lock was built with masonry culverts around upper lock pockets; masonry culverts in berm lock wall are still open and operable; those on towpath side stoned up. Lock 15 was rebuilt by NPS in 1976. Lock had 8' lift.

Two lock houses have existed at Lock 15. First was a stone one on the towpath side of lock, opposite the center of the lock; it existed there until totally demolished in 1889 flood. About 10 yrs. later, a frame lock house was built on the berm, but it was destroyed by a fire within a few yrs. (but still standing in 1900, as was the lock shanty — the latter a shelter to keep the lock tender out of the weather).

LOCK No. 16, SIX LOCKS

13.63 Access: From Lock 20 at Great Falls Tavern (mile 14.30) or from Old Anglers Inn below (mile 12.28) via Berma Rd. Lock 16 is .18 m. above Lock 15 and .36 m. below Lock 18. Built on W. bank of old river channel 100' in width, as was Lock 15. Bypass flume 40-60' wide. Lower berm wing wall extended to cliff in stone-filled wooden cribs as in Lock 15; these were replaced in 1939-42 Service reconstruction with a concrete wall to height of lock and concrete spillway 26' wide, 1' below top of lock. Historic log cribs were simulated below dam on each side of spillway for historic appearance. It is 91' 0" between lock pockets, standard length. Note inscriptions in coping stone mid lock, towpath side, 'J. W. Fisher, Jr.' and 'W. Spong'; Fisher was canal supt. for Georgetown district, Spong, a boat captain from Sharpsburg. On upper berm lock wall coping is canal boat carving. Lock 16 was rebuilt by NPS in 1976. Lock built for a 8' lift. Lock, constructed 1829-1831, originally faced with cut red Seneca Sandstone.

House at Lock No. 16 in the early 1900's.

Lock house here (probably House #10 historically) was erected in 1837, probably from improved specifications adopted in 1836, rather than original lock house specifications adopted in 1828. There are two rooms on each floor in this 2½ story stone house, 18 x 30' 1", fireplaces at each end of building. In c1900 photo, front doorway led to small porch. Birds observed include black, bufflehead, mallard and wood ducks; Canadian goose; great blue heron; whistling swan; and wild turkey.

STOP GATE AND LEVEE

13.74 Access: From Lock 20. In area from Lock 18 down thru Widewater (1.5 m.) canal was built in old river channel, which caused river to override the towpath and seek the old channel during floods, returning to river below Tidewater. For this reason **Canal Co. in 1852 erected a stop gate .36m. above Lock 16 and constructed a stone and earth 15' high 500' levee to the river. A rectangular one-story frame structure for housing machinery for raising and lowering stop timbers was reportedly built at an undetermined date and destroyed in 1889 flood.** Stop gate itself consisited of 2 parrallel stone masonry walls 13' in length, originally 28' apart, towpath wall of which tied into levee running to river and berm wall of which tied into continuatoin of levee back 73' to berm bank. Berm revetment washed out and is repaired with concrete. Walls of stop gate have vertical slots for stop planks which form a wooden dam across the canal and towpath. Stop planks in later yrs. of canal operating period were stored on adjacent platform or in a pile of top of levee. Planks were not in place in recent floods. To help prevent damage to area below in future floods, the Park Service restored the stop gate in fall of 1972, with walkway across top to reach Berma Rd. Stop planks were left in place to be ready instantly for an emergency. This could not have been done, of course, in canal operating period when boats would have needed to get thru the stop gate.

13.83 Just above the stop lock is **Northern or Western loop of Billy Goat Trail**. This popular hiker's route, laid out by YMCA Red Triangle Club between 1918 and 1920, is a spectacular alternate route to the towpath, but very rugged, taking about 3 hrs., so be prepared; this is no place for ordinary street footwear. In a short distance, trail becomes rocky, with steep climbs and descents. Land on this side is Bear Island. Wildlife, wild flowers and geologic formations along the trail are outstanding. View is so exceptional that it must be experienced to be believed. Winds whipping up and down Mather Gorge are a natural air conditioner for the summer hiker.

13.85 Towpath comes onto top of a high, heavy slope wall, in places as high as 56', with a **sheer drop to arm of river in a deep curving gorge —** **a spectacular view.** In original construction, rows of plank piling were driven on inside of such high walls as this. Built on meto graywacke stone.

13.88 Catfish Hole in river and several fine viewpoints reached by trails leading to river. **Cliffs across channel are on Rock Is., which can be reached by foot at low river stages. Extreme care must be exercised. Tho rock climbing and exploring are fun and exciting adventures, many lives have been lost in this area, mostly due to carelessness, recklessness and inexperience.** This area offers fine views across the wild, rocky terrain of the Potomac, below the falls, to the Va. shore.

13.91 Aqueduct overflow on berm hillside. Beyond is rocky promontory fording a magnificent view, reached by trail from Lock 17.

LOCK No. 17, SIX LOCKS

13.99 Access: From Lock 20 (mile 14.30). Lock 17 is located .36 m. above Lock 16 and .10 m. below Lock 18. It is 90' 10" between lock gate pockets. As with many locks, traces of whitewash are visible on lower extensions, turns and wings of the lock. Frame lock house built on berm c1898 by Canal Co. burned or was otherwise destroyed subsequent to 1939. Path on berm leads to high, rocky viewpoint overlooking canal and river. Canal between Locks 17 and 18 widens into a spacious pool 300' long by 100' wide at upper end of which, just below Lock 18, it originally received a feeder from the Potomac. This lock was known to boatmen as 'Crooked Lock.' The lock was built for an 8' lift.

14.05 Site of bridges across river channels leading to Great Falls Vista, destroyed in 1972 flood. Many other bridges have been built on this site, testifying to the frailty of man in attempting to build great and greater bridges to overcome the overwhelming power of natural forces. Numerous side trails and scrambling routes lead to other viewing points. The numerous fish ladders, which can be seen in the river, were built before the turn of the century, but never successful. Despite thousands of visitors each year, an abundant wildlife population calls the falls area home.

Lock No. 18 in the early 1900's. Lockhouse burned, circa 1930. Remains (1974) shown in insert. (Photo by Tom Hahn)

GREAT FALLS, VIRGINIA

Access: Take Exit 13 of Capital Beltway (Great Falls, Va. 193 exit) and go 6 m. to rd. to park entrance, where turn rt. 1.5 m. **Spectacular views of the falls can be had from Va. side — a rare treat and an exceptional scene in Washington. A fine place to take out-of-town visitors.** Site of National Park Service Visitors Center (tel. 703-426-6931). Ample parking. Varied, seasonal programs. This is the site of George Washington's 'Old Potomack Canal,' built 1785-1802. Bed of canal and remains of five locks. See Hahn, *George Washington's Canal at Great Falls, Virginia.*

14.08 Stone arch inlet culvert 1831-1837 fed impounded water from river into the canal under the towpath 16′ below Lock 18. A concrete impounding dam to feed water to the culvert can be seen 81′ above upper towpath wing wall of Lock 18. Towpath end of the dam contained a weir which let impounded water flow along rock walled towpath to entrance of culvert. This structure provided canal below with water at a time when Dam #2 at Lock 23 was not yet built and thought to be used to supplement water supply later.

LOCK No. 18, SIX LOCKS

14.09 Access: Lock 20. Lock 18 is .08 m. above Lock 17 and .10 m. above Lock 19. Compass orientation N. 3.5° W. Lock built originally of red Seneca sandstone with backing of rubble granite and rests on solid rock. Locks 18, 19 and 20 are located just below break of Great Falls of the Potomac. Old river channel once divided at foot of this lock, 1 channel being used for canal below and other going back toward falls. Towpath is often washed out here and canal becomes a river channel once again, which necessitated building of stop lock below. It is 91′ 2½″ between lock pockets. Lock was raised 1′ some time in historic period. Again, as with most of locks from Georgetown to Seneca, this lock built with masonry bypass channels around upper gates. Bypass flume 10′ wide with low, dry laid, battered native stone walls. Flume discharges over stone wall. Bypass flumes vary in design; apparently lock tender had considerable leeway in manner in which he maintained flume. Ruins of 1½ story stone lockhouse 6′ E. of bypass flume. House measures 18 x 30′ 2″; standard is 18 x 30′. House built of native stone with some red Seneca sandstone. House whitewashed on inside for several years before being plastered. **Lock house was one of original stone lock houses on canal, completed 1830 and built according to 1828 specifications. Remained in good condition until about 1930, when it burned.** It was probably historically House #11. Lock shanty previously existed on berm side of lock at upper end. Uphill from Lock 18 is loop of old Washington and Great Falls Electric Railway. In woods hereabout one finds old Civil War gun emplacement, Maryland Gold Mine and thousands of fire ants (Allegheny Mound Builders — their anthills truly spectacular) which sting like the devil if one dares stop too long. Lock has 8′ lift.

LOCK No. 19, SIX LOCKS

14.17 Access: Lock 20. Lock 19 is .09 m. above Lock 18 and .13 m. below Lock 20. Compass orientation N. 3° W. Lock built of red Seneca sandstone, probably on bedrock. **Some of present coping stones possibly taken from older structures: one stone inscribed 'May 24, 1819' and another '1812.'** Lock 15 90′ 11″ between lock recesses and 139′ in length overall. Towpath has rather sharp mule rise; rope grooves extensive along lower towpath wing copings and top of exposed end of wing wall. Lock has 9′ lift. **Only structure**

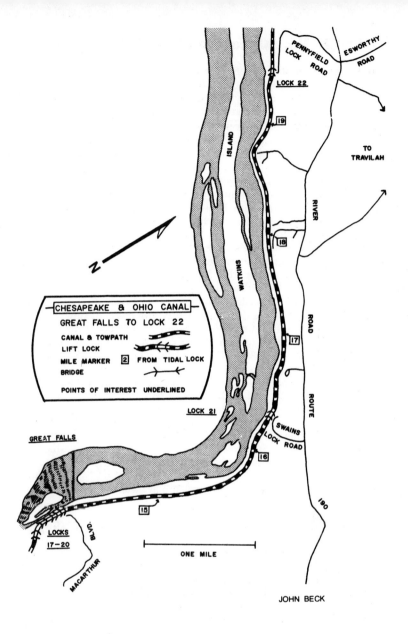

CHESAPEAKE & OHIO CANAL
GREAT FALLS TO LOCK 22
CANAL & TOWPATH
LIFT LOCK
MILE MARKER [2] FROM TIDAL LOCK
BRIDGE
POINTS OF INTEREST UNDERLINED

PENNYFIELD LOCK ROAD
ESWORTHY ROAD
LOCK 22
TO TRAVILAH
ISLAND
WATKINS
RIVER ROAD
LOCK 21
GREAT FALLS
SWAINS LOCK ROAD
ROUTE
LOCKS 17-20
MACARTHUR BLVD.
190
ONE MILE

JOHN BECK

known to have existed at Lock 19 was board and batten shanty seen in c1900 photos. Originally it was intended for lockkeeper in House 12 (present Crommelin House or Great Falls Tavern) to tend both Locks 19 and 20. Supposition that there never was an original stone lock house may be supported by lock house numbering system, House #12 being at Lock 20 and House #11 at Lock 18. Sometime after c1875, the 1st frame dwelling N. of Lock 19 was used as residence by lockkeeper of Lock 19. In c1900 lower end of bypass flume was crossed by narrow board-decked log footbridge with log railings.

LOCK No. 20 (Tavern Lock), SIX LOCKS

14.30 Access: At foot of MacArthur Blvd. Uppermost of Six Locks. Lock 20 is .13 m. above Lock 19 and 2.34 m. below Lock 21. Probably most popular lock on canal being directly in front of Great Falls Tavern, near head of the Great Falls of the Potomac and a part of Great Falls Park. Park has concession stand with light foods, open in summer and on weekends during spring and fall; toilets, water, public telephone. Lock has 8' lift. Canal boat, Canal Clipper II, operates in season.

Lock originally built of red Seneca sandstone but extensively repaired with limestone, granite, concrete and brick. Bypass flume goes under brick patio in front of tavern thru a pipe; old pictures show it existing thru present opening into a sort of wooden trough or flume. Lock is 91' 0" between lock gate pockets; 142' 2" overall length. In river one can see a triangular stone-filled wooden crib across a side channel of river; **remains of a support or pier for an old semi-suspension bridge.** Timbers for crib are said to be timber supports from Md. Gold Mine on hillside near intersection of MacArthur Blvd. and Falls Rd. Original bridge was erected c1880 to Conn. Is. (Falls Is.) from a point abutting towpath at S. end of Lock 20. Bridge was destroyed in 1936 flood and another built and subsequently (presumably) lost in a succeeding flood. Canoeists should avoid the section of the river between Great Falls and Chain Bridge.

Howard Garrett in 1869 built a feedstore on the towpath side of the canal near N. end of Lock 20. Building was replaced by a larger structure in 1879, razed 1910. Two small buildings, a mule stable and a feed house or barn, built c1900 and razed c1913 stood 350' N. of Lock 20 on the towpath. **A telephone line belonging to the Canal Co. was completed during 1879 from Georgetown to Cumberland, a distance of 184 m., plus 16 m. of branch lines to houses of officers of the Canal Co. and to shippers. It had 48 telephone instruments, making it the longest commercial telephone line in the world.** One instrument of this private industrial telephone system was installed in Garrett's store c1879. A small late period frame clapboard lock shanty stood at the N.E. corner of Lock 20 until c1939; records do not indicate a lock shanty here in early days when lock tender apparently slept in N. ground floor room of center of tavern. CANAL BOAT TRIPS LEAVE FROM HERE IN SEASON. Call (301)-299-2026 for details. Charter trips are also available.

GREAT FALLS TAVERN (Crommelin House)

Undoubtedly the most outstanding habitable structure on the canal. It has experienced a long and colorful career as a lockkeeper's house, tavern, hotel and a private club. It is now a National Park Service Museum and Interpretive Center for the C & O Canal National Historical Park. Interpretive programs, tours and walks suitable to the season, tel. 301-299-3613 for general information on the canal from Georgetown to Seneca for the Palisades District Ranger Office.

Central portion of the structure was placed under contract 1828 and was probably finished 1829. The two-story N. & S. wings were added by late 1831. Plastering with " . . . a composition of Sand, common lime if necessary, and Shepherdstown cement" for the exterior of the building and erection of " . . . a porch in front of the stone center of the house" were authorized in 1831. Slatted shutters, called 'Venetian blinds,' were added in 1832 and the structure painted in Sept. 1832, date when enlarged structure seems to have been completed. We know that the building was used for a hotel in 1831 from a report of Cols. John Abert and James Kearney of Topographic Engineers

Old photograph of Great Falls Tavern.

who stated, "At this lock we found an excellent hotel kept by Mr. Fenlon. The house is built upon the ground of the company, and with company's funds, and is a necessary and great accomodation to those who visit this interesting work." W. W. Fenlon was lockkeeper of both Locks 19 and 20 in addition to being a tavern keeper and seems to have had some kind of supervisory responsibility for the rest of the Six Locks as well. Somewhere along the line, prior to 1849, this structure was called 'Crommelin House,' in respect of the Dutchman who was instrumental in effecting Dutch loans to the Canal Co. During the 2nd and 3rd quarters of the 19th C., the house at Great Falls served as hotel or tavern and lock house and sometimes as both. Beginning Aug. 1848, until after the Civil War, the Canal Co. ruled that the lockkeeper at Great Falls could not sell intoxicating liquors. In Sept. 1849, the Canal Co. ruled that Crommelin House should be used as a lock house for the lockkeeper of Locks 19 and 20, perhaps de-emphasizing the role of the structure as a tavern. In June 1851, the Canal Co. allowed the 'Ball Room' (N. wing 1st floor) to be rented as a grocery store. In Jan. 1858, Henry Busey, keeper of Locks 19 and 20, was allowed to re-establish a hotel or 'ordinary' at Crommelin House for the accommodation of visitors to Great Falls. Beginning 1853, the construction of the line of the Washington Aqueduct affected life at Great Falls considerably and by 1861 Crommelin House had been damaged by the construction.

Tavern had no separate kitchen prior to Civil War decade, various occupants using basement under S. wing or parlor (large 1st floor room in S. wing) for cooking. First separate kitchen built was a frame structure erected near E. end of S. wing by Howard A. Garrett when he leased Great Falls House in 1876. Wm. A. Case c1929 replaced kitchen built by Garrett with a frame kitchen (now gone) in the same location. Fences, walks and porches have undergone many changes during existence of Great Falls Tavern. **There have been various buildings in tavern area thru the years.** A carpenter and repair

45

shop existed in various forms to N. from beginning of canal c1830 to c1939. Several other frame structures were associated with construction of Washington Aqueduct between 1853 and 1863 and then razed between 1874 and 1880; **The existing brick and stone residence on hill above tavern belonging to Washington Aqueduct was begun 1874 and completed 1877. The stone gatehouse of Washington Aqueduct opposite N.E. corner of tavern was begun 1853 and completed 1877.** Most famous (or perhaps infamous) of old construction buildings of Wash. Aqueduct was a large 1½ story frame structure N. of tavern near present traffic circle, originally used as a barracks for laborers on the aqueduct. From end of Civil War to 1878 it was occupied and used by Richard Jackson who maintained a notorious saloon and cafe there. Jackson's establishment was conveniently located just outside Canal Co. property where sale of intoxicating liquors was strictly prohibited, so Jackson fell heir to a lucrative canal patronage. Lock House No. 12 historically.

Howard Garrett built 3 houses on berm bank S. tavern between 1883 and 1884. 1st to S. was a frame house; 2nd was a log cabin, used as lock house for keeper of Lock 20 and now the central part of a home near Potomac; 3rd was a frame house used as lock house for keeper of Lock 19. Other buildings stood in area at various times — as these buildings are gone now. No canoeing below the water supply dam. Next safe put-in below Old Anglers Inn (12.27).

14.33 Masonry spillway (now covered over) 70' in length, built 1882-1883, 12' in width, extended from the upper towpath wing wall of Lock 20 to the lower wall of the waste weir just ahead. Photos of later operating yrs. of canal show spillway in use with water 1' below top of coping stones of Lock 20—the normal operating level of water in the canal. While tow animals walked thru water, the mule driver walked along an elevated board walk on river side of the spillway—a modern version is extant.

14.34 Stone and concrete **waste weir.** Just upstream of weir is observation platform overlooking river; platform is atop Army Corps of Engineers Washington Aqueduct Intake; beyond is crest of Great Falls water supply dam, built 1864-1867 and 1884-1886, 2,800' long. Raised from 7½' to 10' in 1896.

14.45 Modern pedestrian bridge leads to parking lot.

15.26 Cool Spring Branch historic culvert #21, 8' span. Up Cool Spring is a shaft of the Ford Gold Mine, one of several opened in hillso on berm in the period following Civil War. Gold was known in vicinity before this, but 1867-1916 saw greatest activity here. Extensive network of trails threads area of gold mine shafts and adits. Trail leading from upper end of upper parking lot is a good starting point. **Gold mine shafts are dangerous and should not be entered.** Culvert has 8' span, 4' rise.

and should not be entered. Culvert has 8' span, 4' rise.

15.98 Intake of Rockville Water Plant. Bed of blue phlox.

15.63 Flat area on berm is **location of old Sandy Landing,** reached by taking Sandy Landing Rd. from River Rd. Informal spillway at 15.76.

15.85 Historic culvert #22, Seneca red sandstone arch, carries stream from ravine in fine, mature woods. Note unusual variety of vines and heights they attain. During summer months, trumpet vines can be seen blooming 40-50' up in the trees. Path leads 200' to river bank opposite lower end of **Bealls Is.** (formerly Trammel Is.), with numerous small islands downstream. Culvert has 8' span, 4' rise.

16.30 Attractive sheer rocks on berm, but prevents good canal level berm path.

16.43 More rock-walled cliffs on berm, **Cedar Bluff,** tho only about a dozen cedars remain. **Lock Is. begins in river. Towpath directly on river bank.**

LOCK No. 21, (Swains Lock)

16.64 Access: From River Rd. (MD190) (Exit 16 of Capital Beltway) 2 m. past Potomac, Md., then left .3 m. on Swains Lock Rd. Limited parking, telephone, water, concession stand with canoe, rowboat and bike rentals. Tel. 299-9006. Lock is 2.34 m. above Lock 20 and 2.99 m. below Lock 22.

Lock built of Seneca red sandstone, boated down from Seneca 6 1/3 m. Original face stones were pebble finished with a 2″ wide ax finished border. It is 90' 7" between lock recesses, Lock built with masonry culverts around upper lock gates. Stump of lower snubbing post (rare) (there were 2 originally) is 7½' away from inner face of towpath wall and 14' 4" above upper end of lower gate pocket. Original stone, 1½-story lock house has fireplaces on upstream end, both floors. Upstream end of house has been removed (probably because of a major flood) and extended 14' 6" in length. Note beautiful rope grooves on lower towpath wing wall. Concrete, covered bypass flume is between lock and house. Lock has 8' lift. Lock house historically No. 13.

Bridge across lock (formerly known as 'Oak Spring Lock') to the lock house occupied by Fred Swain and family, including his mother, Virginia Swain, widow of Bob Swain. This family has long been associated with the canal. Bob's father, Jesse Swain, was lock tender here when canal closed down in 1924. His uncle, John Swain, was lock tender downstream at Seven Locks. A grandfather, born c1817, worked on some of the original canal construction jobs. Swains' house was flooded in each of the classic floods: 1889 (Johnstown yr.), 1936 (when Harpers Ferry and Shepherdstown bridges went out) and 1942 and 1972 floods. Note flood markers on upstream end of house. Stream in ravine on berm above the lock formerly flowed under canal thru a culvert. Historic records show 2 additional small culverts on this level which are no longer in evidence. Oak Spring is on the berm just over the bridge across the ravine, now with a wooden cover. Culvert #23 just above lock washed out in 1831. Put-in/take-out for Potomac River crossing.

16.67 Waste weir, concrete, 6'. Has date of 1906 — earliest known date of use of modern concrete on canal. Site of culvert #23 which washed out in 1831.

17.02 Historic milestone, top broken off, originally read "17 MI. TO W.C." Other known historic stone mileposts are at miles 7, 9 and 22. If there were others, we would certainly like to know about them.

17.36 Beginning of Washington Suburban Sanitation Commission Filtration Plant. Modern stone-faced building ahead built 1968. Ends 17.54. Deer sighted 27 April 1979.

17.60 Cross gas pipe line of Transcontinental Pipeline Co. At 17.78 cross pipeline of Columbia Gas System and Atlantic seaboard.

17.74 Historic culvert #25, length 115', 20' span, 10' rise above spring line, arch of gray Seneca sandstone carries **Watts Branch.** This winding stream, with its numerous branches, drains an extensive and varied terrain 5 m. back from canal. Much of the valley is now developed and there are fewer and fewer trails. Opposite is Watkins Is. Island nomenclature here is somewhat confusing. Watkins Is. was formerly divided into numerous small islands — in fact it still is at high river stages; portions of it are designated Clagett and Harris Islands. Lower end, opposite Swains Lock, is now called Gladys Is. on Seneca topo, was long known as Herzog Is.

17.98 Beginning of 1 m. of beautiful cliffs with occasional houses on crest. Thus greater part of distance between Swains and Pennyfield Locks, the embankment on the river side of the towpath is sustained by a beautiful

House at Lock
No. 22 (Pennyfield),
circa 1900.

and well built sloping stone wall of dry masonry, rising to top of embankment. One continued line is 2 m. long. Stands of blue phlox and golden ragwort.

18.30 Many islands in river between shore and Watkins Is.

18.86 Canal makes sharp bend around 70' cliff attractively decorated with cedars and pines.

19.48 Picturesque rocky berm makes nice approach to Pennyfield Lock ahead.

LOCK No. 22, (Pennyfield Lock)

19.63 Access: From River Rd. (MD190) (Exit 16 of Capital Beltway) 5 m. W. of Potomac, Md. turn left .9 m. on Pennyfield Lock Rd. to bottom of hill where turn left .32 m. to Pennyfield Lock and across pedestrian bridge to towpath and lock house. Parking along rd. to lock. Lock 22 is 2.99 m. above Lock 21 and 2.49 m. below Lock 23. Lock walls built of red Seneca sandstone boated down river 3½ m. from Seneca. Lock originally had lift of 7', but at some time in the historic operating period it was raised 8" by wooden timbers bolted onto the coping of the lock. In a later period, wooden timbers of towpath side were largely replaced with concrete. Raising of the lock probably was necessitated by silting. Lock was built with masonry culverts around the upper gates inside the lock walls. Wicket stem opening (a wicket stem is an iron rod used to open and close wicket gates) was sleeved thru the concrete used in elevating the lock. This meant that the culvert in towpath wall here was used after concrete came into general use on the canal in 1906. **Where masonry culverts were still operable, they probably were used in conjunction with the 4 cast iron wicket gates located in the bottom of the lock gates to speed up locking thru.** Here at this lock as at most, there appears to have been no set pattern to construction of bypass flumes, each of which consisted simply of a ditch on the berm side of a lock, running behind the lock house where one existed. Each flume had a stop plank arrangement of one kind or another, usually at the head of the flume, to bypass water in excess of normal operating level. Each flume had some kind of tumble or waterfall to help prevent erosion. The tumble of the flume at this lock is the stone and concrete riprapped floor itself. General care and maintenance of flumes was probably the responsibility of the lockkeeper. The 8' drop (lift of lock) here in the relatively short distance of the flume (140'), meant plenty of erosion and plenty of repair.

Lock house (No. 14) on river side of towpath is a 1½-story stone house over a full basement, built of roughly coursed greenish gray shale except for cut red Seneca sandstone window and door sills and lintels. House is 18' 2" wide by 32' 2" long. First floor has 2 windows front and rear but none on ends — this certainly must have been a disadvantage to a lockkeeper who needed to see up and down the canal — maybe he took care of his business from upstairs bedrooms, each of which had a window. Note so-called 'Cornish turn' of roof line into gable ends. This area of the river was a favorite base for Pres. Cleveland's bass fishing expeditions. He stayed often at the post Civil War white frame house, back on the berm, with the Pennyfields.

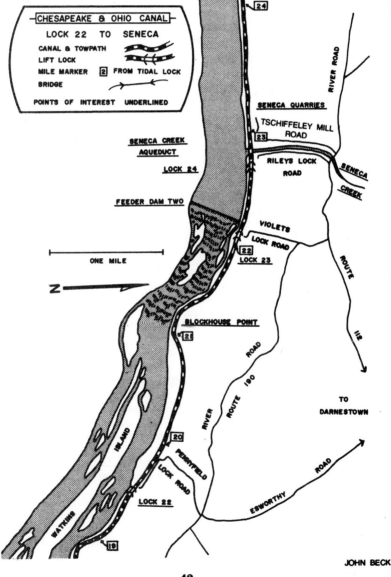

JOHN BECK

49

Lock No. 23 (Violettes) on the right and Inlet Lock #2 at left, 1970.
(Photo by Tom Hahn)

Tradition has it that 'Ma' Pennyfield once called up the stairs to ask, "Mr. President, do you want your eels skunned or unskunned?" (In case you are wondering, he wanted them 'skunned.') An old quarry is located on hill just below the lock and a Civil War outpost (said to be a signalling station) is on the hill above the lock. Put-in/take-out point for Potomac River crossing.

19.67 Waste weir

19.95 Granary site and landing area

19.96 John L. DuFiefs mooring basin and dock. When canal was drained for laying of Potomac Interceptor Sewer in bed of canal, the **remains of a canal boat were found;** they were still visible in period after Hurricane Agnes when canal was unwatered, at which time they also served as home for a large copperhead (or two). Basin and dock were operated by John L. DuFiefs.

20.01 Historic culvert #30, 16' span, 8' rise. Muddy Branch. Sandstone arch badly damaged in 1972 flood. Rebuilt 1979. Inflow end of culvert is strikingly **beautiful across the meadow coming down Pennyfield Rd. — one of only a handful of culverts which can be seen easily. Region is favorite haunt of bird watchers. In spring a morning's tally of 70-80 species is not uncommon. In winter, the river and intervening pools attract many ducks.** Not too long ago, red-headed woodpeckers were often seen here, but they seem to have disappeared since the construction of the sewer (yes, I am trying to make a connection). Withal, prothonotary warblers remained.

20.08 Levee on river side marks beginning of 1st passing pond of **Marshall Bidwell Wildlife Management Area.** Ponds are watered from the canal. Sanctuary ends at mile 20.90.

21.02 Blockhouse Point Regional Park. Beautiful area. Opposite milestone 21 are the lovely cedar-topped cliffs depicted in Justice Douglas' book,

MY WILDERNESS: EAST TO KATAHDIN (Doubleday). Portion of this dramatic cliff 'fell' into canal during blasting for sewer in 1968.

21.07 Towpath comes directly onto river bank. Rapids in river here popular with canoeists. Much of embankment on this level is protected from the river by a well laid stone wall, founded upon a broad footing.

21.12 Sheer cliffs on berm reach 150'.

21.55 End of passage around Blockhouse Point; cliffs recede, giving way to broad, flat area on berm.

22.02 Historic milestone, '(obscured) MILES TO W.C.'

22.04 Culvert #33, 6' span, washed out in 1863.

LOCK No. 23, (Violettes Lock) AND INLET LOCK No. 2

22.12 Turn left off River Rd. (MD190) (Exit 16 of Capital Beltway) 7 m. N.W. of Potomac, Md. onto Violettes Lock Rd. and go .7 m. to parking lot. Lock 23 is 2.49 m. above Lock 22 and .68 m. below Lock 24. Compass orientation N. 85° W. Nearby was **community of Rushville,** a small settlement named for Richard Rush, one-time Secretary of the Treasury, whose success in arranging Dutch loans helped the Canal Co. in one of its frequent financial crises. The prospects of Rushville soon faded with the westward expansion of the canal. In 1890s, thirsty quarrymen gathered here to buy moonshine from one Aunt Pricilla Jenkins. This is now a favorite fishing and canoe launching area. Below this point (barring canal repair from floods) canoe in quiet waters all the way to Georgetown, while more experienced and adventuresome canoeists set off down river in white water of the Potomac. The last lock tender in post-operating period was Mrs. Alfred L. Violette.

Violettes Lock and the inlet lock have adjoining wing walls and are very similar in construction. Violettes Lock runs N. 68° W. in line with canal above and below, while inlet lock runs N. 85° W., a difference of 17°. As the inlet lock is between the towpath and Lock 23, a mule crossover bridge was located across the inlet lock at the lower end. Modern vehicular bridges now cross the inlet lock and Lock 23. Both locks built of red Seneca sandstone, but Lock 23 is smoothly cut and evenly coursed, whereas inlet lock is roughly cut and coursed. Both type stones interlock at middle of connecting wall. Lock 23 was built with masonry bypass culverts around the upper lock gates; 3 culvert openings are visible in bottom of each lock wall. Upper gates were not restored in the 1939-42 restoration, consequently, this is the upper limit of the watered portion of the canal. Lock has no bypass flume, though one is shown on old maps. Lift of lock 8½'. Frame lock house (No. 15) on berm built 1830, burned in the 1930's.

Purpose of the inlet lock was to take water into canal to feed 17.10 m. of canal lying between Dam #2 and Lock 5. Historically it was known as the 'Seneca Feeder.' It also served as a river lock, letting boats in and out of slackwater above Dam #2. Inlet lock was in very active use when this was the only watered section of canal. Larger, standard 92' C & O Canal boats could not use this lock, since it is only 88' 5" between lock pockets, tho 15' width was retained. The numbering of this inlet lock can be confusing, as it was known as Lock 24 in 1831 when this was the upper limit of the canal. Later it became known as Inlet Lock No. 2 and the lift lock at Seneca just upstream became Lock 24. Sometime after original construction, inlet lock was elevated 39" on upper end, probably at same time Lock 23 was raised; both of them served as guard locks to protect canal below from high water. Lock No. 23 rebuilt by NPS 1978-79. Put-in/take-out for canoeing in the river. Drinking water, picnic area. **51**

Feeder Dam No. 2, near Lock 23 (Violettes Lock),
(Courtesy of Dave & Marta Kelsey)

A portion of the Potomac Navigation, the Seneca Cut, a 1,320-yard channel, is on the Va. side of the river at the far end of the feeder dam across the river. Known to canoeists as the 'Seneca Break,' or 'Washington's Cut,' one can make a round trip down the Seneca Canal and up the C & O Canal to avoid needing two cars.

FEEDER DAM No. 2

22.15 The 2500′ arched stone dam (Old Seneca Dam) originally built to raise water 4'. Contract for dam was let in 1828, 1st yr. of canal construction. Dam was originally built of stone filled wooden cribs. Original dam snaked across river, taking advantage of small islands and rock outcrops. Much of original dam is now reduced to scattered rubble and rebuilt in places; lower end now of recently laid stone capped with concrete. One stone of a later rebuilding has date '1902.' Dam impounds a 5 m. slackwater lake, 5' deep, which supports heavy (and noisy and smelly) recreational use of the river. Indications are that the guard dike here was elevated 3½-4½' at same time as upper ends of Inlet Lock 2 and Lock 23 were elevated 3' 4". The dike begins at the high point of land on towpath side of canal near old house ruins, continues upstream to the head of the locks, crosses locks and continues up berm to turning basin at Lock 24 at Seneca, gradually increasing to height of 5' or more. Upper end of dike was obliterated by enlargement of parking lot near the lock house. Canoeists should be wary of unmarked dam.

22.34 Modern concrete waste weir built 1971. Change in runoff patterns of Seneca Creek and golf course on berm between Locks 23 and 24 dictated need for construction of a waste weir to dispose of storm water. At time of construction a beautiful cross section of towpath and portion of canal bed liner was exposed, presenting a fine opportunity to study original towpath and canal prism construction here. Indications are that the location of the new waste weir was site of a historic informal towpath spillway or 'mule drink,' as the towpath was 2' lower in elevation for 100' and armored with stone chips and one-man stone. **22.41** Picnic area.

52

LOCK No. 24, (Rileys Lock) & SENECA AQUEDUCT - (Aqueduct No. 1)

22.82 Access: Via River Rd. (MD190) (Exit 16 of Capital Beltway) 8.5 m. N.W. Potomac, Md., then turn left .4 m. on Rileys Lock Rd. (which parallels Seneca Creek on E. side) to parking lot at Lock 24. **General merchandise and food supplies available at Pooles General Store just N. of Seneca Creek ridge. Tschiffeley Rd. on opposite (W.) side of Seneca Creek leads to quarries and remains of Seneca Stone Cutting Mill.** The local flood in Sept. 1971 and flood from hurricane Agnes in June 1972 badly damaged Seneca Creek area below River Rd. This area is under study by the State of Md. and the National Park Service as to how best to interpret the history of Seneca and yet enjoy the recreational aspects the area offers. Private concessions supply bikes, boats and canoes and light refreshments. Public boat ramp near aqueduct is in poor condition and only induces more and more moise and fumes into an already over-utilized area. Toilets and water available near Lock 24. Picnicking areas, but no camping. Because some horses are spooked by the hollow sound of the wooden bridge over the aqueduct, riders may want to enter the towpath via Tschiffely Road from River Road and cross the canal via the causeway.

Historically this region played an important part in early Canal Co. dreams. Expected canal trade and available water supply just downstream encouraged settlement of area. **For a time Seneca area was head of canal navigation and enjoyed a temporary boom.** Seneca's dreams faded as canal construction pushed on up river. In 1839, when agitation for a canal extension to Baltimore was at its height, one of proposed routes was from Seneca to Baltimore via

Lock No. 24 (Rileys Lock) circa 1918. (Hahn Collection)

53

Seneca Creek Aqueduct (No. 1) circa 1918. (Hahn Collection)

Rockville; this 'Maryland Canal' or 'cross cut' canal was never built and hopes for Seneca prosperity disappeared. **Seneca remained famous for another reason — it was just upstream that unique red Seneca sandstone was quarried, cut and shipped by canal** for use in many of C & O Canal structures and numerous buildings in and around Washington.

Lock 24 is .68 m. above Lock 23 and 8.04 m. below Lock 25. Compass orientation S. 83° W. **Structure here is unique in that it is a combination lift lock and aqueduct.** Lock on lower end of aqueduct lifted canal boats into aqueduct which spans Seneca Creek. Lock and aqueduct were built of red Seneca sandstone. Lock measures 90' 4" between gate pockets. Immediately upstream of upper gate pockets the canal bed is floored with large stones and the canal becomes the 3-arch Seneca Creek Aqueduct. Several upper courses of facing stones are same for both lock and aqueduct and other courses interlock. Aqueduct is 126' between upstream and downstream wing walls. Piers are 7' wide; support is 2 piers in water and 1 abutment on either side of Seneca Creek. Three shallow arches rest on the piers and abutments which are 40' on center. The barrel or arches span 33' clear of spring line and rise 7½' clear at the keystone. Upper berm wing wall of aqueduct has a concrete waste weir/culvert 12' wide by 8½' high which spilled waste water from canal into Seneca Creek. The aqueduct was rebuilt 1873-1874.

Heavy rain on 11 Sept. 1971 raised level of Seneca Creek about 8' above slack water of Potomac River, latter which was not much affected by the local storm. Seneca Creek became a raging torrent and houses, boats, trees and other debris were torn loose upstream and thrown against the aqueduct, blocking E. and middle arches. W. arch then took brunt of heavy objects battering bridge structure and eventually collapsed; **entire arch was destroyed,** leaving only 5 upper courses of stone in upstream flume wall. The stabilization which followed apparently did the trick of preventing further flood damage as no further damage was done by the Agnes flooding in 1972.

Note spur fences on river side of towpath wings, with each picket surmounted by a tall, round arrowhead. Note also ornamental stone cap on lower towpath wing fence on downstream face in which is cut '1889 June 2.' under which is a horizontal line apparently indicating high water mark in flood of that year. A very well restored lock house, 1½ stories over a full basement, is on berm side of Lock 24. Last lock tender here in post operating period was Mrs. John C. Riley. Girl Scouts of America provide interpretations on weekends. Both Lock 24 and Seneca Aqueduct were built 1828-1832.

This point on the canal marks the upper limit of the **Palisades District** of the **C. & O. Canal National Historical Park** with HQ at Great Falls and the lower limit of the **Piedmont District** with HQ at Sharpsburg, MD.

The Darby Mill and a warehouse were below the lock on the berm. There was a country store across the lock on the towpath.

In canal operating days, the canal from Lock 35 to Lock 23 was watered from **Dam 3 above Harpers Ferry.** The **Virginia Free Press** of 27 Aug. 1828 requested bids from contractors for the construction of the canal from Rushville (Violettes Lock) to Harpers Ferry. Progress was noted in a letter dated 1 Nov. 1833 from C&O **Supt. Charles B. Fisk** from Rushville reporting, "The water from the feeder above Harpers Ferry is now within one mile of this place . . . Boats will be able to leave Harpers Ferry in three days." On 14 Nov. he reported by letter to Washington that boats with 2' draft could navigate the canal and suggested draining the canal and making repairs after Christmas.

Historic winter view of Lock No. 6 (Magazine Lock).

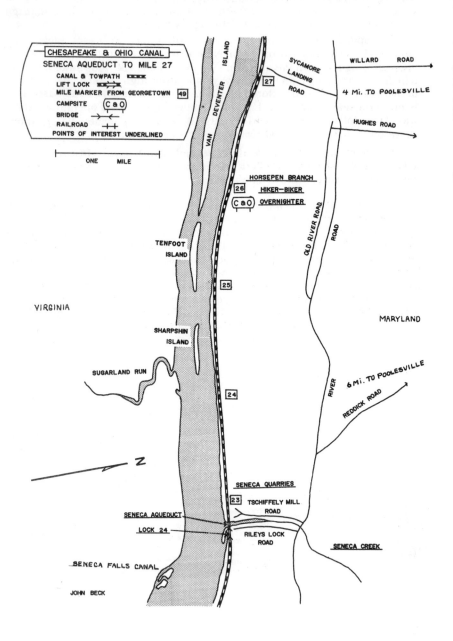

CHESAPEAKE & OHIO CANAL
SENECA AQUEDUCT TO MILE 27

CANAL & TOWPATH
LIFT LOCK
MILE MARKER FROM GEORGETOWN 49
CAMPSITE C & O
BRIDGE
RAILROAD
POINTS OF INTEREST UNDERLINED

ONE MILE

VAN DEVENTER ISLAND

WILLARD ROAD

SYCAMORE LANDING ROAD

27

4 MI. TO POOLESVILLE

HUGHES ROAD

HORSEPEN BRANCH
HIKER–BIKER
OVERNIGHTER
26
C & O

OLD RIVER ROAD

TENFOOT ISLAND

25

VIRGINIA

SHARPSHIN ISLAND

MARYLAND

SUGARLAND RUN

24

RIVER ROAD

6 MI. TO POOLESVILLE
REDDICK ROAD

N

SENECA QUARRIES

23 TSCHIFFELY MILL ROAD

SENECA AQUEDUCT

LOCK 24

RILEYS LOCK ROAD

SENECA CREEK

SENECA FALLS CANAL

JOHN BECK

(Mileage figures from tide-lock are indicated in the small boxes on the maps and in bold face type in the text.)

Flour from the Tschiffely Mill on Seneca Creek was boated down to Washington on the canal. The mill burned circa 1956. (National Park Service)

22.88 The road across the canal goes to several points of interest: at 0.2 mi. from the towpath the road forks; right fork leads to Tschiffely Rd. and to the **old Tschiffely mill site** .8 mi. away at River Rd. The left fork leads around the edge of a swamp, formed by the silting in of an old **boat basin** in the canal, a popular spot for bird observation. The swamp is filling in rapidly; it will eventually reach the point where it could once again be dredged out for a basin without destroying the swamp – nature is taking care of that. On the far side of the swamp are the interesting ruins (off limits) of the Seneca Stone Cutting Mill. Farther along the road, the hillside to the right has many old quarry openings.

22.93 The boat basin was the scene of an accident in 1897 when the passenger packet ANNA WILSON, picking up steam after passing through Rileys Lock, collided with a downstream freight boat loaded with watermelons. The steamboat sank without serious injuries to the passengers, but local people had a ball collecting free watermelons floating in the basin.

SENECA STONE CUTTING MILL

The stone cutting mill was the center of one of the industries associated with the canal. It operated from about 1850 to around the early 1900s. Red (mostly) and some grey sandstone milled here was used in many of the structures of the C & O Canal, the Potomac Company Canal at Great Falls, Va., and many public buildings in Washington; stone for the latter was boated down the canal. The stone cut in the mill was quarried at Goose Creek in Va., Marble Quarry (above Whites Ferry) and Cedar Point Quarry (near Violettes Lock) as well as the quarries in the immediate vicinity.

A water turbine, powered by canal water diverted into a mill race, rotated a shaft running through the center of the building. Belts attached to overhead pulleys transferred water power from the shaft to milling and polishing machines. Gondolas pulled by mules and pushed by men carried large stone blocks along narrow gauge rails to the mill; the remains of the strap iron rails can be traced from a nearby quarry. The stone blocks were shaped by hammer and stone chisels before cutting by toothless saws of tempered steel. The saws were 6' long, 8" wide and 3/16" thick. An overhead pipe dripped water on the

57

saws to keep them cool. A former workman at the mill reported that if a saw cut 1" in 1 hour in a 3'-square block, that was progress! By 1910 the better quality stone from the quarries had already been quarried and cut.

Claude W. Owen, in the **History of Potomac**, said, "When I was quite young I saw the quarry and mill in operation. They had no modern tools for quarrying. Of course no electricity for drilling the stone. I have seen a colored man sit on a large block of stone, sometimes as large as a six foot cube, with three powerfully built colored men armed with heavy sledge hammers striking in rhythm a drill the seated man held in his hands. The slightest miscalculation by either of the three meant a badly broken leg, but it never seems to have happened. The mill was powered by a large wheel propelled by the water overflow from the basin. After passing the mill wheel, the water traveled down hill to Seneca Creek, less than a hundred yards away and on to the river."

A joint development plan is being carried out between the State of Maryland (which owns the Stone Cutting Mill and adjacent property) and the National Park Service).

For towpath conditions or other questions concerning the canal between Seneca and Williamsport, call the Piedmont District Office (NPS) or 301-432-2136.

TSCHIFFELY MILL

Several mills have been located at the site of Tschiffely Mill near the W. end of the River Rd. bridge over Seneca Creek. Earlier mills were the Mitford Mill and (Ulton) Darbys Mill, the latter of which was acquired by W. B. Tschiffely c1900. One of the early mills burned during the Civil War and was rebuilt thereafter from the timbers of the Duffief Mill which had been located on Muddy Branch. The Tschiffely Mill was operated until 1931. Water for the mill was impounded ½ mi. up Seneca Creek, and undoubtedly was carried by a flume to the head race, creating a fall of 13'. The head race remains may now be found in the incinerator of the Pooles General Store on the N. side of River Rd. The mill was located just across River Rd., but was destroyed sometime after 1956. Worthington Tschiffely (son of W. B.) once said that the migration of eels from Seneca Creek to the river would get in the head race in such numbers that they would interfere with the operation of the mill.

23.03 End of the swamp. Quarries ahead were worked from 1774.

23.10 Beginning of the extensive loading and retaining walls of the quarry operations. Quarries in ascending order were John P.C. Peter's, Government's, Peter's, Georgetown College's, West, and Lee's.

23.33 Historic Culvert #35 on Sec. 36, 8' span (Bull Run). Culverts #35 to #71 were built in 1831. The path across the canal bed leads to the **foundations of an old mill** on the left side of the ravine and an old quarry on the right. Quarry openings continue on up the berm side of the canal for some distance. **The first extensive quarrying took place in the 1780s when the Potomac Canal at Great Falls was under construction; some quarrying may have been done in the Revolutionary Period.** Remains of stone masonry walls along the berm testify to **old loading areas.** The sheer cliffs ahead are of red sandstone (Triassic), the source of stone for the Seneca Stone Cutting Mill.

The level from Lock 24 to Lock 25 was known as the 'Eight Mile Level'. (A level is the section of canal between locks.)

23.43 The spring on the berm is accessible but marshy. Caution – on a trip to the spring a **copperhead** narrowly missed daughter Betsy several years ago while picking up a stick across the (unseen) snake (and on her birthday, yet!). Copperheads are common in rocky (usually dry) areas, but also sometimes on the towpath itself. **Blacksnakes** are common on the towpath and adjacent trees.

58

The aggressive **eastern water snake** (which is sometimes mistaken for a copperhead or water moccasin) is common in swampy or watered areas of the canal. The **cotton-mouth water moccasin** is reported by the State of Maryland to exist in swampy areas in Maryland, but I have not as yet seen one on the canal. **Rattlesnakes (Eastern timber)** are very rare in the Potomac Valley. I have heard of only one sighting on the canal.

23.7x Masonry walls on the berm end.

23.81 Pretty river site, previously one of a series of 40 campsites between Seneca and Tenfoot Island, now a pleasant picnic spot. **Caution: Camping is permitted only at designated areas.** The hill on the right recedes as the river flat continues upstream for 6 miles, extending inland as much as 1 mi., a southward shift of the Potomac in recent geological time. The far edge of the flat is followed by River Rd. and is marked by numerous swampy areas where wood ducks, pileated woodpeckers and prothonotary warblers nest. See Fairfax Harrison's *Old Prince William* for information on Potomac River ferries and river lore.

THE POTOMAC RIVER IN MONTGOMERY COUNTY

Montgomery County is entirely in the Piedmont Physiographic Province. The river is generally swift-flowing. One hundred and thirty-six islands are located in the river in this county, 101 of them being smaller than five acres. Primary shoreline woody vegetation includes sycamore, maple, willow, elm, cottonwood, white ash, green ash, hickory, walnut, paw paw and pin oak. Principal submerged shallow water aquatic vegetation includes water willow, pickerel weed, bull rush, lizard tail, spatter dock, rose mallow, cattail and hibiscus.

The numerous undeveloped islands in this region, and the contiguous band of relatively undisturbed shoreline woodland between the canal and the river provide large amounts of excellent habitat for numerous fur-bearing species, song birds, waterfowl, predatory birds and reptiles. The beaver, an animal sensitive to unnatural disturbances, has its highest population concentration on the Potomac River in Montgomery County. Other fur-bearers found along the river and canal include fox squirrel, grey squirrel, mink, raccoon, otter, deer, fox, oppossum and muskrat. The principal sportfish found in the Potomac in this stretch are sucker, perch, carp, catfish, smallmouth bass and sunfish. Believe it or not, the Potomac River in Montgomery County has been declared to have 'excellent' water quality by the Md. Dept. of Natural Resources; at least water quality is gradually improving in the Potomac.

23.92 Historic Culvert #37 on Sec. 37 (Beaver Dam Creek), 10′ span. Worth crossing the canal bed to see the inflow (entrance) of the culvert, and, because of the exposure of the culvert barrel, you can see how part of the culvert is constructed. Nice view of the widewater lake created by Dam No. 2 below Seneca.

24.34-24.64 Wooded Sharpshin Island, aptly describes this little sliver of land in mid-Potomac. The topography of the Potomac islands changes with floods which extend the islands downstream. A comparison of recent topographic maps with those of 80 years ago reveals considerable changes in some of the islands.

24.96-25.63 Wooded Tenfoot Island, larger than its name implies, is probably named for its elevation. During Prohibition, a **moonshine still** was operated on the island, with the smell of fermenting mash permeating the air on both shores on which concrete ramps allowed the unloading of raw materials

59

and the loading of the distilled product. The still was never raided and moonshiner Earl Blatt retired to live happily ever after.

25.01 Fine stands of the uncommon trillium or wake robin (Trillium erectum) bloom in April in shaded areas adjacent to the canal and towpath; also at 25.34). The odor is unpleasant, giving the common names of 'stinking Benjamin' or 'stinking Willie'. Whistling swans and Canadian geese have been sighted along here.

25.63-27.65 Van Deventer Island (known earlier as **Gassaways Island**), on which Curtis Jenkins ran a moonshine still.

25.70 Winslow Archaeological Site – The name applied to an **Indian Village** once located adjacent to the canal. Members of the Southwestern Branch of the Archaeological Society of Md. excavated this area 1950-1962. Hundreds of artifacts were recovered within the stockade of the village: projectile points, knives, scrapers, awls, crude and refined pottery. Both banks of the Potomac and islands in the river reveal Indian cultures from 500 BC to 1500 AD. WARNING: Private digging is against Federal Law in a National Park.

25.91 Wooded **Md. Fish and Game Management Area. Caution – hunting in season.** Note blue phlox and trillium blooming in April.

26.00 Horsepen Branch Hiker-Biker Overnighter; the farthest downstream of this series of camping areas. Nearest road access is Sycamore Landing at mile 22.21. These primitive camps, usually intentionally located away from public road access, consist of a leveled area, fireplace, pump, picnic table, toilet. They are available on a first-come, first-served basis. The next campsite upstream is Chisel Branch at mile 30.5; downstream, a temporary site at Violettes Lock at mile 22.80. Water at Hiker-Bikers available May-October.

26.77 Historic Culvert #38 on Sec. 43 (Horsepen Branch), 10' span. The line of the canal from Georgetown to Cumberland was divided into three

Canal boats going up the canal near Edwards Ferry in the early 1900s. (Thompson Collection, National Park Service)

60

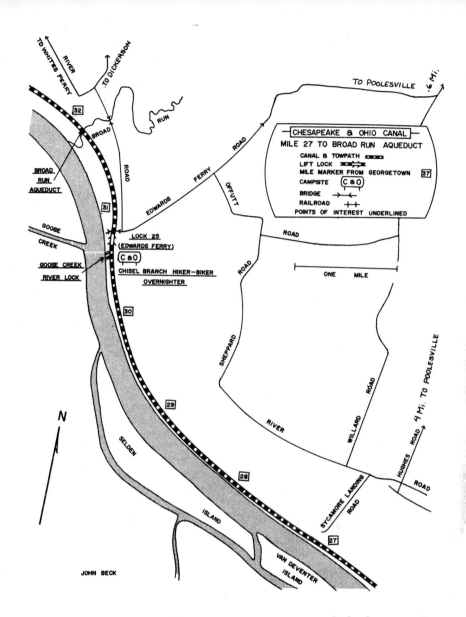

divisions of 120 sections each. A separate contract was made for the excavation of each section, the average section being ½ mi. long. Culverts were similarly identified with the numbers of the sections on which built, this particular one being on Section 43. Up to Harpers Ferry the canal was 60' wide at the top and 42' at the bottom, making for longer culverts than on the 50' wide canal above Harpers Ferry.

26.94 Brightwells Hunting Quarters – a 1,086-acre tract with a 4 mi. river frontage patented in 1695 by Richard Brightwell. The original stone boundary marker was destroyed during the building of the canal; a replacement stone is said to have been sunk later in the canal bed.

61

27.21 Sycamore Island. A footbridge across the canal bed provides access to Sycamore Landing Road through **McKee-Beshers Wildlife Area** – a favored spot for bird observers. Careful, as this is a game management area which has produced record deer. Archaeologists excavated the N end of Van Deventer Island, opposite Sycamore Landing, in 1941 and 1958. To reach **Hughes Hollow**, another favorite spot of bird observers, go up Sycamore Landing Rd and turn right on River Rd. .4 mi. to Hughes Rd. where turn right 1 mi. to old River Rd. For the next 1½ mi. downriver there is a series of small lakes and ponds with paths along the tops of dikes. Bluebirds and red-headed woodpeckers, the latter uncommon and a locally endangered species, continue to be sighted.

27.65-29.86 Seldon Island. Archaeological sites excavated have been identified as 'Woodland Culture'.

27.75 Archaeological excavations at Sheppard (also known as Beshers) site. Work was done on the site in 1936-37, 1952, 1955 and 1959. **A canal bisected the village at a point opposite the lower end of Selden Island** (unverified).

28.36 Ruins of an old building (possibly a barn) on the berm.

28.46 Historic Culvert #39 on Sec. 46, 3' span. Canal bed is lightly watered above; the amount of water varies with the season. Culvert repaired 1985.

29.35 Historic Culvert #41 on Sec. 48. 4' span #40 is missing in the culvert numbering series. This indicates two streams were tied into one culvert or one stream bed ceased to carry water, and a culvert was eliminated. This was a fairly common practice used to save money in culvert construction.

29.86 Historic Culvert #42 on Sec. 49 (Chisel Branch and Cabin Branch), 10' span. Road culverts such as this provided access for vehicles to places on the river side of the canal. Wherever possible, the culvert rested on natural rock. **Culvert foundations were of either stone or timber. Many of the culverts are beautiful masonry structures, the fine architecture of which is unseen by the passing hiker-biker. Take time to view and photograph or sketch them.**

30.5x Chisel Branch Hiker-Biker Overnighter. Nearest access is at Lock 25 (Edwards Ferry) about .3 mi. downstream. Next campsite upstream is Turtle Run at mile 34.4; downstream is Horsepen Branch at 26.0.

GOOSE CREEK RIVER LOCKS

30.64 Access: .2 mi. downstream from Lock 25 (Edwards Ferry). Across the silted basin are the two interesting river locks which admitted boats from the Potomac River and from Goose Creek on the opposite Va. shore. The **Goose Creek and Little River Navigation** (incorporated by Va. on 15 Mar. 1832) was actually a canalization of Goose Creek (and Little River). (A canalization uses the stream for navigation except at rapids, where short canals are built around obstructions.) The canals and locks of the Goose Creek and Little River Navigation are largely obliterated, though there is a guard lock and a two-lock combine near the Potomac River on the E. side of Goose Creek on the Va. side of the river and other locks on up Goose Creek.

River locks – the one opposite the Shenandoah River at Harpers Ferry and the one opposite Shepherdstown and the one at Goose Creek – were demanded by the Va. Legislature of 1833 to provide a market for Va. products in return for the purchase of C & O Canal stock.

The locks here were completed 1837-1838. There are indications that they were built to the specifications of 1837 (the first set of specifications being those of 1828, and the second set of 1830). The coping stones are Aquia freestone; other stones are roughly-cut, roughly-faced, and roughly-coursed Seneca sandstone. The Goose Creek River Locks are a two lift lock combine with a total lift (depending on the river level) of 15½', joined by a middle set of gates. (A combine is a set of two or more locks without intervening basins or levels.) Each lock is 90' 'in the clear', which means that a standard C & O freight boat or two Goose Creek type boats (an assumption) could pass through if the latter were no longer than 45'. Documentary evidence indicates that only one Goose Creek canal boat ever passed through the navigation on the Va. side, and evidence is lacking of C & O boats actually crossing into Goose Creek.

The upper lock appears to have an 8' lift with the lift of the lower lock depending on the river level, but normally 7½'. There is a four-gate waste weir (used to drain the canal for repairs or other reasons) at the upper end of the upper lock, having been put there after the lock was abandoned (otherwise boats could not have passed through the lock). There was a raised mule bridge over the inlet connecting with the C & O Canal, sufficiently high so as to allow boats to pass under. The bridge was burned by General Early's rear guard to prevent pursuit in 1864; the debris from the bridge was pushed into the canal. The C & O Canal prism is wide enough to allow boats to make the turn into or out of the lock, but there is a basin just above the river locks to facilitate that maneuver.

30.78 Ruin of granary on berm.

30.84 Ruin of a canal country store last operated by Gene Jarboe's 'boys', Sam and John. Gene Jarboe drowned in the canal while loading cattle. The store closed in 1906.

LOCK 25 (EDWARDS FERRY)

30.84 Access: From Poolesville 4.5 mi. on Edwards Ferry Rd.; 10 mi. from Seneca via River, Sheppard, Offutt and Edwards Ferry Roads, the latter of which crosses the canal and leads 100 yards to the old ferry landing, parking area, boat ramp and toilets; no water. Lock 25 is 8.04 mi. above Lock 24 and 8.53 mi. below Lock 26. Named for old Edwards Ferry which operated on the Potomac 1791-1836. **Martin's Gazeteer** of 1835 lists an Edwards Ferry post office on each side of the Potomac. The river slackwater here is ⅜ mi. wide.

The Goose Creek River Locks provided access from the C&O Canal to the Goose Creek and Little River Navigation on the Virginia side of the river. Photo circa 1956. (National Park Service)

Lock 25 at Edwards Ferry was a thriving small center of activity during canal operating days. Note the pivot bridge, the rubbing timbers alongside the towpath which prevented the tow-rope from snagging and the whitewash on the bridge and the lock. Photo early 1900s.
(Hahn Collection)

The lock was probably completed in 1831. Bolts in the coping (top layer of stones) indicate that the lock was raised 6″ by bolting timbers on top. This was probably due to a silting problem necessitating a greater depth in the water in the lock. There is also evidence of timbers having been bolted at the lower end of the lock walls to minimize damage to the lock in case a boat hit it.

Lock 25 was the first lock to be extended in length so as to lock through two boats at a time, in one direction. Of the 14 locks so extended, 11 were extended at the lower end as here, and three at the upper end. The lock extensions were done in a period of relative canal affluence under the enterprising engineer, Hutton. All the locks from Lock 25 to 32 were extended as were others on up the canal. Locks extended at the upper ends had drop gates, but the locks extended at the lower end as at Lock 25 probably had swing (mitre gates) as a 15′ drop gate would have been very hard to handle. A drop gate at the upper end would have been 7′ high (5′ depth of water plus 2′ freeboard between the water surface to the top of the lock coping), whereas a drop gate at the lower end would have to have had this 7′ plus the 8′ lift of the lock to account for.

The lock extension was made of Seneca rubble and stone-filled wooden cribs. Little remains of the extension and its lower lock gates except for the windrow (pile of stones) which filled the cribs. Where the stone from these extensions has been pirated for other purposes, leaving no windrow of stones, we still are able to determine which locks were extended downstream by the location of the mule rise (the part of the towpath which goes uphill to the lock) which in the case of the extended locks is 120′ downstream (the overall length of the extended lock) from its normal position. The mule rise accommodates the difference in height (or lift) between two locks; all other points on the towpath are about level.

64

Jarboes store was a typical country store supplying canal boats and neighboring farms as well.
Photo 1971 (Hahn)

Lock 25 was built of red Seneca sandstone. As were all the locks below here, except for Lock 13, this lock was built originally with a masonry by-pass culvert (or a channel) inside the lock walls. These culverts had an opening in the lock wall just above the lock gate to take in water and three openings in the lock walls proper to discharge the water, the purpose being to speed up the locking through process. Unfortunately, these culverts and their openings silted up and were easily jammed with debris, so that this method of filling a lock was eventually abandoned.

The lock house on the towpath side at the upper end of the lock is of brick, 1½ stories over a full basement, 18′-8″ x 31′-6″, a bit larger than the 18 x 30′ standard. The bypass flume (the ditch which carried excess water around the lock) and the area above are grassy and attractively landscaped. There is evidence of a boat basin about 150′ square dug into the berm bank just above the lock. This was probably the location of the canal company scow, which we know from historical records was moored here to provide access across the canal to Edwards Ferry. The scow was replaced with a bridge early in the historic operating period. In 1839 the pivot bridge here (it pivoted on the berm side of the lock) was so decayed as to be unfit for use. The bridge was vital because travelers on an important country road connecting Maryland and Virginia crossed at Edwards Ferry. The bridge was later replaced with a 'small horse bridge', but wagons were compelled to make a detour of six miles to cross the canal at Conrads Ferry (Whites Ferry). No additional difficulty was experienced with the Edwards Ferry bridge until 1850 when stronger abutments had to be constructed. The Civil War was hard on the Edwards Ferry bridge, as it was located at one of the principal crossings of the Potomac. This unusually heavy traffic seriously damaged the structure, and it was rebuilt in a "good and substantial manner." On the return to Virginia from the raid that had carried his corps to the approaches of Washington, Lieutenant General Jubal Early in July, 1864, crossed his infantry and artillery at Conrad's Ferry and his cavalry at Edwards Ferry. Former locktenders John Walters and Charlie Poole ran a store in a wood frame house on the berm side after Jarboe's store closed in 1906.

Waste weirs such as this one above Lock 25 at Edwards Ferry were used to drain the canal in winter and when the level needed repair. Some waste weirs were probably originally made of wood, others of stone, as this one. Concrete began to appear on the canal circa 1906. The weirs were often built near a lock so as to provide easy access to the lock tender.
Photo 1971 (Hahn)

30.89 Waste Weir and Culvert #43, separated by a few feet of stone masonry retaining wall. This 6′ culvert (in 1976 protected from further damage by an earthen dam across the canal bed) was built on a wooden foundation. The stretch beyond here is peaceful; not as exciting in canal features as some others, but offers attractive secluded woods and a nice walk along the old fences alongside the towpath. The hike to Broad Run Trunk (about two miles round trip) makes a nice Sunday afternoon walk. Note field pennycress, harbinger of spring, shepherd's purse, and buttercup above NPS mile marker 31.

BROAD RUN TRUNK (Wooden Aqueduct)

31.94 Access: From Lock 25, 1.1 mi. below. The setting is very attractive with Broad Run flowing clear. **One of the most interesting features of the canal –** a wooden aqueduct. The structure was originally a double culvert built of twin 16′ arches and listed as Culvert #44 – the only two-span culvert on the canal. In 1846 a flood washed out the culvert and a wooden trunk was hurriedly thrown across the span to allow canal traffic to continue. The temporary structure was replaced by another wooden trunk in the winter of 1856. This was burned in the Civil War, but was quickly replaced to permit movement of troops and supplies. In its later configuration it was a wooden trunk about 8′-5″ in height and 30′-2″ in length over red sandstone walls (as it is now). Though it is not classified as an aqueduct, it serves as one and I consider it as such. Rebuilt.

31.95 Concord. An 1106-acre tract beginning 100 yds. above the mouth of Broad Run was patented on 26 April 1721 to Daniel Dulaney.

32.04 We pass the first cultivated field (a turf farm) since leaving Seneca.

Broad Run Trunk (aqueduct) was originally a twinned-culvert, the only one like it on the canal, or perhaps anywhere. Photo taken 1950s. (Hahn Collection)

32.43 **Site of lost Culvert #45** on Sec. 54 (Abrahams Branch), 10' span. Culvert traces are now completely gone except for the outflow ditch from the towpath to the river. The creek now enters directly into the canal bed carrying much debris. It turns and flows 'upstream' for some 1.54 mi., where it has breached Culvert #47. Many of the 'lost culverts' apparently were abandoned because of the tremendous amounts of silt which were carried, making the cleaning out of the culvert almost mandatory after each heavy rain. **One thing we must appreciate in the operation and maintenance of historic canals is that hydraulic control features must be added or deleted (whether or not the canal is watered)** as the surrounding drainage patterns change.

32.73 Pedestrian bridge leads to a farm road.

32.93 **Historic Culvert #46** on Sec. 55, 3' span. There are notable wildflowers the next 3 mi. This is also a good area for observing owls (including the barred owl), raccoons, deer, groundhogs, rabbits, squirrel, moles and flying squirrel. The turf farms ahead (an extensive industry in the area) attract shore birds during fall migration.

33.18 **Hailstone Site** of excavations for Indian artifacts in the flat area between the canal and river, slightly below Harrison Island. (Private digging is illegal.) NPS mileage markers and those in the guide may vary from place to place as they do at NPS mile marker 33 (ours were taken by an accurate measuring wheel)! Canal ahead returns to parallel the river.

33.27-35.1x **Harrison Island,** paralleling the canal for about the next two miles, is perhaps the largest island in the Potomac River. Heater Island below Point of Rocks (mileage 46.85) was closely related to Harrison Island in the days of Indian occupation. Though both islands are on the Md. tax rolls, the approaches to both is by ferry from the Va. shore.

The **Piscataway (Canoy) tribe** fled to Harrison and Heater Islands in the 1690's. The main fort at the upper end of Heater Island was described by Vandercastle and Harrison, representatives of the Governor of Md., as being 50

67

to 60 yds. square and containing 18 'cabbins', with 9 additional cabins outside the stockade. A smallpox epidemic in 1705 decimated the colony. They were no match for the **Tuscarora Indians** who arrived from the Carolinas in 1711, occupying the Canoy Islands (Harrison and Heater) until 1713 when they continued northward leaving behind a legacy of a few place names along the Potomac.

The **Battle of Balls Bluff** on the Va. shore opposite Harrison Island was one of the bloodiest and earliest (Oct. 1861) Civil War battles, with the Union forces failing to take their objective. It is said a flotilla of canal boats (unconfirmed) was assembled by Gen. Charles P. Stone, five boats of which were built at Philip Hauger's warehouse (location unknown). The barges were hauled from

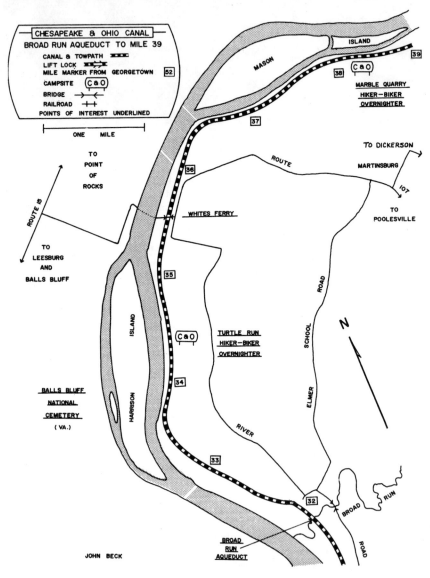

CHESAPEAKE & OHIO CANAL
BROAD RUN AQUEDUCT TO MILE 39

CANAL & TOWPATH
LIFT LOCK
MILE MARKER FROM GEORGETOWN 52
CAMPSITE C&O
BRIDGE
RAILROAD
POINTS OF INTEREST UNDERLINED

ONE MILE

ISLAND
MASON
C&O 38   39
MARBLE QUARRY
HIKER–BIKER
OVERNIGHTER

37
TO
POINT
OF
ROCKS
36
ROUTE
TO DICKERSON
MARTINSBURG
107
TO
POOLESVILLE

ROUTE 15
WHITES FERRY
35
TO
LEESBURG
AND
BALLS BLUFF

ISLAND
C&O
TURTLE RUN
HIKER–BIKER
OVERNIGHTER
SCHOOL   ROAD
N

BALLS BLUFF
NATIONAL
CEMETERY
(VA.)

HARRISON
34
ELMER
RIVER

33
32
BROAD RUN
ROAD

JOHN BECK
BROAD
RUN
AQUEDUCT

68

the canal (perhaps at Goose Creek River Lock?) to transport troops across the river; many drowned when a boat capsized during the evacuation. Canal **legend has it that this area is haunted by the spirits of departed soldiers and** overnight stops on the canal at this point were avoided.

BIRDS NOTED IN THIS STRETCH OF CANAL:

Blackbird, Brewer's
Blackbird, Red-winged
Bluebird, Eastern
Bobwhite
Bunting, Indigo
Cardinal
Catbird
Chat, Yellow-breasted
Chickadee, Carolina
Cowbird, Brown-headed
Creeper, Brown
Crow, Common
Crow, Fish
Cuckoo, Black-billed
Cuckoo, Yellow-billed
Dove, Mourning
Duck, Mallard
Duck, Wood
Flicker, Yellow-shafted
Flycatcher, Acadian
Flycatcher, Alder
Flycatcher, Great crested
Flycatcher, Least
Gnatcatcher, Blue-gray
Goldfinch, American
Goose, Canada
Grackle, Purple
Grosbeak, Rose-breasted
Gull, Herring
Gull, Ring-billed
Hawk, Red-shouldered
Heron, Great blue
Heron, Green
Heron, Little Blue
Heron, Yellow-crowned night
Hummingbird, Ruby-throated
Junco, Slate-colored
Killdeer
Kingbird, Eastern
Kingfisher, belted
Kinglet, Ruby-crowned
Martin, Purple
Meadowlark, Eastern
Mockingbird
Nuthatch, White-breasted
Oriole, Baltimore
Pewee, Eastern Wood
Phoebe

Redstart, American
Robin
Sapsucker, Yellow-bellied
Sparrow, Chipping
Sparrow, Field
Sparrow, House
Sparrow, Song
Sparrow, Swamp
Starling
Swallow, Bank
Swallow, Barn
Swallow, Rough-winged
Swift, Chimney
Tanager, Scarlet
Thrasher, Brown
Thrush, Wood
Titmouse, Tufted
Towhee, Rufous-sided
Veery
Vireo, Blue-headed
Vireo, Red-eyed
Vireo, Warbling
Vireo, White-eyed
Vireo, Yellow-throated
Vulture, Black
Vulture, Turkey
Warbler, Black-and-white
Warbler, Blackpoll
Warbler, Black-throated blue
Warbler, Canada
Warbler, Hooded
Warbler, Kentucky
Warbler, Myrtle
Warbler, Parula
Warbler, Prothonotary
Warbler, Worm-eating
Waterthrush, Louisiana
Waterthrush, Northern
Whip-poor-will
Woodpecker, Downy
Woodpecker, Hairy
Woodpecker, Pileated
Woodpecker, Red-bellied
Woodpecker, Red-headed
Wren, Carolina
Wren, House
Yellowthroat

TREES NOTED:

American beech	Cork elm	Red maple
Ash	Honey locust	Silver maple
Ash leafed maple	Mountain ash	Tree of Heaven
Black locust	Norway maple	Tulip tree
Black walnut	Pawpaw	White oak
Box elder	Red alder	

33.38 Evidence of an **old ford to Harrison Island.** This area is quite secluded giving a feeling of being quite close to nature.

33.68 Historic Culvert #46½ on Sec. 57, 2′ span, box culvert (uncommon). Note the use of '½'. If a culvert needed to be added to the existing system, a '½' was added to the nearest culvert number downstream. Changes in runoff through the years sometimes changed the need for adding or deleting culverts.

34.01 Historic Culvert #47 on Sec. 57, 6′ span. This may be the Hillary Farm Culvert spoken of in old records.

34.28 Historic Culvert #47½ on Sec. 57, 3′ span. Wooden floor is in place. This is the beginning of a notable wildflower area.

34.43 Turtle Run Hiker-Biker Overnighter. Road access at Whites Ferry at mile 35.50. Next campsite upstream is Marble Quarry at mile 38.12; downstream is Chisel Branch at 30.5.

34.50 Historic Culvert #48 on Sec. 58, 4′ span, skewed 20° to the run of the canal. (Culverts are normally at a right angle to the towpath.)

34.82 Historic Culvert #49 on Sec. 58, 10′ span. Believed to have served as a road culvert to Conrads (Whites) Ferry about 1 mi. above; high water in the river limited its use to the dry season

34.90 Harrison Island fish trap extends from the upper part of the island to the Md. shore. A Mr. Nelson reported Indians repairing the fish trap in 1724. Indian fish traps were sometimes used as sluices by the Potomac Company in its improvement of Potomac River navigation, sometimes widening them at the constructed end.

35.03 Historic Culvert #50 on Sec. 59, 4′ span. Generations of farm trash in the inflow. This will someday be a future archaeologist's delight as it contains successive models of stoves, refrigerators, etc.

35.47 Historic Culvert #51 on Sec. 59, 9′ span. **This culvert is unique** and worth stopping to study for those interested in canal structures. The culvert consisted of stone arches under the towpath and the berm banks, with a wooden culvert supported by vertical stone walls in between. The canal bed itself was also made of wood. It has to be seen to be appreciated. (As with most structures winter and early spring are the best times for examining and photographing because of the absence of foliage, and also little threat from snakes and poisonous plants.)

35.49 Pass under an **old iron, wood-planked road bridge on red sandstone.** Until after the Civil War access to Conrads Ferry was provided by a culvert. A year before the end of the war, General Supt Spates estimated that it would cost $700 to construct a wooden bridge to replace the culvert (probably Culvert #49, .67 mile below) which was "very much filled up so that carriages and wagons could not pass through it." Such a bridge was built in 1855 or 1856, but soon proved unsatisfactory because the grade was so steep that it was impossible for

Whites Ferry Road Bridge was built to accommodate traffic which originally had to pass through a road culvert. This bridge saw much traffic in the Civil War. Photo taken 1950s. (Hahn Collection)

heavily-laden wagons to ascend. When the condition was corrected in 1871, additional 'trestles' were positioned under the bridge, but a space of 20' was left for the passage of boats. As the bridge had a clearance of 11'-6" and the minimum clearance for bridges was 12', this condition was corrected at the same time. By 1876 a new bridge was needed and the iron bridge now in place was built; it was opened to traffic in June of that year. The new bridge eliminated the piers which were an impediment to navigation, and used instead the present-day abutments. This bridge is an eloquent statement of the iron-railing technology of the mid-1870's.

WHITES FERRY

35.50 **Access:** From Poolesville 6 mi. W. on Whites Ferry Rd. (Md. 107) or from Edwards Ferry (Lock 25) 5.1 mi. on River Rd. Some parking, boat ramp (fee). Whites Ferry Store carries light food and supplies, Towpath Guides (naturally), etc. Telephone. Ferry To Va. operates the year around, 6 a.m. to 11 p.m. Fare $1.75 (1984). Whites Ferry has been in operation close to 150 years. Canoes and bikes for rent. Tel. 301-349-5200.

This granary at Whites Ferry was used to load canal boats tied up to its wall. The building no longer exists, but the foundations have been stabilized. Photo 1960s. (Hahn Collection)

Originally known as Conrads Ferry, it became Whites Ferry sometime after the Civil War when Lt. Col. E. V. White of Va. took over. Gen. Early, after whom the boat GENERAL JUBAL EARLY is named, is thought to have made his main crossing at Whites Ford 3.5 mi. upstream rather than here. The present boat was put into operation in 1954. **This is the last regular ferry operation on the Potomac, where there were once about 100.**

35.53 Site of **Whites Ferry Indian Village #3** is in the flat between the canal and the river. Areas such as this, where the canal bed has been cleared, grow up quickly unless kept maintained. Leaving mature trees in the canal prism is one solution.

Stabilized granary ruins on the berm. Canal boats tied up to iron rings fixed in the granary wall. Chutes from the granary loaded grain directly into canal boats. The building was of wood, 34' wide by 138' long, supported by a red sandstone foundation.

Whites Ferry boat, the GENERAL JUBAL EARLY, provides transportation across the Potomac River between Maryland and Virginia. Though there were originally about 100 ferries on the Potomac, this is the last one in full-time operation. (Courtesy of W. H. Shank)

35.67 Historic **Culvert #52** on Sec. 60, 4' span. Watch for snake plant and ageratum in March and asters and touch-me-nots in Sept.-Oct. Jack-in-the-pulpit in April.

35.74 This may have been the **site of lost Culvert #52½** on Sec. 60, another road culvert, providing access to Conrads Ferry, and abandoned some 109 years ago.

35.79 Historic **Culvert #53** on Sec. 61, 4' span. Osage orange hedge on the river side of the towpath. The canal bed is sometimes sparsely watered. Moss algae, chickweed and water cress form a green cover at times when there is water.

36.00 **Whites Ferry Indian Village Site #2** was on the river flat.

36.25 Site of **Whites Ferry Indian Village #1** on the bluff overlooking the river.

36.42-38.15 **Lower Mason Island.** One of the largest islands in the Potomac, still farmed. Just above here is a fine stand of Virginia cowslip (Mertensia virginica), or blue bell, which blooms in the latter half of April.

72

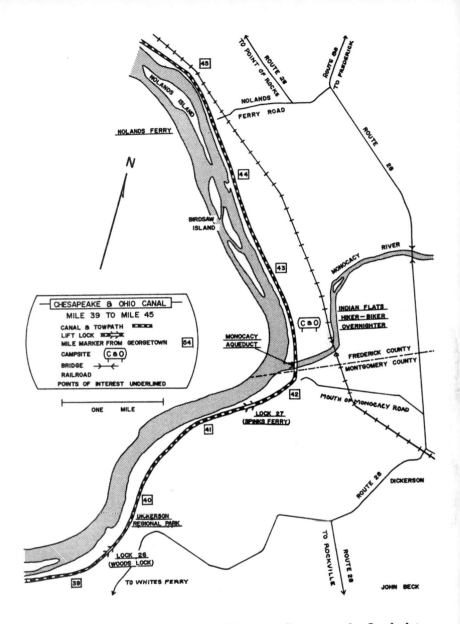

CHESAPEAKE & OHIO CANAL
MILE 39 TO MILE 45

CANAL & TOWPATH
LIFT LOCK
MILE MARKER FROM GEORGETOWN 54
CAMPSITE C&O
BRIDGE
RAILROAD
POINTS OF INTEREST UNDERLINED

ONE   MILE

JOHN BECK

Bluebells are among the loveliest and showiest flowers on the flood plains, their principal habitat.

36.56 Historic Culvert #54 on Sec. 62, rebuilt in 1973. It is important that culverts be repaired and restored, for their operation is necessary to carry streams under the canal whether or not the canal is watered. This is one of the best investments the Park Service can make.

36.93 Historic Culvert #56 on Sec. 63, 6′ span was replaced by the canal co. in 1914 with a 3′ dia. pipe which carries the stream from the adjacent berm fields. Stand of beech trees beyond on the berm at mile 37.15.

37.67 Cliff on the berm, first seen in some miles. These high red cliffs of Triassic sandstone constrict the course of the canal where the Potomac is now only a stone's throw away. Fine stands of Dutchman's-breeches (*Dicentra cucullaria*), blooming in April. Abundant wildlife.

38.15-38.86 Upper Mason Island; a narrow channel separates this from Lower Mason Island. Upper Mason Island is also known as Oxley's Island or Ox Island.

38.17 Historic Culvert #60 on Sec. 65, 4' span.

38.2x Marble Quarry Hiker-Biker Overnighter. Nearest access from Dickerson Regional Park at mile 39.63. Next campsite upstream is Indian Flats at mile 42.5; downstream is Turtle Run at 34.4. Marble Quarry is noted for its fanglomerate (conglomerate) limestone breccia, used in the Statuary Hall of the U.S. Capitol.

38.35 Fine cliff on the berm, with a heavy growth of polypody fern (Polypodium vulgare) and saxifrage (Saxifraga virginiensis).

38.72 Historic Culvert #63 on Sec. 66, 8' span carries a stream from a wooded ravine. This and the two preceding culverts give access to a large, unbroken hilly forest on the berm for further exploration. There were six Indian fish traps in the river from here to Brunswick.

39.17 Waste Weir. Site of lost culvert #64. on Sec. 68. Blue phlox ahead. Bald eagle sighted 1984.

LOCK 26 (Woods Lock)

39.37 Access: Fm MD 28 1.1 mile S of Dickerson take Martinsburg Rd. .2 mi., then take dirt rd. .3 mi. to parking lot; Lock 26 is .28 mi. below. Lock 26 is 8.53 mi. above Lock 25 and 2.09 mi. below Lock 27. Lock is built of red (and some grey) sandstone boated 17 mi. up from the Seneca quarries. The lock house, which was wood frame over a red sandstone rubble wall basement, burned in 1969. An old road leads up from behind the lock house ruins .9 mi. to Md. Route 419. Lock is temporarily filled in.

Lock 26 (Woods Lock) is in a peaceful rural setting. The lock house burned a number of years ago, but the foundations have been stabilized. Photo 1959. (Hahn Collection)

Lock was probably completed in 1831, apparently to the 1828 lock specifications in its lower portion, for the three culvert openings are visible in the lower course of stone in each lock wall. However, the upper portion of the lock seems to have been built according to the specifications of 1830. Locks 26 and 27 seem to be the only locks known to have been built to the specifications of both 1828 and 1830. Lock 26 was extended on the lower end by stone-filled wooden cribs in 1875. Lock has an 8' lift. Note wood replacements for a stone in the 2nd course (2nd row down) on the berm. We see this occasionally – and brick and concrete as well.

39.49 Abandoned waste weir is a good example of an old masonry and wood waste weir no longer needed at some point in the operating period. **May be an original.** Most, if not all, were replaced with concrete after 1906. The barely visible riprap and lowering of the towpath of about 1' here gives some indication that the abandoned waste weir may have been used as an informal overflow after being covered up. **The informal overflows were used to get rid of excess water and were known as 'mule drinks'.**

The river here is the possible site of old **Whites Ford,** which was the favorite crossing of the Potomac by Confederate armies. It was probably at Whites Ford (not Conrads Ferry) where Gen Lee crossed from Va. on 6 Sep. 1862; 'Jeb' Stuart on 12 Oct. 1862 and Gen Early on 14 July after his raid on Washington. Arrowhead, duckweed, and water plaintain in canal.

39.63 Historic Culvert #65 on Sec. 68, 12' span, located just below the parking lot for Dickerson Regional Park and the Potomac Warm Water Fishing Area. **This culvert is both 'skewed'** (at a diagonal to the canal rather than perpendicular as with most culverts) **and 'rifled' – the only one like it on the canal.** It has a springstone at the inflow with 1832 cut in the face; worth stopping to see. The path on the other side of the pedestrian bridge leads to a fishing hole in the Potomac. The canal bed is lightly watered above, with bass propagating nicely.

40.04 Historic Culvert #66 on Sec. 70, 6' span, at the lower end of the PEPCO Dickerson Generating Plant, long a site of controversy over fly ash dumped in the canal through the years, expansion of the plant and location of a sewage treatment plant. The fly ash was removed in 1974 and the **canal watered and landscaped in a better setting up to Lock 27.** Cliffs nice as well.

41.34 Historic Culvert #68 on Sec. 72, 6' span. Nicely restored in 1974. Hearts-a-bustin' shrub upstream.

LOCK NO. 27 (Spinks Ferry)

41.46 Access: From Monocacy Aqueduct .7 mi. upstream. Lock is 7.47 mi. below Lock 28 and 2.09 mi. above Lock 26. Referred to as 'Campbells Lock' (sometimes corrupted to 'Camels Lock') in old records. ('Old Man' (Jim?) Campbell was an Englishman.) Lock built of Seneca red sandstone in 1831, "Boated down 5 miles from a quarry near the river below the Point of Rocks, with the exception of the coping which is from Lee's Quarry near Seneca." (Yet other stone came from a quarry 2½ mi. inland which supplied stone for the Monocacy Aqueduct.) An old road grade parallels the canal on the berm. No traces of the pivot bridge which once crossed the lock and led to Spinks Ferry. Lock has 8' lift and was probably completed in 1831. Like Lock 26, work done prior to 1830 included laying culverts in sidewalls (Lock 27 is the uppermost so built) under 1828 specifications, with the breast wall above the upper gate recesses under 1830 specifications, due to lapses of contracts and work begun anew under different contractors. Lock stabilized by NPS in 1985.

75

Lock 27 (Spinks Ferry). This 1961 photo was taken prior to the rebuilding by the Park Service. (Historic American Building Survey)

This lock was extended a lock's length on the upper end – one of three (Locks 29 and 30 being the others) to be so extended in 1875. Upper extensions required that the breast wall and all walls above the breast wall be removed and the canal bed excavated an additional 8′ for the 100′ extension before the rock-filled, wooden cribs could be constructed. No such excavation of the canal nor change of original lock walls was necessary below a lock. Perhaps the explanation for an expensive upstream extension is that topography required it in certain places. Apparently, locks extended on the upper ends were equipped with drop gates in the extension and the stone-filled, timber cribs were double-planked with 2 layers of 2″ planking. Little remains above ground except for the windrow of stones with which they were filled. It is likely that the wooden cribs and planking are largely intact a few inches below soil level. The lock extends some 128′ above the upper end of the upper gate pocket. The remains of a cast iron wicket gate (of the extension's lock gate) appears about 98′ above the upper end of the upper gate pocket – about where one would expect to find it. Lock extensions probably were used for only a few years after declining use of the canal and mounting maintenance costs led to their abandonment.

The lock house is a 1½-story stone house over a full stone basement with end chimneys, on the towpath side of the lock at mid-lock. The level above (to Lock 27) was known as 'Eight Mile Level' though actually 7.47 mi. long. The tenant of a berm house once here said, "John Whalen was lock-tender here and Henry Collier was the level walker [the person who walked the towpath looking for leaks in the canal caused by muskrats or other problems]; Whalen's wife was found dead in the lock."

There was a canal co. move to discharge Lock-keeper Thomas Walter for collaboration with the Confederates during the Civil War, but a petition from his neighbors citing his efforts to save Monocacy Aqueduct prevented such an

This old building was once the Mouth of Monocacy Post Office and the Spellman Store at Monocacy Basin. Photo 1971 and the building has deteriorated rapidly since that time. (Hahn)

action. The story goes: Thomas Walter, upon hearing that Gen Hill's forces were to wreck the lock and Monocacy Aqueduct, pleaded with Hill not to destroy those structures but to cut down the bank instead and drain the canal. Hill finally agreed after learning that he had insufficient tools and gun powder to destroy the aqueduct, so he concentrated instead on Lock 27 where a hole was drilled into the masonry and a charge of powder detonated. Having destroyed Lock 27 (at least to the point of disrupting service), and having breached the Little Monocacy Aqueduct (between the lock and the aqueduct) and having burned a few canal boats trapped in the level, Hill recalled his troops on the evening of 2 Sept. 1862 and marched northward to Harpers Ferry. An unsuccessful attempt was made on 9 Sept. to destroy Monocacy Aqueduct when a detail of MGen Walker was unable to drill sufficient numbers of holes in the aqueduct in which to place powder in a short period of time.

41.52 Typical three-opening **waste weir.** These waste weirs were used to regulate the water level in the canal by providing an outlet for waste water and to drain the canal in winter. They were generally located on the towpath side of the river, though there were some waste weirs on the berm bank which voided excess water through a culvert, that is, such waste weirs were built at an existing culvert. Foundations of weirs on the towpath side were laid 2' below the bottom of the canal, with the top of the waste weir at towpath level. Slots in the walls of the weirs held stop planks for controlling the amount of water let out. Some weirs have wood floors and other concrete. The original waste weirs were made of stone (some may have been made of wood), later replaced with concrete or had concrete appliqued over the original masonry. Additional waste weirs were constructed (or abandoned) as the need arose.

41.59 Possible location of Spinks Ferry on the Potomac; the ferry probably operated before the canal was built and may have ceased operating in the 1830s. Wild flowers above here to the aqueduct: dead nettle, gill-over-the-ground, grape hyacinth, phlox, squirrel corn, Star of Bethlehem, veronica (speedwell), violets and yellow cordyalis.

41.80 Historical significance of the foundations and parts of walls of the house on the river side of the towpath unknown. Let me know if you find out!

41.97 Historic Culvert #69 on Sec. 73, Little Monocacy, 20' span, completed 1832. Fine broad wooded valley. This stream drains the area around

Dickerson and the S. side of Sugar Loaf Mountain. Hurricane Agnes badly damaged this already weakened structure in 1972, but it was rebuilt 1974-75. The berm bank carried a road from Lock 27 to Monocacy Basin. During the Civil War Little Monocacy was breached by Gen Hill, draining the canal below. The berm and towpath banks were cut down, the ditch corduroyed and the artillery and supply trains rolled across the canal bed without difficulty. On 5 Sep. 1862, 'Stonewall' Jackson's corps forded the Potomac and crossed the canal. The damage here and at Lock 27 was repaired by 14 Oct. 1862.

42.07 Site of dwelling house, still and mill on the berm built by Dr. Boyd in the late 1700s. Verification is needed of this information.

42.10 Monocacy Basin, 500' long and 100' wide, with stabilized **granary ruins** on the berm bank, near the parking lot for the aqueduct. Otho W. Trundle built the granary. Frederick O. Sellman was a farmer and a merchant who boated and loaded wheat at the granary. Back of the granary is another building, still standing, which housed a store and the Mouth of Monocacy Post Office, established by the mid-1850s, with Sellman as the postmaster.

42.1x Parking lot and picnic area for Monocacy Aqueduct.

42.17 Cross unmarked **Montgomery Co.-Frederick Co. line.**

Colorful characters have abounded along the canal. 'Squirrelly' Lambert, a squatter on Park Service property with his chickens, goats, and mounds of trash defied eviction from the 1940s through 1967 when he died. 'Squirrelly' bequeathed a treasure of anecdotes to the more recent history of the canal, of which one is repeated here: Arrested and hailed into court in Frederick, he was convicted of selling intoxicating beverages at the aqueduct. Pronouncing a sentence of a $500 fine as a habitual bootlegger, the judge asked Squirrelly if he had anything to say to the court. He replied, "Yes, Sir! I'm going to have to raise the price of my liquor to pay for this fine!"

MONOCACY AQUEDUCT (Aqueduct No. 2)

42.19 Access: From Dickerson (where supplies and prepared food are available at the Dickerson Market) take Md. 28 .3 mi. N. of RR overpass, turn left on Mouth of Monocacy Rd. and go 1.2 mi. to fork. Take the left fork .1 mi. to the parking lot. Telephone, toilets, boat ramps; no water. Road continues along the picnic area and under the (downstream) arch of the aqueduct.

Monocacy Aqueduct, 516' long with seven 54' arches, is the largest of 11 stone aqueducts, and is undoubtedly not only one of the two finest features of the C & O Canal (the other being the Paw Paw Tunnel), but one of the finest canal features in the United States. The aqueduct was begun Mar. 1829 and was finished Apr. 1833. It was damaged in Hurricane Agnes in June 1972, losing much coping stone and railing, but was undergoing extensive repair work 1975-77. NPS did extensive stabilization 1975-1979.

The white and pink quartz sandstone are from Nelson's quarries 4 mi. distance at the base of Sugar Loaf Mtn.; some was boated down the Monocacy and the remainder transported to the construction site by a rude tramway and by wagon. The tramway probably consisted of oak rails covered with strap iron, with the cars having iron wheels and axles and wooden platforms. Horses hauled the cars, which had cogs on the wheels in which an iron bar was inserted for braking on downhill grades. Sugar Loaf can be seen in the distance upriver from the aqueduct.

The Supt. of Masonry in 1831 reported the following work force needed at the aqueduct: 60 men quarrying at the white quarry; 100 men cutting the white

The beautiful Monocacy Aqueduct as it appeared in the early 1900s. In spite of damage by Hurricane Agnes in 1972, the aqueduct remains the most beautiful structure on the canal. (Hahn Collection)

stone; 13 four-horse teams, transporting the white stone; 33 masons, including tenders, drivers, etc.; two four-horse teams hauling cement; 1 boat and 5 men transporting sand; 10 men procuring backing [stone]; 10 carpenters; 235 total number of men. Note the interesting dedication plaque at mid-point of the aqueduct.

The towpath was on the side toward the Potomac river (to the left when you are proceeding up the C & O Canal). There was a towrope riding timber on the canal side of the towpath to keep the towrope from catching in the stonework. Wooden rubbing rails were bolted horizontally on the inner walls of the trough (canal) to minimize the shock of boats bumping the walls. There are remains of a fine charcoal wrought iron fence, particularly interesting at the ends of the aqueduct where the towropes wore grooves in it. The main posts of the fence were capped with hollow, cast iron decorative tops set on the spike of the post with sheet lead to wedge in the tops. Downstream of the aqueduct toward the Potomac River on the near side of the Monocacy was the first settlement on that river, established by Louis Michel, a Swiss prospector, in 1708.

42.3x A systematic exploration of the river terrace for historic and prehistoric artifacts and traces of human development above the aqueduct was carried out by Catholic University in 1966-67 and is described as "**A Woodland Site in Piedmont Maryland**". Recorded settlement in the area did not begin until 1740, at which time Charles Carroll of Carrollton began development of Carrollton Manor, a 17,000-acre tract on which this site is located. Among potsherds found were four named pottery series: Marcey Stone, Stoney Creek, Albemarle and Chickahominy. Stone artifacts included projectile points, a knife, choppers and unworked flakes. Indications were that quartz (readily available in the form of river cobbles) was the most popular artifactual material. Samples of artifacts indicate that the site was occupied from Early Woodland times through Late Woodland. The historic period of occupation on the basis of artifact analysis was from 1715 to 1865. The heaviest period of occupation was probably around 1825.

42.40 Indian Flats Hiker-Biker Overnighter. Nearest access from Monocacy Aqueduct parking lot about .25 mi. below. Next campsite upstream is

Calico Rocks at mile 47.6; downstream is Marble Quarry at 38.2. The berm dike (the berm canal wall) here is nicely shaped and narrow (2-3' at the top).

42.44 **Historic Culvert #70** on Sec. 73, 6' span carries the stream from the flat wooded area. The canal bed is usually dry and carpeted with wild flowers most of the distance to Nolands Ferry: chickweed, corydalis, Dutchman's-breeches, garlic mustard, ground ivy, pokeberry, spring beauty, stinging nettle, white trout lily, Virginia bluebell, violets and waterleaf. Shrubs include bladdernut, burning bush and spicebush. Vines include five-leaf ivy, honeysuckle, poison ivy and wild grape. Trees (in approximate order of abundance): silver maple, sycamore, box elder, paw paw, tulip poplar, elm, hackberry, bitternut hickory and black walnut.

42.58 Remains of the **original 'Macadam' towpath,** particularly of the armored 4' on the canal side where the mule would have walked. 'Macadamized' in the historical use of the word means that the towpath was covered first with a 6″ layer of 2″ stone, then a 4″ layer of 1″ stone and then a layer of fines which was replaced periodically.

42.90 Several stands of white trout lily (Erythronium americanus), an uncommon plant blooming in April. Two shrubs conspicuous in late autumn are bladdernut (Staphylea trifolia) and Eastern wahoo or burning bush (Eunymus atropurpureus). There are **three Indian fish** weirs (rock dams) visible at low water in the Potomac within a ¾ mi. stretch, one at about NPS mile 43 marker.

44.04 **Historic Culvert #71** on Sec. 78, Tuscorora Creek, 16' span, carries the stream from the wooded depression between cultivated fields.

44.08 Upper end of **Birdsaw Island.**

44.25-45.45 Nolands Island.

44.40 **Beginning of Nolands Ferry Area.** Boat ramp. Picnic area, toilets; parking area above. No drinking water. No camping.

NOLANDS FERRY

44.58 **Access:** Above 4 mi. E. of Point of Rocks take either Water Plant or Nolands Ferry Rd. .8 mi. to canal and parking lot. Here was one of the most ancient crossings of the Potomac, the **Monocacy Trail,** a variation of the 'Warriors Path'. The Treaty of Lancaster of 1744, with the Six Nations, provided for Indians to travel unmolested from the Susquehanna River southward through Maryland to the Carolinas on the 'Indians Road'. This traffic tended to keep the Monocacy Trail maintained. When 30,000 Hessians (mercenaries hired by the British from many German States), captured at the **Battle of Saratoga** and paroled on their honor, were ordered to march south to Charlottesville, Va., they followed the 'Indians Path'. The discouraged army crossed at Nolands Ferry on Christmas 1778 in a snow storm with ice floating in the river and continued to Leesburg for the night. 'Mad' Anthony Wayne, with a detachment to join Lafayette before Yorktown, also crossed here in 1781.

The Nolands Family operated the ferry as early as 1758. Produce from the Shenandoah Valley was shipped across the Potomac by ferry as the shortest route to Baltimore. A thriving community of stores, blacksmith, wagonshop, tailor, shoemaker and taverns was established around the ferry. Highway robbers waylaid farmers and drovers enroute to market. Captain Harper, the notorious Robin Hood of Loudoun, generous to the poor and gallant only to the young and beautiful maidens, reportedly made his largest hauls on the ferry approaches. The nickname 'Rogues Road' spread and travellers avoided the crossing. Picnic area, boat ramp.

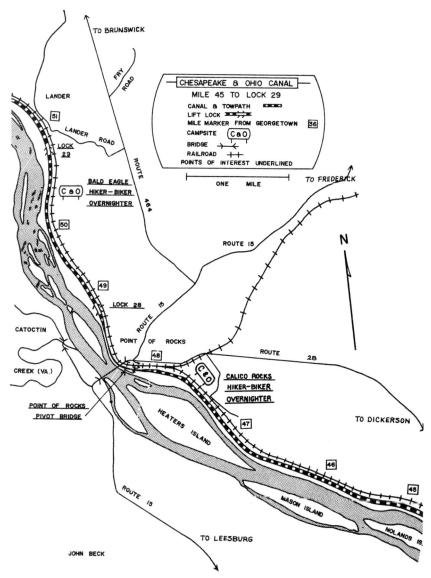

Construction of the canal interfered with traffic across the river. A Buck-eyestown, Md. merchant and flour miller wrote two letters in Nov. 1833 to the canal co. complaining that canal construction had cut him off from his customers in Va. He demanded that a bridge be constructed across the canal. The Annual Report of the canal co. for 1848 noted that the boat previously used for crossing the canal was unfit for further use and a substantial bridge (the abutments for which can be seen upriver from the ferry crossing) had been erected over the canal, but the bridge action was too late to assist in the resurrection of Nolands Ferry. With the erection of the Point of Rocks Bridge across the Potomac, Nolands Ferry became an almost forgotten place name.

Shirley Jackson, self-appointed guide at Harpers Ferry who died in 1950 at age 68, and who claimed that his father had been the valet of Gen McClellan, told of treasure buried near Nolands Ferry and Monocacy Aqueduct. The key to finding the treasure is to follow the ghost of the person hiding it; either a robber who operated at Nolands Ferry or one of Mosby's men sharing in the loot of the robbery of the payroll train upriver, who is seen from time-to-time on moonless nights crossing the Monocacy Aqueduct carrying a lighted lantern.

The berm dike here is built as high as a guard dike, probably because of the additional water which entered the canal from the Tuscarora Feeder above.

44.76 The large, interesting stone building on the river side houses the **Frederick County Water Treatment Plant. A fine example of how a modern service building can blend well with a historic site.** Large patches of periwinkle (Vinca minor) near here.

45.10 TUSCARORA FEEDER. About 150' below the first cabin of a river settlement, cross the dry canal bed and the RR tracks and look inland for the row of trees which marks the path of the feeder canal. The inlet of this historic auxiliary feeder has been covered with soil. Few people know of the existence of the feeder from Tuscarora Creek or have viewed it. It is filled with large trees, but still about 5' deep. The dikes rise about 3' above the level of surrounding fields. It is about 33' from the top of one dike to the other.

45.45 Ahead is a beautiful stretch of canal with frequent views of the river, and, as one nears Point of Rocks, the **Catoctin Mountains.**

46.55 Old wooden flume in canal bed is the remains of former fish propagation area of Kanawha Club. Similar structures divided the canal bed into a series of pools. Spectacular wildflower display above here, including Dutchman's-breeches, squirrel corn, toothwort, violets and wild ginger.

46.80 Beginning of **calico rocks,** a conglomerate – Frederick limestone breccia. Also called Potomac breccia, calico marble and Potomac marble. Conglomerate is composed of coarse and fine pebbles in a matrix of fine gray to red limestone containing grains of quartz. First use of stone may have been in the rotunda of the Capitol, pillars of which are 3' dia. and 20' high. Area also abounds in small red sandstone quarries, products from which were shipped by RR and canal, with a wharf on the berm near here.

46.85-48.25 **Heater Island** has a rock-walled canal connecting the river on the S. side with farm buildings in the center.

47.10 Footbridge across the canal and RR (**CAUTION**) to private Camp Kanawha, concealed behind the **picturesque formation of calico rocks.** Wallrue spleenwort (Asplenium Ruta-mumaria) in this area.

47.20 Houses of the settlement of Rock Hall known c1847 as '**Woodland**'. Ahead is a fine upriver view of the Catoctin Mtns. with Furnace Mtn. across the river.

47.57 **Kanawha Spring.** A large circular dam or dike was built around the spring in the 1950s by the Park Service to divert the spring water to the canal via a concrete trough, but it didn't work out. Large patches of Star of Bethlehem (Ornothogalum nutana).

47.65 **Calico Rocks Hiker-Biker Overnighter.** Nearest access from Point of Rocks about a ½ mi. above. Next campsite upstream is Bald Eagle Island at mile 50.31; downstream is Indian Flats at 42.40. Cross unmarked town line of Point of Rocks.

47.75 **Historic Culvert #72** on Sec. 84 completed 1832, 16' span, drains the lower eastern slope of Catoctin Mtn. Outflow of the culvert under the RR track feeds into the inflow of the canal culvert. RR culvert has sidewalls of stone with an arch of patterned brick, well worth seeing. Grape hyacinth (Muscari

The charming Baltimore & Ohio Railway Station at Point of Rocks is now on the National Register of Historic Places. Photo 1971 (Hahn)

botryoides) on both sides of the towpath ahead. The cornfield on the river side of the towpath is representative of the use of land in the historic canal operating days and as such is historically correct today.

47.79 Washington Junction and the picturesque Point of Rocks RR station, on the National Register of Historic Places.

48.01 Historic Culvert #73 on Sec. 84, completed 1831, 6′ span, carries the stream flowing between the fields.

48.16 Historic Culvert #74, on Sec. 84, completed 1831, 4′ span, carries a small stream coming from the center of town.

THE UPPER POTOMAC RIVER IN FREDERICK COUNTY

The Potomac River flows through 16 miles of Frederick County. Here, the river flows from the Blue Ridge Mountain Physiographic Province to the western division of the Piedmont Province. The river is predominantly moderate to swift-flowing. There are no slackwater regions. Some whitewater occurs in the vicinity of Knoxville.

The high ridges of South Mountain in Maryland and the Blue Ridge Mtns. in Virginia rise up from the banks of the river in the vicinity of Weverton and Knoxville. The Catoctin Mtns. abut the river, forming spectacular cliffs at point of Rocks, Md. The major tributary river to the Potomac in Frederick Co. is Catoctin Creek. It has its confluence with the Potomac near Lander, Md.

Forty-one islands are located in the Potomac River in Frederick County – most of them in the lower one half of the river. Twenty-six of the islands are smaller than five acres. Primary shoreline woody vegetation includes maple, sycamore, willow, white ash, green ash and river birch. Principal submerged aquatic vegetation includes wild celery, water star grass and various pond weeds. Emergent shallow water vegetation includes waterwillow, hibiscus and lizard tail.

Numerous fur-bearing species, song birds, waterfowl, predatory birds and reptiles reside along the immediate shoreline of the Potomac River in Frederick Co. The stretch of river between Catoctin Creek and the Monocacy River offers particularly well protected wildlife habitat because of the numerous undeveloped islands in the area.

Principal fur-bearers include beaver, fox squirrel, grey squirrel, mink, raccoon, otter, deer, muskrat, fox and opossum. The principal sportfish found in this stretch are sucker, carp, catfish, smallmouth bass and sunfish. The water of the Potomac River in Frederick Co. as measured at Point of Rocks is of variable quality.

OLD PIVOT BRIDGE (Point of Rocks)

48.20 Access: At W. end of town at Point of Rocks take last road before US 15 bridge, go toward the canal and cross RR tracks. Road continues .18 mi. to boat ramp under US 15 bridge where it meets the narrow towpath. Provisions at the Mobil station. The pivot bridge no longer operates nor is there anything left of the pivot mechanism; only the center pier and abutments remain. Built in the early 1830s, the pivot bridge was rebuilt as a permanent bridge about 10 years later. As a pivot bridge, boats had 22½' clearance on either side and 11' overhead. The bridge was elevated in 1852 for a 17' clearance. **The other known pivot bridges of this type were at Ft. Frederick and below Antietam Aqueduct.** The present bridge has been lowered to provide a clearance of 9'-4" above the towpath. This bridge was used by vehicles to get to the original highway bridge over the Potomac which washed out in 1936. Of 20 floods of the Potomac from 1896 to 1942, six covered the towpath. The 1936 flood was 17' above the towpath, covering it for 54 hours – the worst flood here on record.

Point of Rocks is important in canal history because of its position at the point where the Potomac cut through the Catoctin Mountains leaving a ledge at the foot of the cliffs wide enough for either the canal or railroad but not wide enough for both. This problem became a major issue in 1831 with the courts ruling in favor of the canal, four years later. The struggle between the railroad and canal involved not only this particular location, but three other points between here and Harpers Ferry; the longest 3,052' and shortest 1,126' according to the Annual Report of 1831. The B & O built the double-track Point of Rocks Tunnel through Catoctin Ridge just after the Civil War. However,

The pivot bridge (now permanent) at Point of Rocks is the only one remaining on the canal. Boats could go on either side of the central pier.
Photo 1971 (Hahn)

when the B & O deeded canal lands in 1938, to the federal government it retained sufficient canal land to construct tracks around the tunnel, which was done in fact in the 1960s, leaving no room in the canal. At that time the double track in the tunnel was replaced by a single track in the center of the tunnel, thereby allowing passage of larger freight cars.

48.38 Pass under US 15 bridge over the Potomac. Other bridges (destroyed by floods) have crossed here in the past. The canal prism is constricted with rocks from the RR here (where the B & O actually owns land in the canal prism and several places ahead). Public boat ramp.

48.40 Point of Rocks RR Tunnel; RR rebuilt in 1909.

48.44 Wooded Patton Island.

48.55 Upstream portal of Point of Rocks tunnel. Steep mountainside continues. Large stone wall (RR) in the canal bed. Nice river views along here.

48.90 Waste Weir; date of 1917 in the concrete.

LOCK NO. 28 (Point of Rocks Lock or Mountain Lock)

48.93 From the pivot bridge .73 mi. downstream. Lock 28 is 7.47 mi. above. Lock 27 and 1.96 mi. below Lock 29. One-seventh of the stone was brought 46 miles on the B & O Railroad (at 6 cents per ton per mile) from the granite quarries of the Patapsco to the Point of Rocks, and thence by wagon nearly one mile to the lock. The other six-sevenths of the stone was transported in wagons from a quarry of hard flint stone in Va., 4 mi. away.

The lock has only a 6' lift. Except for Lock 13, Lock 28 is the most downstream of the locks built entirely to the specifications of 1830, which varied from the original specifications of 1828 mainly in the elimination of bypass culverts in the lock walls and the placement of the breast wall at the upper end of the upper gate recess. As with several others in the vicinity, Lock 28 was extended on the lower end in order to pass through two boats at a time in one direction. Nothing remains of the wooden cribbing used for the extension except for piles of rocks with which they were filled. The lock was completed in 1833, and was destroyed by the Confederates in 1862.

The lock is 140'-4" in total length and 90'-9" between the gate recesses. The latter is a critical measurement for handling boats. A typical 92' boat had to ship (turn) its rudder to the side to fit in the lock.

The bypass flume, which helped to control the proper operating level of the canal (2' below towpath level, 1' below the top of the lock coping) seems to have been a shallow ditch paralleling the lock and terminating in a box culvert. Generally when there is a bypass flume covered over, it indicates a roadway passed over the lock. Though there is no evidence of a pivot bridge here, there are well defined road traces leading from the lock to the river and from the covered section of the flume into the woods. The lock house sits back of the towpath some 34' from the lock, oriented perpendicularly to the run of the lock. The house measures 18'-0" x 30'-3", nearly standard size. It is 1½ stories in height over a full stone basement, and is made of brick. The original chimney in the center of the house has been removed. Note the clump of bamboo above the lock house.

48.96 Waste weir.

49.02 Indian camp site on the bluff.

49.29 Historic Culvert #75 on Sec. 87, 8' span, built 1831 (as were all the culverts through Culvert #94), carries a stream from a deep wooded ravine.

49.66 Historic Culvert #76 on Sec. 88, 4' span, Bottom Branch.

49.70 Informal overflow. Many of these overflows, which were built into the towpath itself are now difficult to detect. One clue is to watch for a gully (without a culvert) such as one sees here, just beyond the towpath. Another clue is the presence of stone on the river side of the towpath, often covered over. Yet another clue is the lowering of the towpath itself. Though often covered with soil, the stones can usually be found a few inches under the surface of the soil. A glint of stone can sometimes be detected in the towpath, and once spotted, you will be an experienced overflow detector for life and can astound your friends with your knowledge! This overflow is about 54' long – a relatively short one. **Culvert #77** was planned here but not constructed. Instead, water was let into the canal and excess water was taken care of by the overflow.

49.88 A stone wall encroaches into the canal (legally so). The smoky overhanging cliff ahead is rather nice.

49.99 RR enters **Catoctin Tunnel** of B & O RR, built just after the Civil War. The canal bed ahead is filled with stone from RR construction. Fine overhanging rock beyond.

50.11 RR emerges from the tunnel. The B & O rebuilt here in 1902.

50.31 Bald Eagle Island Hiker-Biker Overnighter. Nearest access at Lander (Lock 29) at mile 50.80. The next campsite upstream is Huckleberry Hill at mile 62.90; downstream is Calico Rocks at 47.65.

50.67 Historic Culvert #78 on Sec. 90, 12' span carries a large stream from the wooded valley beyond the RR.

50.80 Many cabins of the **settlement of Lander** on the river side of the canal and others on the berm hill.

Lock 29 (Catoctin Lock) at Lander is now used for an occasional ranger contact station and the nearby building for park maintenance. Photo circa 1971 (Hahn)

LOCK NO. 29 (Catoctin Lock), LANDER

50.89 **Access:** From Point of Rocks take U.S. 15 N. 1 mi. to Md. 464 where turn W. toward Brunswick for 2.8 mi. to Lander Rd. which take S. (left) toward the river and go 1.5 mi. to Lander, also known as **Old Catoctin Station.** Cross RR tracks and follow the berm side of the canal to the lock, about .2 mi. Lock 29 is .96 mi. above Lock 28 and 4.11 mi. below Lock 30.

Capt. McNeill's report of 1833 states, "Two-thirds of the stone was obtained from the granite quarries of the Patapsco [transported by B & O Railroad] in the same manner as the last lock. The distance of land transportation [by wagon] from Point of Rocks was 2-2/3 miles; the other third of the face stone

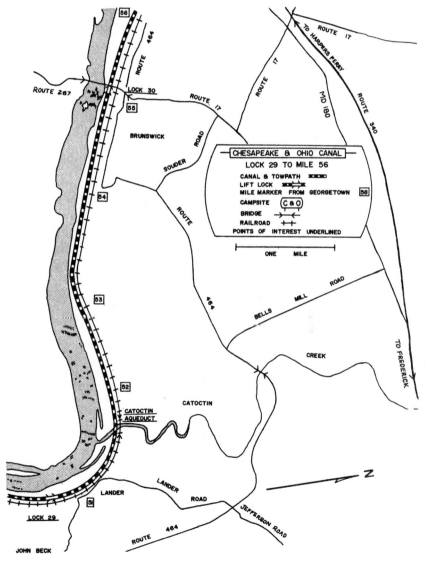

[hard, white flintstone] was obtained from the quarry in Virginia [4 miles], referred to in the last lock."

This lock was once extended by timber cribs, filled with stone on the upper end; the remains are about as good as we find and the position of the wooden lock sill is still apparent. This lock, Lock 28 and all locks through Lock 44 above were built according to the lock specifications of 1830. There are indications here that the bypass flume and the lock were always bridged, even though there are no pivot bridge traces remaining. As with many locks, the lower walls were whitewashed in historic times and traces of the whitewash remain today. The turns of the lower wing walls bear bolt holes and bolts, as is common, indicating that they once held vertical fender timbers to keep boats from bumping the lock walls.

The lock house is on the berm at mid-lock, 20' back from the bypass flume. It is 1½ stories of brick, over a full basement, and has a center chimney. A boat basin extended about 100' below the lock. Locktender L. H. 'Bugs' Cross lived in the house until 1962. William H. Fulton was an earlier tender. The lock house is now an occasional Park Service contact station. The metal (ugh!) building is for maintenance, and certainly out of place in an historic setting. There is a possible boat basin above the lock.

51.06 Waste weir, late period, concrete appliqued over the original stone walls.

51.09 Historic Culvert #79 on Sec. 90, Sugar Tree Branch, 10' span, carries the stream from the valley along Lander Rd. The daughter of lock tender 'Bugs' (Lavenia Waskey Brus) said of this culvert, "How different since the days when we would walk or drive through this culvert in buggies or wagons."

51.35 Fine specimens of large white oak at the edge of the towpath. A day in May finds a plentiful supply of birds calling: the intricate song of the indigo bunting, the tinkling of wood warblers, the busy calls of vireos, the rattle of cow birds and the clarion call of the wood thrush. At 2:30 p.m. on a sunny day a barred owl lights on the horizontal limb of an oak, peers indistinctly about through his wide eye rings and from time-to-time exercises his wings without flying. A young rabbit hops leisurely down the towpath. (Grant Conway)

CATOCTIN CREEK AQUEDUCT (Aqueduct No. 3)

51.53 Access: From Lander at mile 50.89, or at the point where Lander Rd. crosses the RR tracks park along the road and walk across the dry canal bed to save a bit of walking. **This 130' aqueduct is considered by many as the most beautiful on the canal.** The sharp bend in the canal on the upstream side gave rise to the term **'Crooked Aqueduct'.** Of the three stone arches, only the downstream one remains. A local flood on 31 Oct. 1973 caused a very weakened aqueduct to collapse. Stabilization work has been done and a foot bridge now permits safe passage across the creek. The B & O RR crosses Catoctin Creek just above the aqueduct on a handsome two-arch bridge, making a pair of fine structures. The auto graveyard on the flat along Catoctin Creek upstream is the **site of an Indian village** excavated by the Pennsylvania Archaeological Society.

51.85 A very large silver maple, locally called 'river' maple. Ahead the canal bed is silted for ½ mi. to a height **above** the towpath from silt from a RR culvert. This long tree-arched straightaway of the canal is a good natural area until river cabins resume near the mouth of Little Catoctin Creek.

51.88 There is a **buried culvert** here; now served by a metal pipe.

Catoctin Aqueduct (known also as 'Crooked Aqueduct') had been sway-backed for many years prior to the collapse of the upstream and central arches in 1973. Photo 1961 by the Historic American Building Survey

52.27 Historic Culvert #81 on Sec. 93, 4' span, drains a small stream from the ravine on the berm.

52.50 Site of Indian Village on the downstream side of Little Catoctin Creek.

52.51 Historic Culvert #82 on Sec. 93, Little Catoctin Creek, 16' span, restored 1976. The towpath is bad from here to the end of the RR yards W. of Brunswick, due to heavy vehicle use. As bad as it may seem, the quality of the environment over the past 20 years, starting from a very low quality, has improved. Beginning of Brunswick RR yard.

53.17 Historic Culvert #83 on Sec. 93, 4' span.

53.21 Informal overflow. The towpath is well riprapped here to resist water erosion from the overflow. It is 59' long, has a well-defined channel to the river and the towpath is about 1' lower here – all good signs of an earlier overflow.

53.51 Unmarked boundary line of the **town of Brunswick.**

53.59 Historic Culvert #84 on Sec. 95, 10' span, possibly a road culvert.

53.7x The lineup of cabins, abandoned buses, shacks, old trailers, etc. with 'Potomac Flats' sub-division beyond phased out.

53.92 Brunswick town dump on the bank of the Potomac phased out in the early 1960s – one sign of progress; now covered with shrubs.

53.97 Historic Culvert #85 on Sec. 96, 4' span.

54.0x 200-acre **Brunswick Recreation Area,** municipally operated. Portion of an old airfield was converted to picnicking and camping area (200 sites); overnight charge; (ph. 301-834-8050). Permits at the Town Hall or in season at the site. Well water, toilets, boat ramp, boat rental. Area features good fishing for both small and largemouth bass, crappie, catfish, carp and sunfish.

54.56 Water Pollution Control Facility for Brunswick.

54.57 Historic Culvert #86 on Sec. 97, 6' span. Large patch of Star of **Bethlehem** (*Ornithogalum unbellatum*) ahead. **This road on the towpath is terrible, don't you agree?**

54.69 Brick B & O RR 'roundhouse' is an enclosed semi-circle. Limited locomotive service was previously provided from open pits on the un-enclosed side, away from the towpath. The major function of the Brunswick yards today is the repair of freight cars. The first RR station in Brunswick was built in 1834 – one of the earliest RR stations in this country.

54.81 Historic Culvert #87 on Sec. 97, 8' span, carries the stream from the center of Brunswick.

54.95 Waste Weir. Site of old flour and feed mill buildings. The first mill at this site was built 1845. In 1890 the mill had a daily capacity of 85 barrels of flour, buying water from the canal co. to power the mill wheel. One of the mill buildings is said to have been used for Union Army courts martial during the Civil War and was used later for several murder trials. The mill was abandoned as a commercial enterprise in 1862 and burned 1972.

The first mill at Lock 30 in Brunswick was built in 1845. The mill in the photograph burned in 1972, having ceased milling operations in 1962. Photo 1960s (Hahn Collection)

LOCK NO. 30 (Brunswick)

55.00 Access: From the center of Brunswick (Potomac & Maple) go S. across the RR tracks, then turn right 1 block to the lock. The road across the canal at the head of Lock 31 leads to the boat ramp and to Brunswick Park. Groceries in town and restaurants. Canal guides and other publications and RR items are available from the **Potomac Foundation** on W. Potomac Street. The museum is open Fri. and Sat. 10-5, Sun. 11-5, in season.

Lock 30 is 4.11 mi. above Lock 29 and 3.01 mi. below Lock 31. The lift is 8'. Capt. McNeil stated in his 1833 report that, "One-seventh of the stone [is] of the Patapsco granite, one-seventh of the stone found scattered through the neighborhood, five-sevenths of the red sandstone boated 32½ miles from Seneca." The lock was completed in 1833. Lock 30 was extended in 1875 on the upper end so as to lock through two boats at a time in one direction, the 2nd of three to be extended on the upper end, the other 11 being extended downstream. The timber cribbing for the drop gate of the extension is still visible here. Water is

Lock 30 at Brunswick in the early 1900s. Note the pivot bridge in the open position, the lock tender's shanty and the extension of the lock upstream so as to lock through two boats in one direction at the same time. (National Park Service)

sometimes retained just below the lock by an earthen dam for an ice skating pond.

Louis Wernwag built the first pivot bridge across the waterway at Berlin (Brunswick), for which he was paid $401. The bridge was rebuilt in 1841 and again in the 1870s. The pivot was probably on the berm side of the lock. There was a lock house here, but no remains at the present time.

55.03 Pass under the bridge carrying Md. 79. The first wooden bridge was built here by the Loudoun and Berlin Bridge Co. about 1859 and was burned 9 June 1861 by the Confederate cavalryman Drake. A pontoon bridge was used by Union Generals Hooker and Meade. An iron toll bridge was built in 1893 and remained until the 1936 flood.

BRUNSWICK

Brunswick is one of the three largest towns on the canal with a 1970 population of 3,515. The town is located on a portion of a royal landgrant made in 1753 under the delightful name of 'Hawkins Merry-Peep-O-Day'. The town was laid out and named Berlin in 1780, though locally it was called 'Eeltown'. Ferry operations across the river began sometime prior to 1822 and 10 years later (1832), the post office was established under the name of Barry. A Union supply depot was established along the river bank, and during the remainder of the war, pontoon bridges were maintained. Ferry service was resumed after the war until 1894 when another bridge was built on the piers burned in 1861. During the war years the town increased in population to 500 but dwindled to 200 by 1890. The town was officially named Brunswick in 1890, the year when the B & O RR built its eastern switchyard center and repair shops, at which time Brunswick became the busiest RR town along the Potomac until the B & O shifted many of its activities elsewhere. As emphasis turns from the railroad, it gradually turns to the canal, the river and the recreation potential. The town is becoming aware of its historical significance and its potential in attracting visitors to the area. First Potomac River bridge built 1859.

55.10 Abandoned autos, bus bodies, shacks have been characteristic of the river area of Brunswick for some time, but now, gratefully, finally gone as civic pride begins to take hold and acquisition by the Park Service helps to preserve scenic views. **Using the towpath for vehicular use and access to the Brunswick area makes the canal particularly unattractive. Some alternative will have to be found to this intrusion on the historic scene before the Brunswick area becomes attractive to townspeople and visitors alike.**

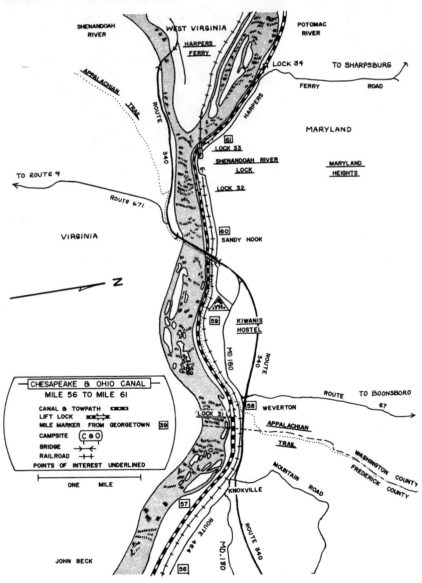

55.45 Historic Culvert #88 on Sec. 99, 8′ span.

55.60 Patch of Miami mist, a light purple flower blooming mid-May.

56.01 Historic Culvert #89 on Sec. 100, 8′ span. Red sandstone ring stones.

56.17 The marshalling hump for switching cars on the RR is no longer very active, but rail fans continue to gather along the road above the track to watch. The black color of the canal banks is due to soot from over a century of use by coal-burning switch engines.

56.45 Historic Culvert #90 on Sec. 102, 6′ span.

57.01 Historic Culvert #91, Knoxville Branch, 12′ span. The area shows much improvement since the 1930s, though the debris along the RR visible from the towpath is disgusting. The general area between the RR tracks and the canal and the river was once one of the largest 'hobo jungles' in the Middle Atlantic states, home for free-loading, free-wheeling freight train riders between World War I and World War II.

57.06 Knoxville. Site of Knoxville Basin ahead.

57.37 Historic Culvert #92 on Sec. 103, 6′ span; the stream drains the E. slope of the tip of South Mtn. The road on the berm continues to Lock 31.

57.39 Pedestrian bridge crosses the canal and provides access and parking. Ahead a path to the river passes through an open field with Star of Bethlehem and Miami mist in mid-May. Good view of the rapids and small tree-covered islands. Also a nice panorama of the N. end of Short Hill on the Va. side, the S. end of South Mtn. in Md. and the river gap between. A fisherman's path at the edge of the river provides a diversion from walking on the towpath from about mile 56.34 to the mouth of Israel Creek.

57.66 Ruins of a small factory bldg.

57.85 Cross unmarked Frederick Co.-Washington Co. line. Old road (now a path) on the river side leads across a ford in Israel Creek to the Potomac River and the **Weverton ruins,** the intakes for the power system of which are intact and worth seeing. When the Savage Distillery on Israel Creek at Weverton burned in 1916, 650 barrels of whiskey spilled into the creek, setting it on fire, burning all the way to the Potomac.

This large structure at the edge of the Potomac River is what is left of the intake for water to power the mills at Weverton. The water in the Potomac was impounded by a 15′ dam. Photo 1974 (Hahn)

WEVERTON

57.8x Access: From Lock 31 at 58.01. Extensive stone walls 20-30' in height sit on the river's edge just above the remains of a stone-filled log dam in the Potomac. The 15' high dam, following a ledge of rocks angling upriver, was completed by Charles B. Fisk, Chief Engineer of the Canal Co. This is about all that remains of the ruins of Weverton, c1830-1877. These walls are part of three river intake sluices designed to take water to 15' in depth to water the Weverton Mills. The tailrace paralled the canal for some distance and was troublesome to the canal in time of high water. The Canal Co. purchased the land and destroyed the dam in 1877.

The story of Weverton centers on its founder, Casper W. Wever, a dreamer who combined politics and engineering, leaving a heritage to Potomac Basin engineers who continue to combine the same activities. The dream of being his own boss (after working for the Federal Government on the National Road and as supt. of construction on the B & O Railroad) came late in life to Wever when he reconnoitered the location for the railroad on Weverton Flat. A small village was already there. Wever estimated a drop in the Potomac of 15 feet in the 2½ miles downstream from Harpers Ferry. He believed this waterpower would turn 300,000 to 600,000 spindles, equal to or greater than provided at Lowel, Mass., and turn the wheels for other industries which he would attract.

He purchased land at the foot of Pleasant Valley for factory, home and town sites and chartered his Weverton Manufacturing Co. in 1834. Wever had his first conflict with the C & O Canal Co. in 1832 when his land was condemned for the canal right-of-way, and the court awarded the utmost damages obtainable from the canal company. Wever then obtained an injunction to stop construction of the canal on his property until he was paid in full.

Wever's plan was to build stone-walled, two-storied factory buildings along his raceway and rent the buildings to manufacturing companies. Because lease charges were high, most of his buildings lay idle. When Asiatic cholera struck the canal in 1832, Gen Mercer of the canal company negotiated with Wever for the renting of a vacant mill building for a temporary hospital. After Wever died, and after 1847, a new company was formed and promotion of Weverton was revived.

A last gasp effort on behalf of Weverton was made in 1858, when a bill was introduced in Congress to establish a National Foundry. Action was not taken on the bill by Congress. A utopian experiment in communal working and living was established at Weverton before the outbreak of the Civil War. Three large buildings constructed of Harpers Ferry shale were built and a fourth was to form a quadrangle. The people lived and worked in the same buildings equipped with running water, which was the envy of neighbors. The communal group was clannish and reportedly used secret processing at the Weverton Cotton Mills, which operated only a few months before the Civil War erupted, and the Union Army took over the buildings for barracks.

After the flood of 1877 further damaged the surviving buildings, the canal company acquired the property from the Potomac Company, which had succeeded the Weverton Manufacturing Company. The principal purpose in acquiring the property seems to have been to demolish the dam which was diverting flood water, destroying portions of the towpath embankment.

The mid-19th century town spreading over this plain has disappeared with scarcely a trace and reverted to its natural environment, laying to rest the dream of Casper Wever to found an industrial town.

Cast a tear for Engineer Wever;
Worked he like an eager beaver;
Turned victim of his own deceiver;
Fell his firm to hands of receiver.
(Grant Conway)

LOCK NO. 31 (Weverton)

58.01 Access: You can't get there from here! This is one of those places not hard to get to particularly, but hard to describe, and I would just as soon skip it, but – from U.S. 340 going W., take the Md. 67 exit, turn left back over U.S. 340 and then take old U.S. 340 off the cloverleaf about .6 mi. back to the RR crossing to park your car. (I assume no responsibility for these lousy directions!)

Lock 31 is located 3.01 mi. above Lock 30 and 2.22 mi. below Lock 32, where it was but a few feet from the Frederick and Harpers Ferry Turnpike (old 340). Capt. McNeil in his report of 1833 says, "Built of stone from different quarries; a part from the hard flintstone quarry in Virginia, mentioned in Locks No. 28 and 29; a part was obtained within a half a mile, and a part from a granite quarry in Virginia; the land transportation of which was one mile, and water transportation one and one half mile." The lock was completed in 1833.

In the mid-1830s a pivot bridge was built at the lock, primarily for access by the Weverton Manufacturing Co. No trace of the bridge is now visible. This bridge caused difficulties between the canal co. and the Frederick and Harper's Ferry Turnpike Co., the latter complaining that persons traveling between Weverton and Harpers Ferry were taking advantage of the bridge to use the towpath, thus avoiding the road and its toll. In an unsuccessful effort to curb this traffic, it was ordered that the pivot bridge over Lock 31 be turned and locked when not in use. In 1850 a Weverton industrialist, George Rothery sought and obtained permission to erect a footbridge over the canal below the lock as the distance between his factories and the boarding houses via the pivot bridge was so great that it was an inconvenience to the workers. The bridge was to have been 17' above the canal (the accepted standard), but there is no record as to whether or not the bridge was built.

The lock is unique in that a **mill race culvert** goes under the upper part of the lock. **A mill was obviously in use when the canal was built,** and the canal crossed the tail race. The culvert was built to carry waste water from the mill wheel, and the lock was built very close to the mill. Apparently the mill took water from Israel Creek and provided a head of about 15'. Most of the head race was obliterated in construction of old and new U.S. 340. As water provided from Israel Creek was insufficient to operate the mill in the dry season, an arched intake from the canal was provided for the mill to augment its water supply by buying canal water. The 6' span culvert under the lock, which provided for the tailrace from the mill, was undoubtedly built by the contractor of this lock and the cost included in its footings. This lock was the most expensive of the first 32, except for the tidelock, costing nearly $4000 more than the average.

Lock 31 is believed to have been built on a wood timber foundation. The tilting of the lock walls toward each other over the years caused the canal co. to cut back the face of the local ashlar (finished stoned) to maintain sufficient width for the passage of boats; more than 95% of the stone face was so treated. Eventually this was not sufficient and the towpath wall ashlar was removed and replaced with concrete. When the upper towpath gate recess was re-placed with concrete, a wooden gate bumper block 4x6" was placed in the concrete to prevent damage to the cast iron wicket gates and the lock itself when the wicket gates were accidentally left open. This is common on up the canal. When the stone ashlar was removed from the towpath wall, the stones were piled in two piles on the river side of the towpath. Their placement indicates that they were removed with a crane in two sittings.

The concrete facing of the towpath wall was formed in several pours. There was a poor bond between the pours as indicated by extreme cavitation along the pour lines. The length of the lock varies (89'-11" on the towpath side and 90'-1" on the berm side). The overall length of the lock is 141'-1". The lift of the lock is 8'. The canal is quite wide below the lock for about a half mile; remains of several stone docks are visible in the berm dike. The berm dike is quite wide and a well-used road trace leads from the lock to Knoxville. A dry laid stone wall some 42' in present length on the berm above the lock serves as a berm dike retaining wall and was probably used for a loading dock.

Lock 31 was an extended lock, as were all the locks #25 through #32. This one was extended on the lower end. The towpath rise is quite abrupt here and begins just below the lower end of the lock extension. The towpath (or 'mule rise') seems to be more abrupt from here on than the normal 150' gradual rise at the locks downstream. There was once a stone-filled wood timber crib in front of the berm wing wall, used to help line up boats for entering the lock and to prevent them from bumping the upper wing walls. They are more common on the berm, as the towpath itself serves as a sturdy base for the upper towpath wingwall. As with most locks, there are stop plank slots in the upper extension walls (the portion of the lock wall just above the upper gate recess) about 2' above the upper gate recesses. Such slots were used to hold planks to dam off water above the lock when repairs were underway in the lock. The fact that they were not formed in the concrete walls indicates their lack of importance in the late operating period.

58.06 Waste weir. Typical concrete over original stone walls.

58.07 Appalachian Trail. The 2050 mi. Maine-to-Georgia trail joins the towpath from this point to Sandy Hook Bridge at 59.58. A good overlook of the Potomac River can be had by taking the trail N. across U.S. 340 up to Weverton Cliff, the southern terminus of South Mtn. Short Hill Mtn. on the Va. side of the Potomac River is the continuation of South Mtn.

58.08 Informal overflow. When water rose above the desired operating level, it simply flowed over the towpath through this low spot and back to the river. To prevent washing, the towpath surface and the river side of the towpath dike were well riprapped. This overflow was 320' in length, a rather large one. It appears on old maps. These overflows today are usually covered with soil and vegetation and, therefore, the only indication of their presence is the outflow flume (or ditch) that extends from the towpath to the river at these points. The towpath elevation at the overflows was historically two feet below the normal towpath level. Where river floods have silted in or covered the outflow flume, these dips in the towpath might be the only clue to their location. Canalers referred to them as 'mule drinks'.

58.18 Historic Culvert #94 on Sec. 107, Israel Creek, 20' span, drains the beautiful Pleasant Valley between South Mtn. and Elk Ridge. About 60' above the inflow of the canal culvert is the beautiful RR bridge over the creek.

58.33 Trail to the river leads to the open shelter of the Potomac Appalachian Trail Club for the use of through hikers on the trail. The Sandy Hook Bridge and Harpers Ferry Gap are ahead – an **outstanding river view.**

58.91 The towpath is directly on the river bank, walled in many places. Fine high cliff on the berm. Sandy Hook Bridge and Harpers Ferry Gap are ahead, an outstanding river view.

59.09 Sizable **cave** on the berm 20′ above the RR. Harpers Ferry is in view as the canal follows the bend of the river.

59.44 **Blue Ridge Hiker-Biker.** Has been closed indefinitely.

59.50 Probable **abandoned culvert,** now covered; the present metal pipe was placed in the canal several years ago to water the canal prism for fishing pools. Possibly Culvert #93, on section 105. 6′ span. Built 1833.

59.58 Pass under Sandy Hook Bridge, carrying U.S. 340 and the **Appalachian Trail** (which has left the towpath at this point) across the Potomac River, and provides access to those wanting to go to Harpers Ferry. The **Kiwanis Youth Hostel** is a short distance back up the road on the berm; overnight fee. (For AYH membership requirements, use of hotels, etc.: Potomac Area Council, AYH, Rm. 451, 1332, I St. NW., Washington, DC 20005). Sandy Hook River and Trail Outfitters up the berm road and on the far side of U.S. 340 has bikes and canoes for rent, provides river float trips, and has hiking and river guides. Ph. 301-834-9950. Youth Hostel (Tel. 301-834-7652). Open 1 April to 1 November.

SANDY HOOK

59.60 The Village of Sandy Hook with its row of old houses facing the railroad and the canal was once a busy town. Before the railroad was centered in Brunswick, Sandy Hook had repair shops and a station between the tracks and the canal. Across the street from the Sandy Hook Station was the Post Office, known earlier as 'Keep Tryst'. The town has maintained the 'old time' flavor through the years. Two stores provide light refreshments and supplies. At Harrison's Store I learned that ice cream and bread were brought into town from Hagerstown by train, and that a RR spur carried fruit from the orchards into town. Better stop here for supplies if you are going upstream, as the next

Israel Creek Culvert (#94) is one of the largest on the canal with a 20′ span. These 'works of art' (as they were called in the canal construction days) are often unnoticed and unappreciated by passersby. Photo circa 1960. (Hahn)

place to stop is Shepherdstown; going downstream there is good access to the towns of Brunswick and Point of Rocks. According to legend, Sandy Hook was named for a quicksand deposit at the edge of the river which took the lives of a teamster and his horses. Present-day canoeists taking out at Sandy Hook report mud but no quicksand. There is still danger on the river, however, and the stretch between Dam #3 and Sandy Hook is recommended only to expert canoeists. The Frederick-Harpers Ferry Toll Road (chartered 1805) passed through here. The road today (the Harpers Ferry Road) leads to Sharpsburg through delightful, rolling countryside. Several paths cross the wet canal bottom to the village, but be careful in crossing the tracks as there are frequent trains.

59.71 New metal pipe culvert under the towpath replaces a complete break in the towpath several years ago.

59.83 A stone foundation on the berm marks a ruin of the railroad. Just beyond are several large red sandstone blocks which puzzled me until recently when I learned that they were dumped off a disabled RR car. A bit beyond on the berm is another foundation (concrete), again marking the presence of the RR.

59.91 The 'Long Wall', built to resist flood damage to the canal, extends from the head of Lock 33 to this point, a distance of .82 mi. Built on the river side of the towpath opposite the mouth of the Shenandoah River, the face of the wall rose from the bedrock of the river to as much as 12' above towpath level. On the canal side, the towpath was riprapped with one-man stone throughout much of this distance, though little remains in view due to the floods of 1924, 1936, 1937, 1942 and 1972.

60.16 Elk Ridge (or Maryland Heights) on the berm overlooks Harpers Ferry. The area below the confluence of the Potomac and Shenandoah Rivers was called the 'Bull Ring' because of the circling turbulence at flood stage when the Shenandoah's flow exceeds that of the Potomac. Many **Indian camp-sites** have been excavated in the vicinity of Harpers Ferry. Indian tribes reportedly shared the fishing grounds during the spring run of yellow suckers.

60.20 Just below Lock 32 are the fragmentary remains of what may be the only **extant section of the Potomac Canal Co. sluice flume around Harpers Ferry Falls**. This flume was blasted out of rock on the Md. shore from above Dam 3 to below Lock 32, over 2 mi. in length. Elsewhere, the construction of the C & O Canal has destroyed all traces of the channel. A rock outcrop about 20' out in the river is believed to mark the river side of the channel.

The Grant Conway Historical Trail begins upstream of Sandy Hook at steps just off the road. A 3½-hour hiking trip to the overlook cliff and Civil War fortifications. Trial is marked with orange blazes.

LOCK NO. 32 (SANDY HOOK)

60.23 Access: From Lock 33, ½ mi. above, or .65 mi. from Sandy Hook Bridge, Limited parking along the road. Carefully cross RR tracks to lock, out-of-view from the road. Lock 32 is .47 mi. below Lock 33 and 2.22 mi. above Lock 31 and just opposite the mouth of the Shenandoah River. The canal, RR and Harpers Ferry Rd. are crowded between the river and the cliffs. Of all the locks on the canal, Lock 32 is the most subject to flood damage, particularly from floods of the Shenandoah. The Shenandoah in flood overrides the Potomac, dashes against the Md. shore, turns and runs down the canal scouring everything in its path. The construction of the canal bed at Lock 32 causes floodwaters to wreak havoc on the lock walls. This would be a difficult section to rewater.

Capt. McNeil reported in 1833, "One-fifth of the stone [is] from the granite quarry referred to in the last lock; the transportation from which was in wagons, distance two miles, crossing two rivers, Shenandoah and Potomac. Four-fifths of the stone was from different limestone quarries up the Potomac, varying in distance from 2 to 12 miles, the last mile of which was land transportation, the rest water transportation." The lock was completed in 1833. Lock 32 bears evidence of much rebuilding, particularly in its upper courses. It seems to be built on solid rock as there is little tilt in the lock wall remains. The towpath wall of the lock has been severely damaged, but because of the damage this lock is a good one to study for period construction, as the backup walls are open to view. Under the 3' deep coping stones, the total wall thickness is 4'. Five feet below the coping, the wall steps out 18" for a total thickness of 5'-6". About 5' below the first stepping, the wall base steps out an additional 18" to become a full 7' in thickness. Around the gate recesses the walls are a full 7' thick all the way up from the footings through the coping stones. It is 89'-8" between gate recesses. The lock had an 8' lift. The towpath was elevated behind the 'Long Wall' so that there is no towpath rise at this lock.

Lock 32 is the uppermost of a series of eight extended locks, continuous from Lock 25. Little remains of the stone-filled timber cribs except for a shallow windrow of rubble rocks. Much of the canal bed has been scoured to bedrock above the lock by floods. Adjacent to the berm side of the bypass flume are high stone walls which are the remains of a canal carpenter shop, last run by Greenwald Keyser. The long rapids in the river are called "White Horse."

60.25 Directly across the river is the N. end of the Blue Ridge Mtns. at the Va.-West Va. state line; the Appalachian trail ascends the ridge at this point. The W.Va. portion of the ridge is part of Harpers Ferry National Historical Park, as is the lower part of Elk Ridge on the Md. side.

60.34 High old dry wall on the berm side, supports the RR grade. This is one of three sections between Point of Rocks and Harpers Ferry where the canal and the RR shared the narrow right-of-way. At one time the B & O was to have built a high board fence between the canal and the RR from the Point of Rocks so as not to unduly frighten the tow animals. The fence was never built, but for a brief period locomotives were unhooked at Point of Rocks and the RR cars were pulled by horses, The first 'iron horse' to reach Harpers Ferry was the 'Arabian.' Across the river are the cliffs of Loudon Mtn.

60.51 The original towpath has been completely obliterated by floods with the towpath now at the bed-of-canal level. During one repair from a flood, stones were taken from the Shenandoah River Lock just ahead and used to carry the Long Wall across the lock. The Potomac River below Harpers Ferry was called Cohongoroota (River of Wild Geese) by the Indians.

SHENANDOAH RIVER LOCK

60.62 Access: From Lock 33, .08 mi. above. This was the first river lock to be constructed, being completed in 1833. The tow animal was to have continued up the towpath and onto the railroad bridge while towing the canal boat over to the Va. shore at Harpers Ferry, and then tow the boat up the Shenandoah River to the quieter waters of the Potomac Canal bypass of Virginius Island where the Hall Rifle Works and several mills were located. However, the RR did not keep its part of the agreement to allow tow animals to pass over the RR bridge, cutting the use of the river lock. The Winchester RR also cut into the once heavy traffic down the Shenandoah River. The result was that the river lock was abandoned early.

99

Little remains of the lock above ground except at the lower end where boats entered the river. The lock left the canal at N. 80° W. or about the same angle that the canal runs from Lock 32, so that the canal did not have to be widened for boats to enter the lock. About 57' of the outlet end is in view on the river side whereas only about 20' of berm lock and wing walls are exposed. Much of the lock, is covered by the protective 'Long Wall', built after the abandonment of the lock. A portion lies under the towpath, which continued on grade after the abandonment. The lock was 15' in width and this measurement still exists at one point.

The 1889 flood greatly damaged the Long Wall and the river lock, and, as the lock had not been used for many years, much of it was taken down and the stones used elsewhere. When the Long Wall was repaired, it was built across the top of the old river lock.

THE FREDERICK AND HARPERS FERRY TURNPIKE

The Frederick and Harpers Ferry Turnpike Co. was authorized by Md. to construct a toll road between those two towns. The western terminus of the road connected with the Wager toll bridge over the Potomac River at Harpers Ferry. On the Md. side of the bridge it followed the edge of the river east to a point downstream of the present-day U.S. 340 bridge, where it ascended the hill, then known as 'the hill above Millers Narrows'. As was usual, whenever the construction of the canal interrupted or displaced a road, the canal co. was forced to build a substitute road at its own expense.

The turnpike co. charged a variety of tolls for wagons, carts, horses, for droves of cattle, pigs, sheep or turkeys, for a rider on horseback and even a toll on pedestrians. The canal co. was plagued with the complaints of the turnpike co. that pedestrians were allowed to use the towpath to avoid paying turnpike tolls. The canal co. did strictly forbid the use of the towpath for wagons, carts and horses for other than company use, but found it difficult to limit the use of it by pedestrians. At one stage the complaints were so strong that the canal co. ordered the pivot bridges over the canal from the Point of Rocks to Harpers Ferry to be locked in the open position to minimize use of the towpath by pedestrians. This was more of a nuisance than value as pedestrians simply used the closest culvert under the canal.

Flooding in this area is caused primarily by the steep gradient of the Potomac River, the narrow gorge below Harpers Ferry and the confluence of the Potomac and Shenandoah Rivers. Records from 1889 until recently show that river water reached the towpath every two years and rose five feet above the towpath every five years. Floods reached 21' above the towpath in the 1889 and the 1936 floods. Great damage was also done in the floods of 1843, 1852, 1877 and 1890, as well as more recent ones.

60.66 Old bridge piers leading across the river to Harpers Ferry are the remains of the highway bridge which washed out in 1936. Many earlier bridges have occupied this site. **What would be nice here would be a foot bridge connecting Harpers Ferry with the C & O Canal!** Right on these same piers.

60.67 Pass under two RR bridges; the first is the Shenandoah Valley Branch of the B & O and the second is the main line of the B & O. Both bridges lead into the tunnel. It is illegal to cross on these bridges. If you do so at your own risk (and without my advice), at least use the one downstream and not the main line of the B&O. Louis Wernwag designed and supervised the construction of the first bridge here in 1836.

This is an 1859 photo of Harpers Ferry and the covered bridge which connected Maryland and Virginia and which was burned early in the Civil War. (Hahn Collection)

No one seems to know the age of the Salty Dog Tavern at the Harpers Ferry Lock (Lock 33), but its reputation for the easiness of its women and the potency of its liquor was well known. C & O Canal boatmen have stated that the saloon was not known as the Salty Dog in the canal operating period.

Lock 33 at Harpers Ferry (but on the Maryland side of the river) was once a busy place. Note the covered bypass flume necessitated by the large head of water passing through from Dam No. 3 above. (Photo National Park Service)

HARPERS FERRY

Access: To reach Harpers Ferry National Park, follow US 340 over Potomac and Shenandoah Rivers 2.7 m. to park sign where turn right .7 m. to parking lot.

Harpers Ferry is perhaps the most significant attraction adjacent to the C & O towpath, combining scenery and history. Here the Potomac and Shenandoah Rivers break through the Blue Ridge Mountains from the west and join at Harpers Ferry, located at the apex of the triangle where the two rivers meet. Here also is where the land across the river changes from Virginia to West Virginia. Surrounding mountains overshadowing the village are protected in parklands, and their natural scenic splendor remains relatively unchanged through almost two-and-a-half centuries of permanent settlement. Maryland Heights, immediately above and across the canal extends along Elk Ridge to beyond the Stone Fort (Loudoun Mountain across the river) and the lower part of Harpers Ferry on the Shenandoah River side are included in the Harpers Ferry National Historical Park. The area beyond the old cemetery above the town is separately administered by the Stephen Mather Training Center of the National Park Service. The C & O Canal National Historical Park bisects the Harpers Ferry National Historical Park.

Rounding the bend on the towpath the vista across the river is of the top of the old buildings along Shenandoah St., partially restored by the NPS. Above the street is the steeple of St. Peters Catholic Church, and in the

Early view of Harpers Ferry. (Courtesy of John Frye)

immediate foreground of the church is a long row house. Construction on the church site was started by Robert Harper, for whom the town was named, and additions made by the Wager and Marmion families, successive private proprietors of the commercial ventures of the town. This tradition has been revived by D. H. Kilham, proprietor of the Hilltop Hotel, which overlooks the Potomac.

Gone are the federal buildings: U. S. Armory on the Potomac side, U. S. Arsenal on the Shenandoah side of the apex, Halls Rifle Works on an island in the Shenandoah, and private forges, iron sheet rolling mills, textile and flour mills, woodworking plants and many smaller industrial, commercial and dwelling structures which once clustered on the flats along the two rivers. Location and growth of this 19th century industrial town, estimated at close to 5,000, was decided by water for power and cheap transportation to markets by water and rail. Two young British travelers in 1835 viewing "a most abominable village" from the overlook from Jefferson Rock beyond the Catholic Church wrote of "smell of coal smoke" from the factories, "and the clanking of hammers obtrude themselves on the senses and prevent your enjoyment from being unmixed".

Natural growth of trees and shrubs has replaced most of the sites of the once industrial-complex located along the flood plain of the two rivers. A closer exploratory examination reveals foundations and the ruins of a complex of millraces. Where archaeological excavations have not exposed remnants of the primitive technology, layers of alluvial soil deposited by earlier frequent floods conceal the remains of man-made improvements. Contributing to the silt-laden floods was the erosion of the steep slopes of the mountains after the climax hardwood forests of the upper Potomac Basin had been removed to fuel the iron furnaces and blacksmith forges before the advent of cooking coal which was introduced into the area in the 1840s. Marginal hillside farms which followed forest clearing were gradually abandoned with repeated soil runoffs. Pictures of the mountains surrounding Harpers Ferry through the Civil War period, when additional clear-cutting for defense

103

purposes took place, and to the turn of the century, reveal a stark panorama of exposed rocky ridges. Regeneration of natural growth provides a more pleasant vista of the environs of Harpers Ferry.

Historically, according to legend, Indian tribes considered the meeting of the two rivers as a shared neutral zone. In early spring Indians converged to spear and net the yellow sucker (also known as the northern hogsucker) on their annual run up the rivers to spawn. Dip net platforms, similar to the Indian structures, and frequent along the upper Potomac until about 1950, continue to be erected by fishermen across the Potomac on the Virginia shore.

Peter Stephens, the first permanent settler at Harpers Ferry, established a trading post and crude ferries in 1733. Robert Harper, house builder, millwright and merchant, purchased "squatters rights" from Stephens early in 1747, and by October the approach routes to Harpers Ferry were posted with the following sign:

NOTICE

"To the farmers in Maryland and over the Blue Ridge in Loudoun County. This is to certify that all persons bringing grist to my mill, under the charge of William Griffith, will be ferried over the Potomac and Shenandoah rivers free of expense."

Robert Harper
Proprietor of the Harper's Ferry Mill

Physical operation of the ferries in early years was usually entrusted to Negroes. Harper's first ferryman, known only by the name of "Uncle Gabe," and one of the eight residents of Harpers Ferry in 1747 whose names have survived, may have been a Negro. The first free Negro of record in Harpers Ferry was Tom, who operated ferries for upwards of 20 years prior to his emancipation in 1803, according to Jefferson County records. Ferries continued to operate until the first bridges, and intermittently during periods when bridges were destroyed by flood, fire, faulty construction and one by windstorm.

The two railroad bridges across the Potomac obscure much of the view of Harpers Ferry from downriver on the towpath and below the bridges. The first bridge across the Potomac opened in 1829. Many replacements have followed over the years.

Rivalry for land rights between canal and railroad between Point of Rocks and Harpers Ferry was intense, involving holdup prices in competitive bidding for land, legislation and court battles in the 1830s before agreement was reached for railroad (tunnel was constructed many years later), canal and wagon road to share the narrow shelf of land along the downriver approach to Harpers Ferry. Competition for freight and passengers continued until the B & O gained shareholder control over the canal. An advertisement appearing in the Virginia Free Press of June 16, 1859, is an example. Under a picture of a sidewheeler steam packet with two smokestacks is an announcement that, "the steam packets "Antelope" and "Brongle" offer cheap, safe and delightful passage from Washington to Harpers Ferry; fare, $1.50; meals, 25¢; remodeled cabins for the 12 hour trip. Fare is 3 or

Lock #33, C & O Canal at Harpers Ferry, 1876. (Courtesy National Park Service)

4 times less than B & O R.R. Boats leave Harpers Ferry at 6 am on Monday, Wednesday and Friday and the return voyages from Georgetown leave at 7 am on Tuesday, Thursday and Saturday. The Saturday boat continues on to Shepherdstown and Williamsport." An editorial in the same newspaper advocated the restoration of right-of-way of passenger boats over freight boats.

SHENANDOAH NAVIGATION

Located in Harpers Ferry is perhaps the best remaining section of Shenandoah Navigation, built by Patowmack Co. Report of company for 1808 describes bypass canal of 580 yards with drop of 17 feet. There were two locks, each 100 feet long and 12 feet wide. One had a lift of 9 feet and the other 8 feet, a third lock may have been added later. After early use as a canal, principal use was for millrace which fed many side races for numerous and changing industries on Virginius or Herrs Island. Early records refer to rapids as Sawmill Falls, and more recent, Shenandoah Staircase, which form many step ledges crossing the river. Diversion dam extended from Shenandoah City, presumably destroyed by flood in 1889 to below high waterfall of sidestream called Drunkards Dell during Prohibition days. Portions of rubble dam encasing steel bars remain in place on south side of river. Guard lock gate remnants at entrance of millrace-canal at upper end of Overton Island and below ruin of Ritenhauer flour mill covered by fill by B & O in 1946, when millrace was blocked with high fill for approach to Shenandoah River bridge for US 340, which opened in 1947. Thereafter, water in lower raceway limited to seepage and became stagnant, with NPS blocking lower outlet for walking access to Virginius Island. Tender lived in neat frame house at upper end of Overton Island. Guard lock could be opened for passage of boats, described as 9 feet wide and 76 feet long, with crew of 14 to 18 men. Boats were beached at foot of Union Street and sold

105

for lumber. Around 1920 Kaplan, HF merchant, had 25 dismantled "gundalows" (local name), stored in a barn. Lumber used in many of early houses in area, including Camp Hill Methodist Church and Iron Horse Inn. Actual origin, structures and operation of the canals in Harpers Ferry area remain obscure.

By formal agreement between B & O and Canal Company in 1835, provision was made for a tow walk on downriver side of first railroad bridge across the Potomac, completed during the following year. From outlet of Shenandoah canal, above the present NPS parking lot, a towpath was constructed along the river bank to the bridge approach. Gerald S. Wager, owner of property crossed by the Virginia towpath approach, and friend of B & O, constructed a brick warehouse in 1837 which blocked towpath access to the bridge. Canal Company was unsuccessful in condemning right-of-way by Virginia court action through Wager property, and railroad dismantled tracking path across bridge in 1841. Tracking path was restored a year later, but toll charge set sufficiently high to discourage use. B & O charge of 50 cents per ton for canal goods hauled across bridge by rail was also prohibitive. Therefore, barges from Harpers Ferry side crossed Potomac, when water conditions permitted, were hand-propelled to C & O Canal intake lock. Later, most traffic to and from C & O Canal and Harpers Ferry was hauled by wagon for reloading at wide basin above Lock 33 and at Sandy Hook.

Harpers Ferry never recovered from John Brown raid in 1859 and the Civil War which followed. This strategic industrial, (especially munitions) and transportation center proved indefensible during Civil War without strong fortifications on ridges overlooking town, tying down a concentration of soldiers and equipment. When in September 1862 three task forces under Gen. Stonewall Jackson (strategy set forth in Lost Order No. 191), surrounded the town in a pincers movement and mounted artillery in heights on three sides, it was like "shooting fish in a barrel," and approximately 12,000 surviving troops of Union army in the Ferry surrendered in time for reinforcements to reach other Confederate troops at Battle of Antietam (Sharpsburg) where armies fought to a bloody standstill.

After the Civil War, fire, flood and epidemics continued to harass Harpers Ferry. Water power was replaced by electricity, making it possible to locate industry above flood plains. Canal failed and Harpers Ferry was little more than a whistle stop on the B & O Railroad.

When National Park Service entered the picture the town was povertystricken and in need of a restorative. In 1944 a Congressional enabling act established the Harpers Ferry National Historical Monument. First land was acquired in 1952 and an act of Congress of 1963 promoted the Monument to National Historical Park status. Park Service presence is firmly established. Scattering of oldtimers remain, supplemented by retired folks, tourist businessmen and a sprinkling of "younger" generation.

Slow restoration of some of the buildings along Shenandoah Street is being accomplished after careful research of structures tracing to pre-Civil War days. Exhibits are tastefully arranged. Economic impact of National Park is evident on Potomac side where commercial buildings and houses have attracted antique, souvenir and snack shops.

Short-order food is available along Potomac Street across from R.R.

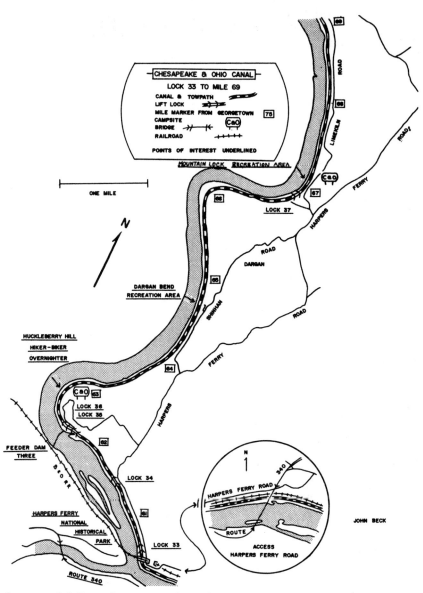

depot, and full meals are served at the Iron Horse Inn and Hilltop Hotel. Grocery shopping for long distance hiker is not as convenient with the nearest store, Tattersalls, almost a mile from the lower town and reached by following High Street which becomes Washington at top of hill.

Easy access from towpath to Harpers Ferry is difficult right now. Lower railroad bridge across Potomac from Maryland has board walkway posted for "No Trespassing" and some pedestrians cross at their own risk. Long range plans of NPS call for rebuilding piers of highway bridge across Potomac washed away in the 1936 flood, and installing a footbridge to connect parks.

TOWPATH GUIDE

*(Mileage figures from Tidelock west are indicated in
bold face type at the left)*

LOCK NO. 33 (HARPERS FERRY)

60.70 *Access:* From I-70 near Frederick, Md. take US 340 (Harpers
Ferry Exit) 16 m. to the road just short of the Potomac River bridge, where
turn left (at the service station) about ¼ m. to the first road to the right which
take about ½ m. down hill to the stop sign. Turn right on paved (possibly
unmarked) Harpers Ferry Rd paralleling the RR and canal on the left 2.2 m.
to Lock 33. Accommodations and restaurant off US 340, in Harpers Ferry
and at the Sandy Hook America Youth Hostel. Limited train service to
Harpers Ferry.

Lock 33 shows terrific pounding of flood waters, leaving river side of
lock as high wall. According to Engineers Report of 1833, most of stone
used in lock is Virginia "flint" hauled 1½ m. by wagon, crossing Shenandoah
and Potomac; small portion of stone from Maryland quarry 1 m. away.
Lock is in fairly good condition. Interesting masonry in elaborate wasteway
thru stone arch culvert. William S. Elgin, locktender and section collector
in 1850, according to 1851 annual report of Canal Company. John Cook,
advance man for John Brown who arrived 15 months before the Brown raid,
married a local girl and tended lock "across the river from Harpers Ferry"
(presumably Lock 33) according to John Penn Warren in his biography
of John Brown. Looking back on river side of lock toward R.R. bridges,
old pictures taken during canal operation show several buildings from
which Reed family sold feed for mules and groceries to canallers for at
least two generations.

Footbridge crosses upper end of Lock 33 to limited parking. Canal parallels Harpers Ferry Rd. for .9 m., separated from canal prism by beautiful
stone wall which is berm bank; some stones have tumbled into canal bed
near beginning. Four wooden footbridges from here to Lock 34 cross to

Lock #33 at
Harpers Ferry
as it appears today.

Lock 33 and Bridge to Harpers Ferry, ca. 1850s.

road and limited parking between road and spectacular rock cliffs which form SW end of Elk Ridge (Maryland Heights). Parking cannot be expanded without damaging natural environment with possible exception of small expansion at Lock 34 where Harpers Ferry Rd. leaves canal toward Antietam and road (61.07) leading to former Weaver residential complex on shelf overlooking canal and river.

A most delightful short hike is from Lock 33 to Lock 36. In 3.58 m. round trip one sees 4 lift locks, an inlet lock, beautiful river scenes, skyline of Harpers Ferry, unique canal drydock, 2 dams and ruins of 3 lockhouses.

60.79 *Footbridge across canal.* Towpath between Locks 33 and 34 has hardpacked, smooth, clay surface on top of river bank. Good walking and excellent views of river and cliffs on berm. Vines have been cleared from high rock wall forming berm side of canal. Canal prism is wide, allowing canal boats to dock along road and pass as well. While Canal Co. specified width of canal, locks and towpath, flexibility prevailed.

60.84 *Limited parking along road.*

60.92 *Sheer cliffs along road are cascade of flowers in April*—especially saxifrage (Saxifraga virginiensis) and moss pink (Phlox subulata). Ferns abound, notably purple cliffbrake (Pellaea atropupurea), woodsia (Woodsia obtusa) and uncommon lip-fern (Cheilanthes lanosa).

61.xx *Skyline of Harpers Ferry* overlooking Potomac from Hilltop House Hotel on left to "Crazy House" at right where Civil War relics imbedded in concrete. Long wooden island is Byrnes and was site of amusement park operated by B & O, destination of passengers on excursion trains. Beautiful view of Potomac River. Byrnes Island was also known as "Island Park," run by B&O RR.

61.07 Prominent rock ledge crosses river in direction of Potomac Edison hydroelectric plant used for peaking power; building not visible when trees in leaf. Overgrown roadway beyond led to Weaver's two building (now gone), one of which was used for winter quarters for 15-20 goats later living wild and occasionally sighted and, *old military road in circuit route to Maryland Heights and Elk Ridge trails passing naval battery* on slope of ridge overlooking Bolivar. Main wall of battery was 200 feet long with gun positions and two magazines, manned by Washington Naval Yard crews in 1862. A Barbary ape, belonging to Spence Weaver's widow, escaped and lived in the wild part of one winter.

61.27 *Footbridge to limited parking along road.* Stream flows into canal from pretty cascade beyond road on berm. Canal without water from Lock 33 to this rivulet which seeps into canal bed. From here to Lock 35, intermittent pools of water in canal; one large one just beyond this point.

61.37 Evidence of *comparatively recent rock slide* from sheer cliff next to road on right; freshly-broken rock 60-75 feet long extends upward about 100 feet.

61.52 *Intersection of Hoffmaster and Harpers Ferry Roads* to right; stream enters canal from ravine.

LOCK NO. 34 (GOODHEARTS LOCK)

61.57 *Access:* See Lock 33; Lock 34 is .87 m. above via Harpers Ferry Road. Also reached south from Sharpsburg 10 m. on Harpers Ferry Road. Parking on berm limited to 8 cars. Wooden footbridge and motor vehicle bridge over lock and flume at lower end. Cable across roadway to lock unfortunately blocks pedestrians and cyclers crossing from road or parking lot, as well as unwanted motor vehicles. Drinking water.

John Brown and his men descended this road from their HQ at Kennedy Farm for the raid on Harpers Ferry between 11 p.m. and midnight on the night of 16 Oct. 1859. Same road was used by Col. Ben Davis and his 1300 cavalry to escape the trap at Harpers Ferry on the night before Gen. Miles surrendered 12,000 soldiers to Stonewall Jackson on 15 Sep. 1862.

Stone foundation of lockhouse remains; lockhouse washed away in 1936 flood. Lock constructed of limestone with a few blocks of red sandstone at upper end, possibly replacements.

On a Christmas Eve, sometime before 1919, locktender shot in self-defense man by name of Smith who demanded entry to lockhouse and tried to break open door. After flood last locktender, Willard "Coon" Goodheart sat in rocking chair which he salvaged. He commented philosophically, "We would swap belongings at flood time—lose some, gain some." In interview in 1946, he commented, "The lockhouse withstood many previous floods. Sometimes water came into the first floor and belongings were moved to the second floor. During the 1936 flood, water rose higher and higher and we moved our possessions to the second floor. Even the chickens were carried upstairs. It was a brick house with stone foundations and appeared to be firm against the swirling waters. However, we could hear the walls cracking, and we escaped by boat without our possessions before the house collapsed."

According to river survey of 1822, *canal bed ahead was location of Patomack Co's. "Long Canal."* This section may have been one described in survey, ". . . a broad wall at foot of Rocky Mountains is used for a towpath along which the boats are dragged up."

61.61 *Pretty stream* (except for litter) enters canal to right. High bluffs begin.

61.68 Breaks in towpath here repaired with towpath bridge, repaired with heavy rock and surfaced with crushed rock. Canal has shallow water filling prism from bank to bank. Painted turtles weighing up to 10 lbs. seen in summer. *Area adjacent in river is called "The Needles."*—navigating narrow rocky channels with sharp turns beginning below Dam No. 3 is compared to threading a series of needles by whitewater enthusiasts.

61.91 Extremely steep bluffs; *interesting rock formation.* Rock face of bluffs plunges into canal bed forming berm bank in places. *Round drill holes for early powder blasting can be seen.*

62.xx *Canal widens* beyond NPS mile 62 marker, giving appearance of sluggish river.

62.20 *Abutment of New Armory unfinished dam* started in 1859 to replace Dam No. 3 for diverting water into raceway for turning water power wheels in Harpers Ferry Armory, latter destroyed in 1861. Interesting view of river at low water stages by scrambling over rocks just below unfinished dam to middle of river. Probable channel of old Potomac Company canal begins above bridge abutment.

FEEDER DAM NO. 3

62.27 *Access:* From Lock 34 7 m. downstream.

Break in towpath of long standing. *Towpath traffic is routed on service road along protective semi-circular guard bank, regaining towpath above Lock 36.* Just beyond break (at point where service road goes to left toward river), one sees the lower end of Lock 35 ahead. "Mule crossover bridge" to reconnect break in towpath over feeder intake canal is under construction. *To take route which most closely approximates what towpath would be if restored (that is what one would see from the towpath), cross over narrow stream of water (conditions permitting) below Lock 35 and scramble up to berm of lower end of lock and across canal bed to towpath and on up to Lock 36.* Mileages herein are those with towpath considered intact. Route normally taken by hikers (and certainly best for cyclers) is service road to left. Area is so interesting that both routes should be taken for full appreciation.

Dam comes into view as one walks along service road on levee parallel to feeder canal and up to Inlet (Guard/Feeder) Lock No. 3. Road crosses upper end of inlet lock on wooden bridge. Lock is in excellent condition with wooden partition across upper end and part of lower gate still intact at lower end.

Dam, built in 1799, supplied water for Harpers Ferry Armory. Dam rebuilt in 1809 and 1820 "Government Dam" was repaired frequently thereafter. Local residents who remember when canal company suspended operations in 1924, recall that canal barges loaded with rocks were sunk above dam on the Maryland side in vicinity of Locks 35 and 36 in about 1927 to divert more water to raceway serving hydroelectric plant across river on West Virginia side.

As you proceed along service road note ruins of two-story brick lockhouse with center house chimney, fireplaces on each side. This was house for locktender who tended both Lock 36 and inlet lock. House was destroyed in 1936 flood. Last locktender was John W. Ault, grandfather of Level

Feeder Dam No. 3 above Harpers Ferry in 1936, showing construction detail
(National Park Service)

Walker Lavenia Brus who described the house as follows: "Grandfather's house sat in a sort of semicircle. This high guard protecting it from the high waters of the Potomac River gave it a look of seclusion so different from the other lockhouses. A two-story house consisting of two bedrooms upstairs, a living room, large kitchen, and a frame summer kitchen built on. Also a porch the length of the house with many steps. A two-room size basement where grandmother stored all her canned vegetables, and pickles. Not to mention alll the potatoes, apples, pears, etc. When viewed from the towpath, it presented a picturesque scene, with its unusual type of house, and scattered buildings, which housed chickens, hogs, a shed for garden plows, and tools. There was a pond alive with ducks, frogs and fish. A beautiful well-kept garden, fenced in from chickens. There was even a cow to provide milk and butter, and an old white horse which was a family pet and a source of enjoyment for my cousins and myself, when I was lucky enough to visit. To me this birthplace seemed like a small estate, secluded, yet homey. Verily a scene of tranquility." As you continue on past this house you will come to Lock 36, from which it is but .11 m. downstream to Lock 35.

Canoeists should avoid unmarked Dam 3. Canoeing is no recommended between Dam 3 and the US 340 bridge. Extremely dangerous.

LOCK NO. 35

62.33 *Access:* From Lock 34, .76 m. below. This lock and Lock 36 built of limestone brought by water 5 m. from Knotts Quarry on opposite shore. Lock gates missing. Locks 35 and 36 known as "Two Locks" in late 1800s. On berm side of lock note interesting structure—drydock used extensively for repairing canal boats in 1800s. There was inlet with lock gates. Concrete beams supported boats when water was let out of enclosure via now-vine-covered drainway. Boats rolled on trucks built in under water. Space enough for a man to stand and repair leak with tin and tar. To river side of lock is feeder canal, with water flowing from Inlet Lock 3 and slackwater above Dam 3. Member of Cross family was locktender

Feeder lock and canal at Dam No. 3 above Harpers Ferry, with mule crossover bridge in the background.

in 1800s. Last locktender for Lock 35 was "Jap" Smith, who lived in a frame house on hill above lock; only foundation remains. John Kercheval was locktender for locks 35 and 36 in 1850.

LOCK NO. 36

62.44 *Access:* From Lock 34, .87 m. downstream. Lock in good condition with footbridge across. Road on hill behind lock leads to Ft. Duncan, built 1862 by Union to protect Harpers Ferry. Both lock gates down and nearly rotted away. Frame house on hill above lock unoccupied since late 1950's, noted for "ghosts". Early occupant (Lavenia Brus as a girl) tells of her father and mother hearing sobbing sounds and moaning night after night and finally sound of heavy shoes on the stairs and dragging of a chain, ending with her father yelling, "Walk all night, damn you, I'm going to bed!" after which everything was quiet for the remainder of the night. Climax of ghostly activities came when Mrs. Brus' mother saw a ball of fire crossing her (Mrs. Brus') bed, after which she ran down the hill with the little girl in her arms to her father's house, never to return. In later years Mrs. Brus' grandmother said that lights would be shining in the empty house but would go out suddenly if anyone went to investigate. A path on the berm side of the lock leads upstream to the Maryland One Bank.

62.56 *Cross concrete waste weir.*

62.90 *Huckleberry Hill Hiker-Biker Overnighter;* nearest road access Dargan Bend at 64.9. Next campsite upstream Mountain Lock Carry-In Camp Area at 67.2; hiker-biker upstream is Killiansburg Cave at 75.2; downstream is Bald Eagle Island at 56.31. Campsite situated on bend of river; exposed to brisk winds in winter and gentle breezes in summer. 100 yards downstream on river side of towpath is clump of Dutchman's-breeches, with border of squirrel corn predominating in April. Water, toilet.

63.05 Low cliffs along berm support *beautiful rock garden of wildflowers:* squirrel corn, Dutchman's-breeches, Star of Bethlehem, rock columbine. Canal bed dry. Fine sycamores.

113

House at
Lock 36.
(Historic American
Building Survey)

63.29 Canal rounds rocky point, river side dropping straight to water. *Beautiful views of river.* Lovely walk or bicycle ride.

63.68 Small stream flows into canal from forked ravine to right. Male yellow-throated warbler noted here several years ago quite far up river for this southern species. This is warbler suspected of hybridizing with parula warbler. (There's no accounting for tastes!) to produce controversial "Suttons warbler." Observed Canadian Geese, chickadee, Carolina wren, downy woodpecker, mallard duck, ring-billed gull, whistling swan, and roosting area of about 40 turkey vultures. Abundance of sliders (turtles)—sometimes 7 to 8 to a log. Canal bed swampy after being filled with several inches of water. Wetness of bed varies widely in most sections of canal, depending mostly on season, unless some body of water feeding particular area. Straightaway in canal for ½ m.

64.20 Stream enters canal. Site of lost culvert #95. *Path leads across canal bed to Shinhan Road* which comes down far side of ravine and continues ahead along berm to Dargan Bend. Canal bed filled with water to that point. *Here as elsewhere along canal, inadvisable to drink from side streams.* This stream, for example, provides drainage for Washington Co. dump (solid wastes), located between Dargan and canal.

64.68 Culvert #96, Sawmill Run, 8' span, rebuilt ca 1980. 100 whistling swans sighted 1954.

DARGAN BEND RECREATION AREA

64.89 *Access:* From Lock 34 (Goodhearts) proceed 2.3 m. on Harpers Ferry Rd. to graveled Shinhan Rd., where turn left .8 m. to parking area. Can also be reached from Sharpsburg by taking Harpers Ferry, Dargan, and Shinhan Rds. Parking for 25 cars. Upper lot of 14 spaces for vehicles with boat trailers. Footbridge spans canal near parking entrance. Vehicular bridge at lower edge of upper parking lot crosses canal to asphalt boat launching pad. Dargan one of many power boat-oriented recreation areas constructed along canal by NPS in 1969-1971. Camping not permitted. Area has dozen picnic tables with one fireplace for every three tables. Toilets. Summer and year around houses scattered along flood plain of W. Va. side of river.

64.99 *Culvert #97*, 8' span. Whistling swans sighted here. Many large sycamores and maples. Recreation cabins ahead.

65.10 Beginning of *ruins of Potomac Refining Co.* Original quarry opening for manganese, discovered during construction of canal. Manganese operation discontinued when formation led under canal bed and company developed limestone quarries. At one time, crusher and kilns operated with steam power generated by coal delivered by canal boat. Operating company abandoned site in 1912 when it reestablished operations near Staunton, Va. Lime produced through the 1950's.

65.21 *Two old, abandoned limestone kilns* on bank above berm. O. J. Shinham operated kilns until about 1960. Dirt road upstream connected several quarries.

65.34 Slide has obscured downriver entrance of 50 foot-long vehicular tunnel through high ridge at edge of canal. Upstream portal seen from towpath is clear of debris and provides dry but drafty shelter from rain. Old road upstream leads to other quarries with high cliffs and loose rocks.

65.37 *Cave opening* about 25 ft. from floor of quarry; requires rock climb to reach from below; cliff rises above opening. *Exploration by other than experienced rockclimbers with equipment not advised.*

65.38 *Cave opening at base of quarry wall.* Cave-ins near entrance make it *unsafe to explore.*

65.60 Across river cabins and trailers can be seen along flood plain with more substantial dwellings on heights above overlooking river.

65.65 Open pasture dotted with red cedar. Stone foundations and cistern on knoll 150 yds. from canal. Across river, stream from ravine drains watershed surrounding Bakerton, with extensive abandoned manganese and limestone quarries.

65.78 Open field on flat along berm.

66.00 Opposite this point on W. Va. side is extensive cut from which iron ore was obtained for Antietam Furnace prior to canal days. At this point was Cow Ring Sluice, on opposite side, one of river improvements of Patowmack Co.

66.02 Lower end of narrow island, 100 yds. from Md. shore for .5 m., covered with shrubs and trees up to 25 ft. high. Drift wood lodged on shore indicates it is subject to overflow.

66.03 End of field on berm. Towpath beyond cuts across upper end of Dargan Bend. Distance of river from towpath exceeds 100 yds. in some places. Sycamore predominant, with scattering of beech, oak, silver maple and infrequent persimmon, wild cherry and shadbush (also called service berry) and juneberry which bloom in March and April. Pawpaw, spicebush, honeysuckle and grapevines provide an understory for taller trees.

66.30 *Towpath rejoins river.* Ducks noted: blue winged teal, common merganser, green-winged teal, mallard and wood. Also osprey (rare) pileated woodpecker and whistling swan (migratory). Beautiful view.

66.32 Hillside along berm rises and rocky outcrops protrude from slope. Rocky hillside soon becomes cliff.

66.61 Ravine enters canal with drainage providing water in canal for 100 yds. downstream; broad path leads up ravine. Very scenic area.

Lockhouse
Number 37
(Mountain Lock)

66.86 Path leads across canal to road ending at limestone quarry.

LOCK NO. 37 (MOUNTAIN LOCK)

66.96 *Access:* See Lock 33 (60.70) from which take Harpers Ferry Rd. 5.1 m. (.3 m. beyond Dargan Village) to Mt. Lock Rd.; take left .4 m. (road takes sharp left at .1 m. where Limekiln Rd. joins on right) past recreation cabins to Lock 37, with practically no parking; or, proceed straight ahead on Limekiln Rd. to Mt. Lock Recreation Area with ample parking and walk .22 m. downstream to Lock 37.

Mountain Lock has one of most picturesque settings along canal with rocky slopes rising immediately behind lockhouse and panoramic view of river in foreground. Lockhouse constructed of red brick with lower 5 feet coated with whitewash; attic has double windows in each gable. Disintegrated front porch replaced by NPS with side steps to front door. Outside entry to cellar with small windows at ground level. Building stabilized with board breather frames in windows. Lower frame wing in rear. Newly roofed and guttered, in good maintenance condition. Wooden lower extension in rear has large stone fireplace with rock chimney extending upward for 14 feet; converted to smaller brick chimney for additional 4 feet.

Deep lock immediately in front of house; lock was extended downstream with wooden extension, one of eleven such locks. Concrete bridge spans wasteway; rock wall on upper river side has collapsed, but otherwise stone work in good condition. Footbridge crosses lock. Blocks of limestone transported from a quarry ¼ m. away on Md. side. Capt. John Moore, Boat No. 9, states that there was also drydock at Mt. Lock. Some capstones retain towrope creases. Remnants of lower gate survive. W. R. Hutton, Chief Engineer for Canal Co. in his report of 14 Aug. 1872 advised that Mt. Lock was in need of repair, "A part of the masonry is loose, and the side walls have been pushed in at top, so that boats cramp in it." On 31 May 1873 Hutton reported that Mt. Lock had been rebuilt.

Wide basin extends north of lock for about 75 yds. before canal narrows to normal width. Basin and canal have built-up berm here as there is stream valley beyond berm.

116

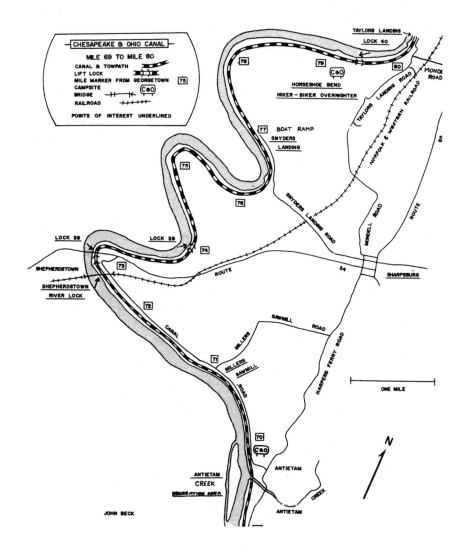

67.02 Informal overflow.

67.07 *Cross culvert #100, 8'-span.*

67.15 *Cross concrete waste weir* (controlling water level between Locks 37 and 38).

67.16 *Mt. Lock Recreation Area* extends 300 yds. along bank between towpath and river with tables, fireplaces, cut wood, pump, covered trash cans, toilets and footbridges at each end over canal bed to parking area just off Limekiln Rd. *Limekiln Rd. leads E. .4 m. to Harpers Ferry Rd. or N. 2.2 m. to Antietam Village. From* this point Limestone Rd. parallels canal, sometimes close by and at other times on slope above from this point to Wades Landing.

67.37 Built-up berm stops and canal widens for next mile as hills and cliffs on opposite side form natural berm. 67.61 Quarry.

67.83 Fine spring (but water not safe for drinking—doesn't sound too fine, does it?); moderate cliffs along berm. Squirrel corn, Dutchman's breeches.

67.93 Steep, dry watercourse to right, "Giant Steps," affords an interesting scramble.

68.05 Beyond very large patches of squirrel corn and Dutchman's-breeches, both blooming in April and early May beyond cabin on hill.

68.25 Large spring flows several-gallons-per-minute stream from base of hill on berm side and north along canal until it disappears in canal bed.

68.45 *Old ruins of lime kiln on berm are probable location of "Sharpless Landing"* of early canal days.

68.52 Lost culvert #101 Briens Road culvert. Site of McShanes Ferry
68.53 Limestone loading wharf.

68.85 Footbridge across canal. *Stone support for pivot bridge has disappeared in last few years.* Stone probably salvaged for ballast in vehicle tracks which crosses here to get boats to river side. *Rd. opposite leads .1 m. to Limekiln Rd. This is Wades Landing, frequently referred to as Shaffers Landing,* popular with fishermen and boatmen. *Limestone for Godeys Limekiln on lower Rock Creek in Georgetown* was boated across Potomac after quarrying on Knotts Island opposite. Berm stone wall beyond.

69.30 *Probable stone-walled water gate through berm to small (2-3 acres) basin. This was "O'Briens Basin,"* canal landing area for *Antietam Village.* NPS access road descends from towpath to canal bottom, through aqueduct, then back to towpath on one side and to Canal Road on berm side. 1877 map of Sharpsburg area in *Illustrated Atlas of Washington County 1877* shows a railroad connecting the village with the canal at this point.

Antietam Iron Works, 1822.

ANTIETAM VILLAGE

Access: Take Harpers Ferry Rd. from center of Sharpsburg 3 m. to Antietam Village. It is .2 m. to right on Canal Rd. from lower end of Antietam Creek Aqueduct Recreation Area parking lot.

Peaceful village gives little hint of teeming activity which prevailed here in pre-canal days. Three lime kiln chimneys, 250 yds. inland on paved Harpers Ferry rd., all that remain of industrial crafts village once extending along both banks of Antietam Creek for ¼ m. up from Potomac. Old Antietam Iron Furnace was located across road from the lime kiln chimneys. Traces of old millrace, which supplied number of wheels, may be discerned opposite chimneys.

The first Battle of Antietam was in 1736, before earliest landgrants in Antietam Valley; only handful of scattered French and other settlers occupied the valley. Delawares, crowded from earlier hunting grounds to north and east, on hunting and exploratory trip far to south of Potomac, invaded home territory of Catawbas and pillaged a few villages. The usually peaceful Catawbas formed a war party and headed north to avenge their vandalism. Where silt-laden Antietam formed a delta extending into Potomac River, Delawares forded and camped on the Md. shore. Here Catawbas attacked, but in ensuing hand-to-hand combat, Delawares ruthlessly vanquished them. Indian artifacts have been found on surface and also uncovered in this vicinity. When canal was dug, tomahawks, bones, pipe stems, beads, and arrowheads were revealed. From nearby burial mounds mortars, pestles and skinning knives have been recovered. Scharf in 1882 mentioned a burial mound on the bluff across from Antietam Iron Furnace.

Iron deposits near Antietam were known at early date, entire valley was underlaid with limestone for fluxing, and hardwoods were available for charcoal; by 1750, before Washington County was formed, land records refer to Antietam as Frederick Forge. First iron furnace was opened here in 1765, and during American Revolution cannon were forged, cannon balls cast and muskets turned out by craftsmen. Products reached lower valley by Potomac longboats. After completion of C & O Canal, pig iron was boated to Harpers Ferry for further working in Federal Armory. Metal parts for Rumsey steamboat were forged at Antietam in 1786. Blacksmiths produced farm and other machinery. At various times village included rolling mill, slitting mill, nail factories, large grist mill, limestone crushing mills, spinning mills, hemp mills, flour mills, sawmill, shingle mill, cooperage factory, a woolen mill and stove works. Water power from Antietam Creek raceway drove the wheels of industry. Dam, diverting water into raceway, was 19½ feet high. Water wheel operating bellows for furnace was 20 feet in diameter and 4 feet wide. Furnace produced 40 to 60 tons of pig iron a week. Forge hammer 21 tons operated by 16 foot mill wheel. Iron rolling mill operated by 14 foot overshot wheel. 16 foot wheel in nail factory drove 19 nail and spike machines, producing 400-500 kegs of nails/week. This industry is hard to visualize today as one gazes across soft green pastures to quiet village of the present. The ironworks employed 260 workers in the 1840s.

As early as 1802 work was underway to convert Antietam Creek in Maryland to canal boat navigation. Engineer making survey recommended 20 dams (they haven't changed!) with locks, and noted low fish dams built by Indians in creek bed. No lock sites have been found to date. Coke by canal boat replaced charcoal for fuel at Antietam in 1860's, as coke proved superior fuel.

Antietam Village fell before the Four Horsemen of the Apocalypse: Fire, Flood, Pestilence, and War. Pestilence alone would have been enough; Sharpsburg Rd. nearby passes along field where 500 Irish canal workers were buried in common grave—victims of cholera epidemic of 1832.

ANTIETAM AQUEDUCT

69.36 *Access: Distance from Sharpsburg 3 m.; from Lock 38 3.15 m.; from Lock 33 (opposite Harpers Ferry) 9 m.* Take Harpers Ferry Road from center of Sharpsburg 2.8 m. to Canal Road (just short of Antietam Village) where turn right .2 m. to Antietam Creek Recreation Area. Reached via Canal Rd. from Lock 38, which see. NPS camping and recreation area from aqueduct to about mileage 69.9. Canal Rd. on berm side paved, with marked parking spaces alongside road. Several footbridges cross canal bed to camp-

Antietam Creek Aqueduct. (Photo 1961 by Historic American Building Survey)

grounds between towpath and river. Toilets, water pumps, firewood. Evening programs in NPS campfire area in season as announced on bulletin board. Tent camping only (34 spaces). Camping subject to time limits as posted. Next camping area upstream is Killiansburg Hiker-Biker Overnighter at 75.2; downstream Mt. Lock Recreation Area at 67.2. Next H/B downstream is Huckleberry Hill at 62.9.

Antietam Aqueduct is 200 yds. downstream from lower end of parking lot. This beautiful 140-foot structure is No. 4 in series of 11 stone aqueducts. Built of limestone from quarry ¼ m. away, it is 108 feet between abutments. The two outside spans are equal. Much of the aqueduct above the arch was blasted down in 1864. Heavy iron railings once protected mules and mule drivers. Antietam Creek, which flows under aqueduct, drains an extensive valley reaching to Hargerstown and beyond into Pa.; famed Burnside Bridge crosses it 4 m. upstream. Creek is favorite of whitewater canoeists in spring. Creek originates in Pennsylvania.

69.48 Improved Canal Road across canal and downstream end of recreation area, comes from Antietam Village, continues along berm to Lock 38 and connects with MD. 34. View back to right includes interesting stone arch of Antietam bridge over Antietam Creek.

69.65 Houses and cabins on berm side of road. Clumps of Osage orange trees follow canal.

69.98 End of developed area. Fields to right.

70.38 Dog-leg in road over natural spring outlet thru culvert #103, 8'-span. Houses along berm road from here through Millers Sawmill area.

70.52 Grassy area begins in front of houses facing canal. Nice river vistas. View back along river includes bulk of Elk Ridge with site where McClellans lookout tower (on Red Hill—dismantled by Md. Forest Service and Park Service) was at its left end.

70.61 American redstart, bobwhite, cowbird, goldfinch, indigo bunting, mourning dove, pileated woodpecker, osprey, whistling swan, pileated woodpecker.

MILLERS SAWMILL

70.68 Access: Via Canal Rd. from Lock 38 or from Sharpsburg on Harpers Ferry Rd. .8 m. to Millers Sawmill Rd. where turn right about 2.5 m. to Canal Rd.

Now summer community, Millers Sawmill was "Millers Basin" of canal days. Canal supplied water to Millers Sawmill until Civil War. Wide area in canal marks location of former wharf and warehouse. Cross culvert #104, 4'-span at 70.78. Note interesting geological formation in hillside behind first house west of Millers sawmill consisting of series of twisted anticlines. Grassy stretch of towpath here marked by fine line of large syca--mores. Beautiful area of W. Va. side from here to Shepherdstown.

71.24 Cross cleared area with road leading up right to Conocoheague Gun Club. Clubhouse was 5th stop for famous "Douglas Hike" of 1954, when party led by Supreme Court Justice William O. Douglas walked the towpath from Cumberland to Georgetown to build sufficient sentiment to block proposed destruction of route by construction of parkway.

Old Canal scene below Lock 38 across from Shepherdstown, W. Va. (Courtesy of John Frye)

PACKHORSE FORD

71.39 *Access:* From paralleling Canal Road directly on berm. Note irregular pattern of rocks forming double "V" ford. Small island (100 yds. in length) below ford, with dam across to island. Path from Canal Rd. leads across canal bed and towpath to lower end of island. Beyond Packhorse Ford to S. on W. Va. side is old Trough Road, route of Confederate retreat after Battle of Antietam. When first settlers—Germans, Irish, and Scotch-Irish from Pennslyvania and Dutch from New York—began to push into Western Md. in 1730's they followed old Indian and packhorse trail from York, Pa. Those who wished to cross Potomac River into Va. found Packhorse Ford. 1 m. below site of present Shepherdstown, W. Va. the one and only good crossing for many miles east or west of it. Md. Historic Commission sign along road reads: Blackfords Ford. Also known as Botelers, Packhorse, and Shepherdstown Ford. According to 3 May 1742 deed from Isaac Garrison to Moses Teague it was called "Wagon Road Foard." "Stonewall" Jackson's Command crossed here enroute from Harpers Ferry to Sharpsburg. Here the entire Army of Northern Virginia withdrew into Virginia, Sept. 18-19, 1862, following Battle of Antietam."

71.55 *Culvert #105,* 4' span. Pull-over parking areas along parallel Canal Rd. connected by foot paths through uncleared canal bed to towpath. Beautiful wooded shelf between towpath and river *formerly* used for camping.

71.63 Riffle running across river here is actually remains of old dam called Boteler/Reynolds Dam) supplying water to mill race of Botelers natural cement mill, remains visible on opposite W. Va. side of river. Cement for locks and other stone structures along canal was produced at this mill. First operated as flour mill then as cement mill until it was burned by Federals in early morning of 19 Aug. 1861. Was rebuilt but damaged in 1889 flood. Next cement mill was Roundtop above Hancock. A dam here allowed boats to go out of canal to cement mill, most cement of which went to Washington for federal buildings, possibly including Washington Monument. This was scene of lively military action following Battle of Antietam. Federal troops pursuing Confederate detachment across river found themselves in untenable position, and retreated across river under fire—some swimming, some wading ford downstream and some trying to cross on the dam. South of old dam on W. Va. side is beautiful example of complete geological fold, rare view caused by erosion over centuries.

71.73 Large *abandoned cement kilns* were in operation 1888 as a part of the Antietam cement company. Active birdlife year around. Level Walker Ken Rollins assigned this section comments that, "This must be the blackbird capital of the world."

71.75 At small *culvert* draining directly in canal bed note almost hidden cedar logs which formed apparent timber cage filled with riprap for *wall of landing, probably for lime kiln because of limestone close by.*

72.23 ˙ Two large pin oaks overhanging river. Oak trees generally are not common along towpath.

72.35 Two large, prominent houses atop cliff on W. Va. side of river; one to right burned out, leaving 3 yellow brick chimneys.

72.48 Pass under high trestle of Norfolk and Western R.R. Park-like slope under trestle to right. Trestle built c 1908.

72.59 *Atop cliff across river in W.Va. is James Rumsey Monument,* erected in 1915 in pretty Rumsey State Park, it has an Ionic column of granite 75 feet high. Remains of Rumsey lie in unmarked grave in St. Margaret's churchyard, London. James Rumsey of Shepherdstown (then Mecklenburg) was a pioneer of steam navigation, designer of the Patowmack Canal locks at Great Falls, and at George Washington's bequest, one-time superintendent (chief engineer) of the Patowmack Co. Rumsey's famous steamboat, utilizing a sort of hydraulic jet-propulsion, made its debut in a gala public demonstration in the slackwater of the Potoamc at this point on 3 Dec. 1787. Hundreds of spectatiors lined the banks when the craft set out from the Shepherdstown ferry landing, headed into the current, and astounded onlookers by making headway upstream at the rate of four miles an hour. By many, this is considered a true "first" for steam navigation. After going for half a mile above Shepherdstown, to a point opposite to Swearingen's Spring, she rounded to and retunred, going for some distance below town, below the Shenandoah Valley R.R. bridge.

72.63 Pass line of 5 stone piers of old Shenandoah Valley R.R. bridge across to Shepherdstown. Piers were built on wood cribbing, visible at low water. When dam below in place cribbing protected by being submerged: now rotting and piers tilting. The Shenandoah Valley was an extension of an earlier local railroad whose northern terminus was at Shepherdstown and eventually became a division of the N & W. The bridge was built, and line opened to Hagerstown in 1880. Piers of bridge, topped by cedar trees, are quite picturesque. Beginning of 100-feet-wide section of canal serving Lock 38 and Shepherdstown River Lock. Directly across river is wall for old wharf area. White-washed brick building was toll gate house; brown streak which sometimes shows thru indicates 1936 flood level.

Old scene at Lock 38-Shepherdstown. (Courtesy of John Frye)

SHEPHERDSTOWN RIVER LOCK

Access: From Lock 38 .15 m. upstream. Boats entered the canal from the river slackwater formed by Botelers Dam below.

72.65 Towpath crosses filled-in portion of lock (and continues on embankment with masonry wall on river side), but originally passed over stone arch or bridge. Much of fine masonry still intact, but obscured by vegetation; no gates survive. Lock once admitted boats from Shepherdstown to canal; operated until 1889. One of several such "river locks" along canal. Directly across river note remains of stone wharf where boats unloaded at Shepherdstown. An item from the *Shepherdstown Register* of 27 Mar. 1858 recalls the former activity here: "The boat 'Susan Barker', George Harris, Capt., left the Chesapeake and Ohio Wharf at this place on Saturday, ladened with 4,000 bushels of corn, 200 bu. of wheat, 150 bu. oats, 128 barrels of flour, 56 bu. of timothy seed—the entire weight of which was 134 tons. The boat averaged 4 feet 6 inches of water in the bow, and 4 feet 5 inches in the stern. This is said to be the heaviest load ever known to leave the wharf of Shepherdstown upon the Chesapeake and Ohio Canal."

SHEPHERDSTOWN

Shepherdstown, on opposite side of Potomac, is oldest inhabited community in W. Va. Thomas Shepherd, founder, may have arrived in 1732, but at least by 1734 when he obtained a grant of 222 acres. By 1736 there was a considerable settlement in the area. By 1739 Thomas Shepherd had established at least one grist mill. Town was laid out before outbreak of French and Indian War in 1754. On 12 Nov. 1762, town was incorporated as Mecklenburg. Popularly called Shepherd's Town from the beginning, it acquired the name legally in 1798. Another charter in 1820 named it Shepherdstown.

Old Market House, so used from 1800 to 1853, now houses very attractive library. A 40 feet-diameter mill wheel installed in 1880 on the site of Shepherds Mill, thought to have been built sometime before 1754. Mill wheel is said to be largest overshot wheel extant.

Lock 38, Shepherdstown; from Rumsey Bridge across Potomac River at Shepherdstown, W. Va. 1962.

BLACKFORDS FERRY

72.77 *Access:* From Lock 38. Recent concrete ferry ramp on river bank to left. Exact site of original ferry not known.

As population increased, Packhorse Ford no longer met needs for crossing Potomac River. Thomas Van Swearingen established a ferry from Md. side and began ferry operations in 1765 with charges of three pence per person and same for each horse. Shepherdstown maintained road to ferry landing on its side of river, and Washington County, Md. constructed road from Boonsboro thru Sharpsburg to Swearingen Landing on Md. side.

According to one source, (A. D. Kenamond — *Prominent Men of Shepherdstown*), ferry passed from Thos. Van Swearingen to his son Benoni to his daughter Sarah, who married John Blackford. According to another (Editor Fletcher M. Green of Ferry Hill Plantation Journal), Col. John Blackford in 1816 purchased from Thos Van Swearingen of Shepherdstown half interest in his ferry and franchise, boats and apparatus, and three tracts of land; later, perhaps in 1828, the remainder from Mrs. Thos. Van Swearingen. Together with lands acquired from Thomas Shepherd, among others, Col. Blackford consolidated them all into Ferry Hill Plantation. Blackford appointed two of his slaves, Edmund and Julious (Ned and Jupe), "Foremen of the Ferry." They did the work themselves, called on other slaves to assist and even hired free labor, both black and white, to assist in rush periods.

Construction of C & O Canal resulted in a court case involving ferry lot of 1 acre, 3 rods, and 17 perches. The Canal Co. condemned the lot and one cent in damages was allowed on 30 Aug. 1832. Col. Blackford and five others retained three lawyers to appeal, and in court thereafter Attorney Price claimed ferry business would be damaged by a lift lock from river which would encourage taking boats from Va. and lifting them into canal and bypassing ferry. Court ruled in favor of Canal Co. and confirmed one cent damages.

Ferry passed to Blackford's son Franklin in 1839, until he (or his brother Henry Van Swearingen Blackford) sold it to Virginia and Maryland Bridge Co. (David Billmyer of Shepherdstown principal stockholder) for $15,000. Company abandoned ferry in 1850, replacing it with a covered bridge which was burned by confederates in 1861. Rebuilt in 1871, it was destroyed by flood of 1889 and replaced by an iron bridge, piers of which are still evident in river; flood of 1936 carried away bridge itself. Present concrete ramp was built when ferry resumed operation in 1936.

AN ASSIST TO JOHN BROWN

Steep road to top of hill was used by John Brown to pull a wagon loaded with iron-tipped pike poles. Henry Kyd Douglas (later youngest staff officer under command of Stonewall Jackson), crossing from Shepherdstown in early fall of 1859, met Brown, whom he knew as Isaac Smith, at foot of hill in a rainstorm. Brown was unable to climb hill with an overloaded wagon pulled by two horses. Young Douglas went to his home, Ferry Hill Farm (large brick house at top of hill now C & O Canal Headquarters), returned with a team of carriage horses and its driver, Enoch, and helped pull wagon to top of hill, only later learning of contraband pike poles which were delivered to B & O station across river (Shenandoah Junction).

72.78 Piers of old Shepherdstown bridge washed away in 1936; abutment's on berm and first pier on river side, between canal and towpath. Canal bed artificially split in later years at this point by dirt embankment in middle of canal bed, running up to lower end of Lock 38, with one channel for canal and other for flume. Area was upper end of loading, unloading and stopover basin for Shepherdstown area. Birds noted include American red start, bob white, cowbird, goldfinch, indigo bunting, mourning dove, pileated woodpecker, scarlet tanager, summer tanager, and warbling vireo.

LOCK NO. 38 (SHEPHERDSTOWN)

72.80 *Access:* Distance from Shepherdstown .5 m.; from Sharpsburg 3.2 m. From Shepherdstown, W. Va. take W. Va. 48 .4 m. from center of town across Rumsey Bridge and go .1 m. to first road to right and go down road .2 m. past 3 old houses, earlier associated with Ferry Hill Plantation. House on south side of road has been in Knode family for several generations. From Sharpsburg take MD. 34 3.1 m. W. and turn left on paved (but unmarked) Canal Rd. .1 m. short of James Rumsey Bridge at red barn opposite Ferry Hill Inn and go down hill .2 m. to Lock 38 parking area. Graveled Canal Rd. (hard surfaced not far below) leads downstream on berm side of canal parallel to and only few feet away from it to Antietam Creek Recreation Area 3 m. below, providing good access to canal, Millers Sawmill and Antietam Aqueduct, as well as good canal views along way. Dirt road crossing wooden bridge over waste weir and downstream end of Lock 38 leads down and back to river to boat ramp located South of old road bridge piers straddling canal. No drinking water or toilets. Overnight accommodations available in Sharpsburg and Martinsburg areas. Restaurant, stores in Shepherdstown. Overnight accomodations at the Bavarian Inn at Shepherdstown and the Thomas Shepherd Inn (excellent bed-and-breakfast).

Lock 38 offers an excellent jumping-off point for nice 3¾ m. walk upstream to Snyders Landing or 3 m. downstream to Antietam Village or Antietam Aqueduct.

Lower end of lock shows well-preserved covered flume is clearer than opposite side which is mostly filled in. Wasteway intact, has nice arches. Lock 38 had unusually small lift of 5 ft. (standard was 8 ft.) Lock had wooden extension to handle two boats at a time. Lock in excellent condition constructed of limestone from quarries on opposite W. Va. shore. Part of one side of lower lock gate in canal bed. Upper gate missing. Two-story brick lockhouse stood opposite upper end of lock on towpath side, approximately 40 feet from lock wall. Feed store, a wooden structure 40 feet long, stood on berm side of lock wall just about centered between lock gates. Both structures removed with no traces left though there are traces of other ruins in area. Until about 1972 opposite lock on berm was old ferry inn constructed in late 1700s and may have been operated as an inn by Franklin Blackford (son of John Blackford-owner of Ferry Hill Plantation) in 1838; later occupied by Knode family which also operated feed store on lock wall.

George Knode (of Shepherdstown) lived in inn building (his home) early in this century. He relates how Level Walker Capt. Dan Soulders (of Sharpsburg) would stop by or pass around 7:15 each morning, carrying a little pack on his back as well as a pick and square-ended shovel (for emergency repairs) as he made his round from Sharpsburg to Snyders Landing to Millers Sawmill to Mt. Lock and back to Sharpsburg. In his pack he carried letters and miscellanous items—a well-known figure for many years.

72.82 Pass under James Rumsey Bridge opened 15 July 1939 (carrying MD. 34) replacing bridge destroyed in 1936 flood at which time canal was under water for 62 hours with peak 22 feet above towpath. Canal bed for next .73 m. completely cleared of vegetation by NPS in 1957. Towpath slightly graveled and in good condition for some distance. Next mile or so popular fishing for bass, carp and catfish. Several trailers are on berm side of canal at bottom of cleared and mowed slope leading up to Ferry Hill Inn .2 m. to right. Birds observed include American redstart, indigo bunting, little green night heron, pileated woodpecker, warbling vireo, and whistling swan.

FERRY HILL PLANTATION

Ferry Hill was built by Col. John Blackford in 1813 and was later home of Col. Henry Kyd Douglas, aide to Gen. Stonewall Jackson. Gen. Robert E. Lee's son was brought here after being wounded at Antietam. Ferry Hill Plantation was closely tied with both the C & O canal and Potomac river. Blackford's Journal for 1838 and a bit of 1839 (Ferry Hill Plantation Journal, published by Tom and Nat Hahn) contains many references to canal, for example:

5th (Jan. 1838)—Exchanged $30 with Franklin for Canal scrip. (The scarcity of small coins in circulation, caused by the disappearance of specie during the panic of 1837, the Canal Co. in 1837 to issue notes of $5.00 or less and later up to $20.00. Scrip circulated widely in Maryland and Virginia and spread also into Pa. and Ohio.)

15th (Jan.)—A Humerickhouse called to request me to make out my acct. against the Packet Coy. for ferriages. (The Packet Co. operated a line of boats from Georgetown to Williamsport. It unloaded goods at Ferry Hill to be ferried across the Potomac to Shepherdstown. Humerickhouse was a boatman.)

21st (Jan.)—Michael called after candlelight has been down at J. Knode's says he is in search of coment stone [lime] that wants to ingage to take down the canal.

127

14th (Feb)—The lock Keeper from the lock above called says Rogers noticed two logs which I have in the Canal. (G. W. Rogers was an official at one of the dams above Ferry Hill. Despite the lockkeeper's warning Blackford failed to remove the logs and on March 11 Rogers himself called on Blackford and threatened action.)

11th (Mar.)—The weater let into the canal. The companys scow and Boarding House Boat came down Rogers with it has made some threats relative to two popler logs which I have in the canal the lower level filled in the course of the day.

Next 11.6 m. to Dam No. 4 takes us along a very scenic portion of canal through an area rife with Civil War history, with pretty river scenes, fine berm cliffs and interesting caves. Beauty of this section can be rivaled by few others. Though close to main roads, it seems far away from congestion.

73.07 Towpath comes directly onto river bank and remains so to Lock 39, with interesting *stone paving of towpath,* designed to maintain towpath during flood periods. To right *berm rises steeply as cliff; beginning of very beautiful, striking stretch of berm cliffs, extending for next mile.* Red, white and yellow flowers add to beauty of cliff face on spring days.

Ferry Hill Plantation at Lock 38, Shepherdstown. (on Maryland side of Potomac River)

73.17 *Across canal is rough footway up hill leading left to excellent viewpoint atop cliff, 100 feet above towpath.* Cliff beyond is often sheer for 90 feet, affording *many opportunities for rock climbing. Cave in face of cliff.*

73.29 *Two small caves 20 feet up berm wall, reached by narrow ledge.* Many cardinals, downy woodpeckers, Carolina wrens, blackbirds, catbirds, and an occasional pileated woodpecker.

73.46 *Culvert #107,* 4'-span, silted in on river side, with only 6 inches of opening left. To right, berm wall is broken by very pretty ravine. Very fine wildflower area in April: bitter cress, bloodroot, chickweed, Dutchman's-breeches, Indian strawberry, pansy violets, squirrel-corn, saxifrages, toothwarts, twinleaf, walking fern and wild ginger, early mendow rue, mitre wort, shepherd's purse.

73.89 *Cliff reaches height of 100 feet.* Smooth yellow violet, Solomons seal, Virginia water leaf.

73.9x *Stone paving of footway ends about 100 yards below Lock 39.*

Killiansburg or Killing's Cave was a place of refuge of Sharpsburg
citizens during the Battle of Antietam.

LOCK NO. 39

74.00 *Access:* From Lock 38, 1.2 m. downstream; or Snyders Landing 2.65 m. upstream. Known earlier as "One-Mile Lock" in Shepherdstown area, and perhaps as "Foot of Sharpsburg Level" in Sharpsburg Landing area, and as Mitchels Lock in 1838. In attractive, remote setting; evidence of old road to lock now gone. *Portion of walls of former lockhouse remains* on berm at upper end of lock. *Remains of snubbing post* near center of lock on towpath side; uncommon. Lock gates gone, though portions of both upper and lower gates were visible in bed of lock in 1970. Some original iron work remains in stonework. Cleared. Stone and concrete flume. High cliff at downstream end of lock. Beyond lock is pleasant, wooded ravine with intermittent stream. Look for veronica (speed well).

74.04 *Culvert #108*, 6'-span. In excellent condition, good example of fine masonry work done on canal culverts.

74.07 *Cross concrete waste weir* (39-40 level). Earlier stone construction of weir can be seen below concrete. Waste weirs were necessary to remove canal water for repairs and to prevent winter ice damage.

74.12 The remains of the old wooden timing marker 150' above the lock has now disappeared.

74.15 *Cliffs on berm end;* rounded hills beyond, with scattered cedar trees.

74.2x Beginning of *40-yard stone wall* at canal bed edge on berm, probably used for 2-3 man repair scow and possibly for loading point for local farm products as well. *Ruins of 2½-story canal company* frame section house, 18 x 33 feet, at upper end of wall. Zimmermans maintained house for repair scow quarters. Ruins of stable and root cellar above company house; 2 buildings on old maps. Hinde Manion was in charge of repair scow to Mt. Lock in later years.

74.28 *Culvert #109,* 6'-span, carries a small stream from ravine on berm. Faint trail leads up ravine to road which connects with MD. 34 on each side of Norfolk & Western R.R. overpass. This shows as road on old maps; road continued up berm ½ m.; an Osage orange hedge, still visible, marks its route.

74.30 *Pumping station* for Sharpsburg water works.

74.60 Typical for next mile are old cedar-dotted cow pastures on berm, with stretches of hedge rows and wooded floodplain with many fine trees to left. Cliffs mark far side of river as canal curves around one of many points caused by entrenchment of former meanders of Potomac. Towpath graveled with intermittent patches of grass and in good condition to Snyders Landing, lightly shaded in summer by fine sycamores.

75.29 Widewater on Sharpsburg Level now made into 3-acre, lightly-wooded camping area—*Killiansburg Cave Hiker Biker Overnighter.* Closest access from Lock 38 at mileage 72.80. Next campsite upstream Horseshoe Bend Hiker Biker at 79.9; downstream Antietam Creek Carry-In Camp Area at 69.3. Next Hiker Biker downstream Mountain Lock at 67.2. Berm side becomes rocky slope and then cliffs. Pleasant walking. Towpath forms a river wall.

75.61 *First of several caves* on berm, known as *Sharpsburg Shelter Caves.* First two caves, whose openings are about 20 feet apart, are accessible from edge of canal bed in interesting rock formation. *Caves are muddy, slippery and dangerous, so be prepared!* Cave to right has winding crawlway reaching back 200 feet.

75.73 *Very interesting cliff,* 75 ft. high, with curious twist and overhangs. Two shallow caves: one to right (Killiansburg Cave) 50 ft. above towpath on cliff face reached by steep climb. Cave about 20 feet high x 30 feet across x 35 feet deep—really only shallow opening; obscured by growth in summer. Visitors should not build fires in cave or leave cave a mess as some do. Second shallow cave to left near canal bed level. Published documents on Battle of Antietam report citizens of Sharpsburg in caves along canal at Shepherdstown, including Killiansburg Cave.

75.78 Towpath supported on river bank by *surface-level stone wall.* Long straightway in canal.

75.8x *Shallow cave* about 30 feet above towpath. At least *20 caves* counted between 75.61 and 76.58.

75.9x River bank is cleared, providing *unobstructed view of river.*

75.95 *Beautiful abrupt cliff* on berm. Spectacular cliffs ahead as well.

76.24 *Shallow cave* on berm; very interesting cliffs about 120 feet high, then steep ravine.

76.5x Canal bed has thick small growth. River 75 yards away. Intermittent stone wall ends. Grove's stone warehouse once stood here on berm.

76.58 *Cliff ends.* Beyond, populated area with road on berm.

SNYDERS LANDING

76.65 *Access: Distance from Sharpsburg 1.7 m.* From MD. 34 (Main St.) at stoplight in center of Sharpsburg turn North on N. Mechanic St. and go 1 block to Snyders Landing Rd. where take left 1.6 m. to Snyders Landing Potomac River Boat Ramp. Limited parking. Entering Snyders Landing (previously known as Sharpsburg Landing), homes appear on berm. Cross culvert, #111, 6' span.

76.73 First structure over canal is footbridge. *Site of Snyder coal and grain warehouse* which washed away in 1936 flood. Footbridge rests on concrete supports, once part of swinging bridge which allowed boatmen to travel from towpath to berm side, thence to Snyders Landing Rd. which headed into Sharpsburg. Flowers observed: bed straw, ball wort, common sea shell, euonymus, Indian strawberry, kidney leaf buttercup, red dead nettle, shepherd's purse, Solomon's seal, spotted touch-me-not (jewel weed), garlic mustard, Dutchman's-breeches, sweet cicely, cream or pale violet.
Bends in river along this point make excellent fishing. Continuing on to half-way point of Snyders Landing, about ½ block past boat ramp is Barron's C & O Canal Museum and Country Store, on the hill on the berm side of the canal, owned by Lee Barron. Open weekends throughout the year. Supplies, bicycle rental. Houses and cabins on berm — next ½ mile.

77.24 For next 2 m. to Lock 40, canal, towpath and river run approximately parallel, with river 150 yards to left, as canal begins its long curve in following river around Horseshoe Bend. Several large fields, farm houses and barns visible on berm. Large numbers of sycamores and maples.

77.38 Profuse growth of Star of Bethlehem (Ornithogalum umbellatum). Wooded floodplain has many wildflowers: mertensia (cowslip), spring beauties and grape hyacinth predominate in April. Others in area are May-apple, wild rose, blue-bells, buttercups and squirrel corn.
This portion of canal was one severly hit by episode of Asiatic cholera in 1832, when construction work was at its height. The "sickly season," term somewhat superstitiously given to Potomac Valley by workmen, was an annual problem; but a truly terrible catastrophe arrived in Sept. 1832 with spread of cholera southward from Montreal. Panic spread among Irish immigrants, and work stopped as laborers scattered throughout countryside. Canal engineer Purcell, writing from Sharpsburg on 11 Sept., said: "Men, deserted by their friends or comrades, have been left to die in the fields, the highways, or in the neighboring barns and stables. In some instances, as I have been told, then the disease has attacked them, the invalid has been inticed from the shanty and left to die under the shade of some tree. Excited by the sufferings of the miserable victims of the disease, the citizens of this place [Sharpsburg] have administered to their wants, and sought to soothe their dying moments, but unfortunately for the cause of humanity, nearly every person who has been with the dead bodies or has assisted in burying them have paid the forfeit with their lives, and it is now scarcely possible to get the dead buried."

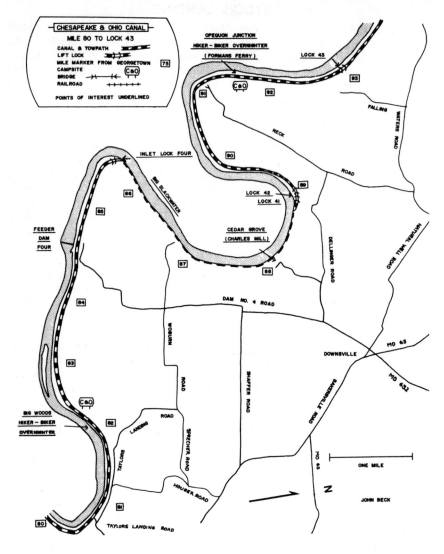

Canal Co. tried to calm panic and help the sick; among other measures was rough "hospital" set up at Harpers Ferry and operated on funds obtained by a form of group insurance; workers contributed 25¢ monthly thru payroll deductions. But interruption to construction virtually halted westward progress of canal, and helped precipitate one of periodic financial crises of the company.

78.15 *Culvert #112, 2'-diameter pipe.*

78.4x *Stone wall begins on berm.* This was a property fence which continues for .8 m. to mileage 79.15. Large patches of blue bells.

78.84 *Prominent cliff on W. Va. side of river.*

79.25 Footbridge over canal. Towpath directly on river bank.

LOCK NO. 40

79.41 *Access:* From upper Snyders Landing, 2.16 m. downstream or Mercersville 1.54 m. upstream.

In little-frequented section. Andrew McCoy was listed a locktender in annual report of Canal Co. for 1851. Foundation of lockhouse on berm, old well and stone cellar remains. Concrete flume. Stones of lock intact. Wooden gates down and falling apart. Small wooden bridge over lock and a wood-and-earthen dam at upper end. Potomac Valley Farms real estate development on berm.

79.65 *Cross concrete waste weir (over original waste weir).* Some of birds noted: barn owl, bluebird, blue jay, cardinal, chickadee, crow, yellow-shafted flicker, grackle, song sparrow, tufted titmouse, turkey vulture, downey woodpecker and red-bellied woodpecker.

79.68 *Horseshoe Bend Hiker-Biker Overnighter.* Water pump, picnic table, toilet. Reached from Sharpsburg via MD. 65 and Mondell Road. Next campsite upstream Big Woods at 82.46; downstream Killiansburg Cave at 75.29.

79.98 Culvert #114 (Roses Culvert), 4'-span, from wooded ravine. Path up right side of ravine leads ½ m. to farm on Mondell Road.

80.52 Hill ends. Houses begin *in settlement of Mondell.*

80.55 Cross Culvert #115 (Mondell), 6'-span. Stream from valley on berm. Paved Mondell Rd. comes down valley on far side and continues along berm to Mercersville. Ruins of stone structure 60 x 25'. Numerous cross paths between river and houses. Trees removed from canal bed, grass neatly cut to 81.6x.

80.95 *Mercersville.* Road junction and store on berm. Road inland leads to MD. 65 (Sharpsburg-Hagerstown Rd.) and to paved road leading into MD. 63 to Downsville and Williamsport; 12 m. to Hagerstown, 9 m. to Williamsport. Road continues along berm, with occasional houses and frequent cross paths to river. Of the three access roads, middle road leads to Dogtown, small community within 1¼ m. of canal. Walled portion on berm here is probably site of Harris Warehouse and wharf of early canal days.

Mercersville (named after Canal Co. Pres. C. Mercer) known locally by name of Taylors Landing. John William (Jack) Taylor was born and spent his 80 years here until he died in 1948. Was superintendent for this section of canal and operated general merchandise store for 50 years in basement of his stone house. Obituary described him as one of the best known and beloved characters along canal.

81.0x Vehicle bridge over canal leads to paved *Taylors Landing Boat Ramp.* Winter cress, winter mustard.

81.62 *Marsh Run Culvert, 10' span* giving apearance of rushing mountain stream from depression extending to Taylors Landing Road, which bears away uphill giving access to Dam No. 4 (via Woburn and Dam No. 4 Roads). Parking just off bend of road reached via path across canal bed. Area designated in early canal info as "Middlekauffs" Basin. Beyond, fields occupy berm side and large trees border towpath.

Nearest bicycle repair shop is Potomac Pushbikes on Taylors Landing Road, tel. 301-223-8071.

81.87 Appears to be *collapsed culvert*. Rocky wooded bluffs on W. Va. side of river.

81.93 Stone house and barn on open slope on berm. Warbling vireas. Corn fields and pasture on slopes continue for some distances.

82.11 Possible informal overflow.

82.24 Old road parallel to towpath for .3 m. with camping/trailer sites apparently laid out, end in turnaround. Road provides interesting variation from towpath route. Bluffs now steep on W. Va. side. Water pump.

82.46 *Big Woods Hiker Biker Overnighter*. Best access from Taylors Landing Road at 81.62. No water. Next campsite upstream Big Slackwater at 85.5; downstream Horseshoe Bend at 79.6. Fine woods between canal and river; tall trees in canal bed beyond; fine sycamores between towpath and canal bed. Water pump located 50 yards below campsite.

82.75 River comes into view here, *opposite lower end of Shepherds Island*. Mallards seen on clear Dec. day. Berm steepens into heavily-wooded hill and then into cliffs. Sycamore, silver maple, American elm, box elder, tulip tree, cottonwood, black walnut and mulberry trees. Rabbits and quail common. Quarry loading dock. Blue bells above NPS 83 mile marker.

83.13 Shallow ravine on right. Towpath on river bank. River, which has been slackwater for some time, contains a few rapids.

83.21 Head of Shepherds Island. Beyond, cliffs on berm reach 100 feet. *Stone wall on berm* possibly a loading platform for quarry directly behind.

DAM NO. 4 CAVE

83.30 *Access:* From Dam No. 4 parking lot 1 m. upstream. Large entrance to cave at canal level. This interesting cavern extends about 200 feet back into Conococheague limestone, with offsets, side passages, flowing stream and 2 pools. From entrance, floor and stream rise to 20 foot pool. Beyond, passage offsets to right, then continues as 4 x 4 foot corridor to low-ceilinged room. From this room, 2 foot-high passage with pool lies ahead,

Winch House at Dam No. 4 housed machinery which lowered this large gate for protection against floods. (National Park Service photo of 1945)

while to right narrow fissure leads into 30 foot-high chimney. At end of offset, side passage leads up to similar chimney, which connects with other chimney by narrow fissure passage. Stalactites and flowstone in chimneys, and deposit of river gravel which has worked down from gravel terrace atop hill above cave. My children (Duane and Betsy) and I found this cave most interesting to explore. As with all caves, proceed with caution, carry ample light (*each* person), wear old tough clothes; it isn't a bad idea to leave large note at cave entrance as to time of entering in event you do get in trouble. *These caves should not be explored by inexperienced persons!!* Good description of Maryland caves in Franz and Slifer, *Caves of Maryland*, Maryland Geological Survey Educational series 3, 1971. Several smaller caves in vicinity between here and Dam No. 4.

83.37 Shallow ravine on berm. Ahead is pretty straightway section, with several small ravines on berm. Earth slide beyond exposes cave opening at top left.

83.47 Site of lost culvert #117.

83.51 Sediment collecting basin on berm.

83.70 Abandoned stone farmhouse beyond old road at top of steep ravine.

83.75 *Fine cliffs on berm,* its ledges decorated with cedars.

83.88 Nice cliff with stone wall and terrace. *Dam No. 4 comes into view ahead;* listen for it as well. Several boulders have fallen into canal bed..

83.99 *Culvert #118 (Hensens Culvert),* 6' span, from wooded ravine. This is a nice picnic area a short distance from Dam No. 4.

84.23 Paved Dam No. 4 road leads uphill to right. Towpath repaired with crushed rock, apparently result of erosion caused by flooding. About 1000 feet below Dam 4 canal bed partially filled in; Park Service maintenance road runs across canal bed, along towpath, up to dam crest and continues on top of protective dike along river above dam. Canal bed has water from Inlet Lock No. 4 for about 800 feet below winch house at Dam No. 4.

84.35 *Cross concrete waste weir.* Magnificent view of masonry structure of Dam No. 4.

FEEDER DAM NO. 4

84.40 *Access:* By following paved Dam No. 4 road to its end 5.5 m. South of Downsville (intersection of MD. 63/632). Williamsport 8 m., Hagerstown 12 m., Frederick 31 m., Washington 76 m. and Baltimore 79 m. Asphalt 11-car parking area. Sign reads, "Big Slackwater Recreation Area and Boat Ramp 1 Mile." Access to Dam No. 4 via footbridge over canal and towpath, alongside winch house. Picnic area, with barbecue grills, picnic tables and toilets. No water. NO CAMPING.

The first dam was begun in 1832 and completed in 1834; opened to this point in 1833. By using slackwater above dam, boats able to reach Williamsport, 15 m. upstream. Original dam rubble-and-brush construction; suffered flood damage and continual seepage. Loss of water was critical in dry years, and at least twice caused suspension of navigation below dam. To correct this, Canal Co. contracted for completely new masonry dam in 1856, said upon completion to be one of finest in country. Yet the disastrous flood of Nov. 1877, which left the canal a wreck, tore a 200-foot breech in the fine, new masonry. (Bad break in 1936 also.) Winches in winch house, recently restored, over canal operated stop gate, which was lowered if break occured in canal downstream, a frequent happening during high water. Note rope burns at each end of winch house foundation on towpath side.

One really has four choices for travel at this point—talk about over-kill—paved public road extending to last house; paved NPS road which goes for .95 m. before crossing over to parking lot; graveled NPS mainten-ance road which runs along levee to Inlet Lock No. 4; and towpath. My choice is naturally towpath along watered canal on lower level. Difference in level is adjusted at Inlet Lock 4, 1.22 m. upstream. Stretch of watered canal between the winch house and the feeder lock. Clearing operations along berm road have left most large trees standing. Canoeists must portage on the Md. side. Dam is marked.

84.73 Footbridge over canal. Wooden steps lead up to river bank. Berm side has playground, picnic area, toilets.

85.21 Across river sheer cliffs drop directly to water as view to those taking levee road.

85.35 Wooden bridge carries berm road diagonally across canal and towpath to river bank.

85.40 Asphalt parking area for 37 trailer-car rigs and 25 cars. 30 foot wide boat ramp into river (concrete ends at slackwater level). Picnic area with 8 tables, 4 barbecue grills, 2 toilets.

85.5x *Two lock gates* rotting on levee bank next to towpath. Bicycling and horseback riding are hazardous upstream to Charles Mill (mile 88.10). Alternate route is Dam 4 Road to Dellinger Road, to Charles Mill Road to Charles Mill. Do not use towpath in high river levels in the slack water area.

INLET LOCK NO. 4

85.62 *Access:* From parking lot .22 m. below, via towpath or levee road. Heavy timber bridge crosses lock, NPS road and towpath across canal and connects berm road and levee road, levee road ending and berm road continuing as maintenance road. Yes, it is confusing! Guard lock (inlet lock) concreted at upstream end, and filled to create river bank across opening.

Guard Lock No. 4 above Dam No. 4. It was here that boats once again entered the canal after 3.28 miles of slackwater navigation in the Potomac River. (Hahn Collection)

Peaceful towpath along "Big Slackwater"

Foundation for lockhouse can be seen just up from inlet lock, along slope. Swans, sometimes geese and ducks often seen on river above this point. Lock passed boats between level of canal below and slackwater of river (called "Big Slackwater") forming 13½ m. lake. Canal resumes at Lock 41, mileage 88.90, 3.28 m. upstream. Boats followed river bank, towpath becoming cleared ledge along shore. There was once a pivot bridge at the lock built c1835.

85.68 Berm road crosses canal supply inlet over concrete bridge. "Towpath" cannot be used as such from here to McMahons Mill because of line of trees at water's edge. Service road serves as "towpath" to about 86.94, at which point towpath road ends.

85.74 "Towpath" crosses shallow depression of former intake channel. Cliffs on right beyond followed by flat area, with fields and stretches of Osage orange tree hedge. Bicyclists are advised that the towpath ahead is sometimes covered in high water and is rough in the approach to McMahons Mill.

86.61 Trail, on old road grading, comes in diagonally on right. Intermittent spring. Hill and then rocky cliff beyond, followed by steep gully.

86.83 "57 Steps" lead up steep berm to owners cabin. Fern-decked cliffs. Presence of much lip-fern (Cheilanthes lanosa) testifies to limestone character of rock. 4 feet above towpath sign, "High water mark Oct. 16, 1954, day after Hazel's visit." 7 feet above towpath, sign, "Hurricane Diane stopped here Aug. 19, 1955."

86.94 "Improved towpath" ends at approximately this point, just short of cliff.

86.96 *Towpath supported on masonry wall as it rounds rocky point, with fine view of river palisades.* This scene should remain as it is, without further improvement. Beyond are several ravines and steep, dry watercourses. Primitive towpath very picturesque as it clings to cliffs.

87.04 Eight-ton boulder on towpath. Towpath difficult going.

87.19 *Towpath is ledge at foot of vertical cliff.*

87.62 Possible quarry.

87.64 *Towpath ledge widens at foot of narrow, wooden ravine*, with pretty cascade (Berkson Run). Footbridge over stream. Towpath paved stone, crossing stream as ford. Ledge-like character of towpath resumes beyond, with occasional portions supported by masonry. Path up hill to South leads to spectacular outlook rock at top of 100-foot vertical wall. Profuse growth of shooting stars in May.

87.76 Several caves.

87.8x Fallen rocks block towpath. Carved rock towpath close to river level at times. Narrow cave.

87.88 Stone dock.

88.xx NPS mile 88 marker. Intermittent spring 20 feet South. Towpath under water at high river stage, but passable to hikers on rocks. Towpath supporting wall nicely restored by NPS.

MC MAHONS (CHARLES) MILL

88.10 *Access:* From Hagerstown take MD. 632 8 m. or from Williamsport take MD. 68 4 m. to intersection of MD. 63/632 in Downsville; take Dam No. 4 Road .7 m. Southwest from intersection to Dellinger Road; turn right .5 m. to Charles Mill Road where go left .7 m. to end of road. Mill just ahead on berm. Mill built on Downey Branch in 1778 produced flour, feed and plaster and was closed in 1922 due to floods. Original wooden overshot wheel replaced by steel wheel in 1920s when waterpower used to generate electricity. *Mill has been known under various names: Shanks, Charles, Avis, Shaffers, Old Flouring, Galloways, Cedar Grove, and now McMahons Mill.* This Charles Mill not to be confused with Charles Mills located above and below Dam No. 5. Most grist mills along Potomac in 19th century from Harpers Ferry to Big Spring operated by Herr, Charles, Middlekauff, and Peacher families, all of whom intermarried. Do not use the towpath in the slack water area during high river levels.

88.12 Cross *concrete bridge over Downey Branch.* Stone steps lead to former owner's house on hill. Towpath beyond rough, narrow ledge at foot of interesting cliffs on edge of river which often covers it. Cliffs are veritable rock garden of wildflowers, with sedum and moss pinks predominant, some gaining nourishment from unbelievably small cracks in rock. The towpath has been tastefully rebuilt for a short distance. River edge is spotted with boat landings; occasional steps lead up to summer cottages on rocks above.

88.28 *Howell Cave,* one entrance (on right) in beautiful grotto. This one (of two Howell Caves) sometimes referred to as McMahons Mill Cave. Large underground stream issues from cave, and another to right, apparently reappearance of stream descending into sinkhole 700 yards north. Cave, in Stones River limestone, previously started as 12 foot-long crawlway, opening into 2 large rooms, 2nd one 20 by 60 feet, with height of 12 feet. End of room, blocked by rockfall, reputed to lead into passage running back to distant sink hole. Numerous small cave openings in cliffs to area below Lock 43.

McMahons (Charles) Mill

88.52 *Interesting overhang,* with flowstone formed below small cave opening. Towpath traverses rough rocky area. Face of cliff gives appearance of enormous, shallow grotto.

88.59 *Cave opening 20 feet up cliff,* best seen looking backward. Towpath here is good walk, except for occasional muddy footway. Nice views of river bend in both directions. Numerous steps up cliffs to summer cabins.

88.6x Round steep, rocky cliff. *Towpath extremely rough.* Under water when Potomac floods. Note drill marks and "rope burns" from tow ropes.

88.68 Cross foot of narrow ravine, with dry watercourse and path leading 300 yards up to Dellinger Road. Beyond, towpath considerably improved and towpath ledge widens in honeysuckle-covered area.

LOCK NO. 41

88.90 *Access:* From McMahons Mill .8 m. below. *Canal resumes after slackwater navigation thru this inlet lock.* Most exposed surface of lock structure concrete, probably later repair work. Lower lock gates intact though in poor condition, as is river side upper lock gate. Small stone foundation to right of lower end of lock. Cleared area above upper end of lock on berm. One has choice of towpath (on berm) or roadlike path along river bank to Lock No. 42; latter gives good view of both canal and river. Towpath crosses from land side of canal to river side at Lock 42, via a mule cross-over bridge.

89.01 Foundation of house on berm. *Several foundations here represent former settlement,* with road running along berm and ascending hill to Dellinger School, on Neck (formerly Opequon) Road.

LOCK NO. 42

89.04 *Access:* From McMahons Mill .94 m. below. Much concrete work in this structure also. Very old foundation on berm probably lockhouse for both locks. Another foundation beyond opposite head of lock. Lower berm gate collapsed in lock bed, as well as both upper gates. Towpath continues road-like, but pleasant, thru nicely-wooded area with river 25 yards away. Numerous cabins on W. Va. side.

89.1x Old foundation back on berm, about 20 yards beyond NPS mile 89 marker. Be careful of copperhead snakes.

89.21 *Culvert #118½, 4'-span*, stream coming from fields to right, with farm buildings in pretty, rolling country beyond. Beautiful Colonial stone farmhouse (circa 1825) one of nicest houses along canal. Towpath beyond is grassy with cedar trees; cedars also provide beautiful borders to fields on rolling hills back from towpath. Pretty rocky hills on W. Va. side of river. Canal bed has some small growth and Osage orange trees. Level Walker Victor Conrad comments that some of his most enjoyable hikes have been in cold, windy weather, as hills, cliffs and great trees provide shelter from wind. One can walk along in comparative calm, listening to wintry blasts roaring through branches high above, imparting a sense of security and peace. Try it—winter hiking is great. Note limestone-loving cedars.

89.63 *Begin broad section of canal bed, formerly ½ m. pool known as Dellinger Widewater.* Interesting cliffs across river on Whitings Neck, another of long necks caused by meandering course of Potomac. River is beautiful green color on cloudy December day.

89.78 Region in April is sea of purple as bluebells or cowslips (Mertensia virginica) come into bloom.

90.24 *Upper end of Dellinger Widewater.* Long straightaway in canal. Line of fine, tall silver maple trees borders towpath again grassy and giving appearance of little-used country lane.

90.52 *Good picnic site* at grassy area to left. Cliffs on W. Va. side.

90.94 *Opequon Junction Hiker-Biker Overnighter Camp.* Access from Lock 43 (92.96) or McMahons Mill (88.10). Next campsite upstream Cumberland Valley at 95.2; downstream is Big Woods at 82.7 (but no water). *Site of Foremans Ferry*, which crossed Potomac River to mouth of Opequon Creek, visible just ahead on opposite side of river. Camp lies between towpath and river on narrow (about 10 yards) terraced area. Fireplace, table, trash can, toilet and pump. Firewood easily obtainable from fairly dense woods joining campsite and from wooded canal bed. Potomac still part of pool behind Feeder Dam No. 4; river quiet and wide. Cliffs on opposite shore drop sharply nto river. Worn groove of very old road comes down slope, probably original route to ferry. Cliffs resume beyond.

91.xx Towpath wooded on both sides of its grassy, groove roadway. Potomac immediately on left about 15 foot below. Canal bed generally dry with good growth of trees. On berm, cliffs rise abruptly and are dotted with columbine and gnarled tree growth. On cool and calm December day one sees red-bellied woodpecker, downy woodpeckers, chickadees, mocking birds, brown creepers, ducks and hawks. Deer tracks common on soft towpath surface.

91.13 *Long straightaway of canal.* Cliff dotted with columbine.

91.19 Cliffs recede for wide ravine. Cliffs resume beyond, exhibiting long slanting folds going up from right to left and are well decorated with wild-flowers and shrubs.

91.46 *Cliffs drop back to rocky wooded hillside.* Power line crosses river.

91.66 Ravine breaks into hillside. *Culvert #119*, 4'-span.

91.70 Summer cabin community on opposite side of Potomac for ¼ m.; beyond them is rolling pasture land.

92.xx *Cliffs in this section, 90-100 feet high,* are beautiful with their folded strata and shrub and tree growth. Moss pinks, sedum, shooting stars and star flowers.

92.05 Good, fast flowing accessible spring issues from foot of cliff on berm side of canal. Lush growth of water cress grows in pool made by spring in canal bed. *Cave opening few feet above canal bed in cliff face connects with main passage of Dellingers Cave* (see 92.11) but is too small to crawl thru.

92.11 Steep sided wooded ravine breaks cliff, with cascade of water coming down into canal bed over lush growth of green moss and cress. Trail leads across floor and up into ravine along stream. Within 35 feet trail is blocked by 2-strand barbed wire fence. (Beyond, about 175 feet is quiet, secluded valley nestled in rocky hills and dominated by very large sycamore tree. Stream here recently dammed and small, still pond adds final touch of reverence to scene.) Crossing stream (but without crossing fence) work up poorly defined trail to right along top of cliff to find *Dellingers Cave*. Entrance to this interesting cavern is very small, inconspicuous hole at top of escarpment overlooking canal and river. From entrance you drop almost straight down some 25 feet into large (almost 4 yard-square) room. *Getting in is the hardest part!*

Dellingers Cave. "Main" passage leads off parallel to cliff face; at first it is only about 2 feet high, but later it generally is from about 3 to 4 yards high and from 2 to 5 yards wide. Passage runs for about 70 feet in this section; one short side passage, several shelves and one place with passages on 2 levels. After 70 foot section, passage becomes fissure, 3-6 feet wide and 35 feet high. Beyond 200 feet (from entrance) fissure reduces in height to impassable low crawlway.

Cave described as "usually dry", but we found steep slope at entrance very slippery and muddy. A ¼ inch line can be strung from convenient tree root over entrance down into cave, as you might have bad time of it climbing out in wet weather. We also found a ¼ inch 20 foot nylon line handy at one place inside cave. Cave formed at base of Stones River limestone layer (which here strikes off at 30 degree vertical dip). A few formations in cave and several stumps of large stalagmites (broken off by former visitors); many of the ceilings covered with mini-stalactites. Floor of large room and several other "basin" points covered with chips of broken limestone. One nice column (really 2 separate columns merged together—joining of stalagmites from floor and stalactites from ceiling). *View from cave entrance looking out over calm river toward mountains in far distance is a striking vista not usually afforded the hiker.*

92.23 Proposed site of dam during construction.

92.25 *Exact mid-point of canal.* Intake lock at Cumberland 92¼ m. ahead; tidewater lock in Washington 92¼ m. behind. Across river, summer community ends.

Boat leaving Lock 42 and heading downstream in the canal operating days.

92.56 Dry cascade interrupts cliff. Just beyond is fast flowing spring at foot of cliff on berm side. In the canal operating period boatmen sometimes filled a bucket attached to a boat hook. Canal partly filled with water from spring; good growth of cress. Spring approached only with difficulty across soft and wet canal bed.

92.63 *Cliffs* end and recede to steep wooded slope beyond. Numerous wildlife: usual birds common to area, squirrels, groundhogs, rabbits, harmless snakes and an occasional deer.

92.73 Towpath goes over a concrete waste weir. Water from spring, flowing up canal in narrow stream, joined by another stream flowing down canal from above Lock 43; together they pass thru drainway into Potomac. Just beyond wasteway is dense growth of young saplings; area between towpath and river widens to 30 feet.

LOCK NO. 43

92.96 *Access:* From center of Williamsport take MD. 63 2.5 m. to Falling Waters Rd; turn right 4 m. or so to the canal. Lock 43 is .92 m. downstream.

Just before lock area, hill on berm side recedes and is interrupted by narrow ravine. Beyond, hillside is some 35 yards from canal. Lock in good condition, with portion of lower gates standing and remains of portions of upper gates. Lock of limestone possibly extended. Stream passes down thru lock. Brick lock-keeper's house stands 10 yards back from lock on berm side; reconditioned, painted white with large screened porch overlooking canal. Unoccupied. Stay out of this and other NPS posted structures! House faces roadway.

93.02 *Culvert #120,* 6'-span, pass thru lawn-like area, part of Potomac Fish and Game Club.

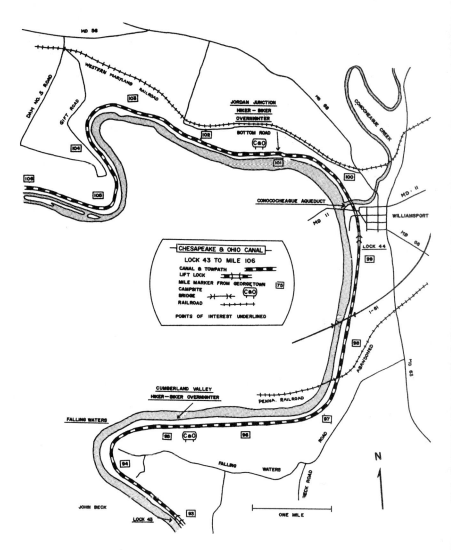

CHESAPEAKE & OHIO CANAL

LOCK 43 TO MILE 106

CANAL & TOWPATH
LIFT LOCK
MILE MARKER FROM GEORGETOWN [75]
CAMPSITE
BRIDGE
RAILROAD

POINTS OF INTEREST UNDERLINED

N

93.29 Begin a long stretch of recreation building which intrudes on the canal. This extensive summer community at Falling Waters is contained in privately owned strip between canal and river, but the "paved" towpath, the unsightly line of electric poles on the edge of the canal bank, and the unbelievable row of toilet houses along the berm add up to one of the least attractive sections of canal route. Settlement extends 1½ m. up canal; unfortunately still being enlarged.

93.56 *Culvert #121*, 6'-span. Road leaves towpath which it paraliels to 93.88.

93.88 Recreation area road which has paralleled canal crosses canal and becomes paved road connecting with Falling Waters Road. Access to recreation area (Potomac Fish and Game Club) sometimes blocked, so don't count on access, but worth a try. *Public access should be provided at*

143

points such as this, as there is really no public access between Dam No. 4 and Williamsport. Canal bed overgrown to Williamsport.

94.0x Double row of cabins ends (Thank God!). Field and single row of cabins on far side of field between towpath and river, continues for next ¾ mile.

FALLING WATERS

94.44 *Access:* From end of Falling Waters Road extension at mile 93.88, .51 m. downstream. Road may have locked gate.

Pass stone piers of bridge one source says this was a pivot bridge formerly carrying road over canal and towpath to river bank at left, *where ferry operated to Falling Waters, W. Va.* Md. Civil War Centennial Commission sign. Village of Falling Waters can be seen across river with cascading stream that gives it its name. Village reached by US 11, 5 m. South of Williamsport. On right of US 11, just past turnoff to village of Falling Waters are some of watercress ponds that dot this section of W. Va.—one of few places in country where this cultivation is practiced.

Canal at this point was scene of intense military activity in July 1863 during Lee's withdrawal after Battle of Gettysburg. Lee's engineers, sent ahead to prepare crossing of Potomac, found river swollen from heavy rains, and ridges at Williamsport and Falling Waters destroyed by Union troops. To cover river crossing, Confederate Army established line from Hagerstown on North to Falling Waters (Md.) on South. Meade's Federal troops soon set up parallel line some miles to East. For several days another major battle seemed imminent, but Meade failed to attack. Lee, impatient at speed being made in rebuilding bridges, ordered warehouses along canal torn down and timbers used to construct pontoon bridges. Night of 13 July, in continuing downpour, Lee's forces crossed river at Falling Waters and at fords along river, and when Meade advanced in force on the 14th he found his enemy safe beyond river.

94.75 More housing development.

95.05 *Culvert #121½,* 6'-span. Path to river on near side.

95.20 *Cumberland Valley Hiker-Biker Overnighter.* Access from end of Falling Waters Road. Next Hiker-Biker upstream Jordan Junction at 101.2; downstream Opequon Junction at 90.9.

95.66 Culvert #122, 6'-span.

96.24 *Culvert #123,* 6'-span. An old road, now path to former Nally Youth Hostel. Path across canal to old platform foundation in front of what appears to be cave. Sighted 5 foot blacksnake across towpath here in spring of 1970.

96.72 *Culvert #124,* 4'-span. Access road. Area on right of road marked "Funkstown Rod and Gun Club-Private". Towpath on river bank.

96.89 *Culvert #125,* 4'-span.

96.97 *Culvert #126,* 4'-span, was recently rebuilt by National Park Service. Ravine leads .7 m. up to junction of Falling Waters and Neck Roads.

97.15 *Area of splendid trees*–fine shagbark hickory to left, many paw-paws along towpath, numerous large walnuts and towering sycamores along river bank. Blue grosbeak, broad-winged hawk, prothonotary warbler, yellow-billed cuckoo.

Superintendent's House at Lock No. 44 in Williamsport (National Park Service)

97.41 Engine House for railroad.

97.42 Masonry wall.

97.44 *Stone wall with timbers on berm, remains of wharf. Beginning of area where canal traffic made connection with Cumberland Valley R.R.* Piers in river mark location of old Cumberland Valley bridge; newer bridge now Penn Central, is farther upstream. Siding on downriver side of old bridge led down to track along berm where unloading of coal from canal boats to R.R. gondolas was made by crane up to closing of canal in 1924 for shipment to nearby points in Pa. and W. Va. Coal loaded only in Cumberland. Old grading and concrete foundation of crane in evidence. Interesting piece of curved masonry work on abutment of old R.R. bridge.

97.54 Pass under *concrete piers of Penn Central R.R. trestle.*

97.95 Culvert #127, 4'-span. Repaired 1985.

98.5x *Pass under highway bridges of I-81.* Steep hillside with rocky outcroppings to 99.00.

98.82 Pass under transmission line coming from power plant at Williamsport.

98.92 *Cross concrete waste weir (43-44 level).* Old transmission tower on left beyond.

99.12 *Culvert #128, 4'-span.*

99.16 Old quarry on berm. Dirt road from quarry leads along berm to Williamsport.

99.23 Sewage disposal plant in fenced area on left.

99.25 Spring on berm bank, accessible from Lock 44. Ahead on left coal supply of power plant begins. Standing water in canal bed up to and beyond Lock 44. Marshy area.

A race course for horse racing was located on a tract of land between the canal and river extending from the mouth of Conococheague Creek to the waste weir below Lock 44; jousting tournaments and picnics were also held there. At the close of the Civil War, baseball was played on the same tract of land, which Gen. Abner Doubleday could see from his observation post on what is now known as "Doubleday's Hill" at the north end of Riverview Cemetery.

LOCK NO. 44 (WILLIAMSPORT)

99.30 *Access:* See Conococheague Aqueduct (99.80). From center of Williamsport at intersection of Potomac and Conococheague Sts. (US 11 and MD 68) take latter 3 blocks to Canal St. where turn right 1 block to Main Street; turn left 1 block to Lock 44. Limited parking.

Lock in fair condition was an extended lock. Well-preserved, large, wooden frame, unoccupied lockhouse to left. Plank footbridge leads across to berm road. Well-kept area. Unmarked town line of Williamsport crosses here. NPS maintenance building beyond on right.

99.35 *R. Paul Smith Generating Plant of Potomac Edison* on left. Coal piles beyond. Canal watered to 7' depth almost to aqueduct.

99.38 Masonry wall once used by Steffey & Findlay Coal Co.

99.59 High wooden fence directly on towpath encloses coal yard of Potomac Edison plant. R.R. siding on berm, with cemetery on hill beyond *where "founder" of Williamsport, Otho Holland Williams, is buried.*

Canoeists should portage on W. Va. side of the power company dam. The dam is unmarked.

WILLIAMSPORT

Williamsport is perhaps most typical "Canal Town" on C & O Canal. Settlement here, called Conococheague (spelled in a variety of ways), was first in what is now Washington County—a true outpost of civilization. First crown grant was "Jacks Bottom" of 175 acres to Jerimiah Jack, who built log cabin near Byron tannery. Charles Friend probably received his grant of 260 acres in 1739; for ''Sweed's Delight.'' Jerimiah Jack deeded "Jack's Bottom" to Jack Friend in 1778 for 568 pounds, 63 shillings and 6 pence. In 1790 Friends acquired adjoining property, "White Oak Swamp," for 130 pounds and "Hear Bargain" for 25 pounds from John Hogg. When Tom Cresap moved to Oldtown in 1750 he sold "Springfield Farm" to Joseph and Prudence Williams. Son, Otho, was one year old at the time. Conococheague settlement was important point during French and Indian War (1753-58) and major supply point for Braddock's illfated march; he crossed Potomac here on 1 May 1755; major part of his army retreated later over same route. Town formally laid out in 1786 by General Otho Holland Williams and named Williamsport in his honor.

Williamsport made an early bid for importance in 1790 with its campaign for selection as location of the new national capital. Washington made an inspection of town in October of that year. In denial of its petition, a prominent reason for rejection was inability of large vessels to ascend river to this point. During Revolutionary War Williamsport was Capitol of the country for 28 hours.

River trade was important to Williamsport long before construction of C & O Canal. With Patowmack Company's improvement of the river and opening of the skirting canals, a lively commerce developed through medium of small river boats and rafts. Boats carried varied products to Georgetown and Alexandria, and sometimes brought payloads back, although arduous return trip was difficult enough for empty boats. Rafts carried much trade, and were dismantled and sold for firewood at lower end of journey. Following advertisement in Hagerstown papers of 1825, quoted by Williams in "History of Washington County," is typical of pre-canal period:

BOATING: The subscriber respectfully informs his friends and the public generally, that he has at present FOUR NEW BOATS in complete order for conveying flour, whiskey and other produce from Williams-Port to the city of Washington, on terms to suit the times. He has appointed Mr. James Shoaff, for his agent to conduct business in Williams-Port, such as taking in loading and securing the same, so that it may be safely delivered, and have punctual returns made to all those that may please to favor him in the above line of business.

Christian Ardinger

N.B.—Any person wishing to have Fish, Plaster, Sale, or any back loading, can be accommodated on reasonable terms.

Canal construction work gave Williamsport some trying moments. In 1832, cholera epidemic had reached town from downstream; next year it recurred, starting this time at Williamsport. For a time, repetition of terrors of 1832 seemed certain, but despite trouble in nearby Hagerstown, where victims among the Irish workers were taken for burial in Catholic cemetery, threat subsided. After some were buried there citizens' protests resulted in priests consecrating burial grounds closer to canal; some were mass burials because of lack of funds and difficulty in hiring grave diggers who were willing to risk exposure to the plague. Next two years brought excitement of another variety, when rivalry between two factions among the Irish laborers erupted into armed clashes during idle winter months. Worse of battles took place in Jan., 1834. Corkonians were working near Dam 5, above Williamsport, opposing faction, Fardowners, or Longfords, were located near Dam 4, below town. Presumably each hoped to oust other from canal and benefit by resultant scarcity of labor and higher wages. Preliminary clash near town resulted in several deaths before militia restored order. Williamsport townsmen set up patrol over Conococheague Aqueduct, then partly completed, to keep factions apart. Week later Fardowners marched up canal, 300 strong, armed with guns and clubs, and persuaded guardians of aqueduct to let them pass. They met outnumbered Corkonians on hill near Dam 5, defeated them in a short pitched battle, and returned to their shanties down the canal. Opposing forces were brought together to sign formal peace treaty following week, and under surveillance of 2 Cos. of troops from Ft. McHenry, hostilities were limited to a few minor outbreaks.

First canal boats reached Williampsort in 1834, coming by slackwater navigation from Dam 4, and canal itself was in operation to town basin next year, bringing period of intense activity and prosperity. Some 50 canal boats arrived thru locks on opening day. In 1850, first downstream boats

The Norfolk and Western bridge at Williamsport to lift the railway tracks for passing canal boats, built in 1923. (National Park Service)

from Cumberland arrived—3 of the 5 which started downstream race following ceremonies marking final completion of canal. Two of the boats grounded near Dam 6, because of low water; a 3rd gave up at Williamsport. Remaining 2, *Freeman Rawdon* and *Southampton*, reached Alexandria in a dead heat, 7 days after leaving Cumberland.

Floods left their mark on the Williamsport basin. The 1889 flood, in notorious Johnstown year, augmented by a local tornado, did tremendous damage, reaching an all-time high and transforming area around aqueduct, according to *Hagerstown Mail*, into huge lake. The 1924 flood, which ended navigation on canal, and devastating inundation of 1936, pounded section unmercifully.

Several Civil War battles were fought in and around Williamsport. The Southern forces tried to destroy Conococheague Aqueduct; difference in masonry at the West end shows where blasting was done. Williamsport used by Union Gen. Patterson crossing on 2 July 1861; Confederate Gen. Jackson moving against Harpers Ferry on 11 Sept. 1862 and Gen. Lee advancing with much of his army to and retreating from, Gettysburg in June and July 1863. Had Union forces been more alert, Civil War might have ended in Williamsport.

Today, Williamsport is a pleasant town with a variety of businesses and attractive, substantial residences; the home of canal author George "Hooper" Wolfe; and the home of the Williamsport C & O Canal Club of 500 members.

99.65 Pass under wood and iron bridge carrying W. Salisbury St. (River Park Dr.) over canal to Williampsort River Front Park. This is perhaps best access point from towpath to Williamsport, center of town, 3 blocks to right.

Williamsport's Cushwa Basin was a busy place in the canal operating days.
(National Park Service)

The bridge is an iron truss bridge, built by Baltimore engineer Wendell Bollman
(1814-1884). He invented the system of bridge trussing first using
iron in all the principal structural members. Of perhaps 100 Bollman
bridges (including the one built in Harpers Ferry in 1852 over which
John Brown and his raiders later passed) the one at Savage, Md. is the
sole survivor of the Bollman truss. "Hooper" Wolfe decided to take a closer
look at this bridge over the canal after reading an article on the Bollman
bridges. After dusting off the cast iron name plate and applying a bit of
red paint, it read 1879-W. Bollman Baltimore." *So, there are at least two
Bollman built bridges.* This bridge, despite its present state of neglect, is in almost perfect condition. It replaced a wooden bridge built in 1834 and rests on the piers
of the bridge used by Gen. Lee to go to and return from Gettysburg.

99.69 R.R. spur crosses canal on interesting liftbridge. Built 1923. This may be
the smallest R.R. liftbridge anywhere.

99.71 *Pass under US 11 highway bridge* crossing Potomac River to
W. Va. Transmission line crosses diagonally to right. Canal widens into
large basin, now partly filled in. This was one of the busiest wharf areas
along the canal; some of the old buildings remain; Cushwa's Boat House
is a landmark, constructed 1835-1838.

In 1744, the Virginia House of Burgesses permitted a ferry to cross
the Potomac between Virginia (now West Virginia) and Maryland. Said
ferry to be operated by Evans Watkins and *became known as Watkins
Ferry.* This ferry landed about 50 yards downstream from what is now
US 11 on the W. Va. bank of the river and at the foot of what is now the
west end of Salisbury St. in Williamsport. In 1775 the ferry was obtained
by Eli Ardinger and continued in the possession of the Ardinger family by
charter from the Washington County Board of Commissioners until the

149

construction of the Washington and Berkley Bridge was completed, when the ferry ceased to exist. *In the spring of 1910 the ferry was sold to the operators of the McCoy's Ferry.*

In the early summer of 1908, construction of the Washington and Berkley Bridge began. On 16 Dec. 1908 the north side of pier No. 10 gave way, when the heavy weight of the steel work on the fresh concrete caused the pier to collapse, throwing 14 men into the river from a height of 60 feet. Four men died instantly or before the morning had passed; five men died later. The Pennsylvania Steel Company Reconstruction was started in the spring of 1909 and the bridge was ready for traffic and dedicated August 1909.

99.7x *Causeway path* to right of downstream end of aqueduct leads thru old wharf area of former canal basin around fenced-off private property to city streets of Williamsport and parking, but best access from River Park (See 99.80). End of rewatered section of the canal.

For towpath conditions and other questions about the canal from Williamsport to Cumberland call (NPS) Allegheny District or 301-678-5463.

CONOCOCHEAGUE AQUEDUCT (AQUEDUCT NO. 5)

99.80 *Access:* Seven m. S.W. Hagerstown to Williamsport on US 11 or from I-70 heading West take I-81 south 1½ m. to Williamsport (US 11) exit and follow US 11 (E. Potomac St.) 1.1 m. west to center of town (Conococheague St.), where turn left 1 block to West Salisbury St.; turn right 3 blocks crossing woodplanked iron bridge on River Park Drive to Williamsport River Front Park. Road continues in U-shape past parking area, toilets, picnic area, beach, boat ramps, and small boat tie-up area (mouth of Conococheague Creek) and dead-ends at end of good parking area just few feet short of towpath below aqueduct. Fine views of aqueduct and Potomac River from parking area.

Conococheague Aqueduct, over Conococheague Creek, completed in 1834, is 5th of 11 masonry aqueducts on the canal. Fine piece of masonry work in poor state of repair though stabilized by Park Service several years ago, with three equal arch spans of 60 foot each, extending 196 feet between abutments. Aqueduct built of limestone obtained "from quarries within 3 miles" according to early engineering reports (High Rock Quarry, now known as Pinesburg Quarry). Has deteriorated badly, but much of interesting masonry remains. Only 15 foot or so of iron railing left near center of lefthand coping. Note rope burns in wood at top of railing and date of 1877 and letters "C. S." carved in stone of pier for first arch. Close to 3rd arch at upper end on Potomac side note slight difference in stone work which was replaced after being damaged by Mosby's Raiders in Civil War. US 11 bridge over Potomac clearly in view. The wooden trunk was placed in the aqueduct and the berm wall rebuilt 1869-1871.

Masonry on right was lost in 1920 when struck by a canal boat. Early on the morning of 20 April 1920 Frank Myers, Captain of Boat No. 73, steering the boat, and his step-son, Joseph Davis, driving a three mule team left for Cumberland. At 5:00 a.m., while going through the aqueduct, the boat struck the east end of the berm wall a light blow. Capt. Myers saw the wall beginning to waver and called to his step-son, who was almost at the western end of the aqueduct, to cut the mules loose, which he did. As

Collapse of Conococheague Aqueduct, 1920, showing Boat #73, fallen into the Creek below. (Courtesy of George "Hooper" Wolfe.)

the wall broke and the boat started to go through the break Capt. Myers jumped from the boat onto the eastern end of the berm parapet. The boat remained in the Conococheague Creek until the 1936 flood, when it floated down the Potomac River and remained high and dry on the towpath, where subsequent high waters caused it to break up and float away. Wooden wall was constructed in place of stone wall and remained in place until 1924.

99.84 *Upper end of aqueduct.* There were once plans to make Conococheague Creek navigable to Pennsylvania.

99.85 Former boat basin for the nearby tannery.

99.8x Archaeological site to west (private property) along river short distance from west end of aqueduct. Indian tribes which roamed and lived in this area were Algonquins, Kruskaraw, Wassawomenkes, Iroquois, Delawares and Catawbas. Bone pins, pottery, arrowheads, bones of buffalo and deer and a quarry for clay used for red and yellow war paints were found in 1956 in excavation in cooperation with the Smithsonian Institution. Area closed to public. "Rafts" of timber brought down the Potomac River were once processed into slab lumber at the Williamsport saw mill, upstream of the aqueduct.

99.93 End of Fenton Ave. leads across canal bed, and provides access to Kaplans Grocery (Melvin Kaplan is President of Williamsport C & O Canal Club) few blocks away and to Williamsport. Short distance from store on Williamsport-Clear Spring Road number of canal workers who died of cholera are buried in plot of ground known as Hospital Hill—cannot be seen from road. Towpath is grass-covered beyond, canal bed filled with young trees and river remains close-by for some distance.

100.23 *Culvert #129, 6'-span.*

100.51 Cabins on left. Path *across canal and up edge of field to Bottom Rd.* along R.R.

151

100.69 *Road connecting with Bottom Road comes into river colony* and continues thru cabin area to left. Towpath cinder then packed dirt to picnic area. *Culvert #131, 4'-span.*

100.91 *Large grassy picnic area* of Hagerstown Filtration Plant begins on left. Picnic tables and fireplaces but no toilets. *Wooded Duck Island* visible in river, near far shore.

101.00 *Footbridge* leads across canal to foot of cement stairs ascending levee around filtration plant. Path to left leads to steps down river bank at concrete intake gates, with river gauge. *Good place for fishing.*

101.10 To right, graded flat area adjoins levee around filtration plant. May have been basin here. Path crosses canal bed to parking area for several cars. Road along canal berm for cabin owner's access short distance above. *Road to right leads .4 m. to Bottom Road and then to Williamsport after it connects with MD 68.*

101.15 End of intensive canal clearing area of 1957. *Towpath and canal ahead arched over by trees and very attractive.* Site of Culvert #133 or #132. Now a concrete pipe.

101.28 *Jordan Junction Hiker-Biker Overnighter.* Access from parking area at 101.10. Next Hiker-Biker upstream North Mountain at 110.0; downstream Cumberland Valley at 95.2. Canal bed continues dry with little undergrowth. Towpath smooth. Cornfields to right. Begin long straightaway in canal.

102.00 *Culvert #134, 6'-span.* Just beyond is end route leading 150 yards to *paved road near Pinesburg Station and then 2.7 m. to Williamsport.* Site of landing and boat basin. Basin is approximately 290' x 100'.

Canal Basin at Williamsport, Maryland.

102.20 *Towpath comes onto river bank,* built up with protective wall. Outcropping of rock on berm.

102.26 Sharp cut in hill on berm side leads to active quarry. Previously known as "High Rock", stone for Conococheague Aqueduct was probably taken from here. Other nearby quarry activity visible. Berm becomes steep slope, then cliff. *Dangerous area-best to keep off cliffs!* NPS warns of loose rocks which sometimes fall when blasting occurs in quarry.

102.45 *Interesting sheer cliff on berm.* Hugh boulder in canal bed; result of blasting from nearby (now abandoned) quarry.

102.65 Culvert #135, 6'-span discharges the stream into river. Cliffs resume beyond. Towpath directly on river bank. Towpath dirt with some roots obtruding.

102.90 Narrow ravine between cliffs on right. Near top of cliff on left of ravine is *entrance to Pinesburg Cave,* approximately 75 feet in length.

102.92 *Stone wall above towpath level.* Towpath shale surface.

103.02 *Very fine limestone cliff* on berm, with bare blocks of rock interspersed with cedar trees.

103.14 Culvert #135½, 4'-span. Stream from wooded ravine goes directly into river. Path leads up ravine on berm. *Beautiful river view.*

103.26 Road comes in across canal and coincides with towpath beyond and *connects with Gift Road and Dam No. 5 Road for access from Hagerstown or Williamsport.* Good views up and down river, especially of sharp "Millers Bend" upstream. *Beautiful section of canal.* Good fishing area for bass and catfish.

Dam Number 5

153

103.45 Two-story house on berm facing canal basin long associated with canal. Member of work crew obtained permission to build house for his family and move away from work crew house above.

103.4x Dock for canal work crew sand and repair boats at foot of large rock; iron mooring bar remains. *Foundation of work crew house back on berm.*

103.53 Cultivated fields begin to right and continue for 1 m. Pretty open river terrace.

MILLERS BEND

104.38 *This is Millers Bend* where many tomahawks have been recovered from river gravel. In 1941 trapper living in shack across river had 3-gallon bucket full of tomahawks which he claimed he had found in river gravel on Md. side.

Cliffs on opposite shore recede to sheer limestone cliffs of abandoned Nestles Quarry. Landmark during canal operations from upriver was *Indian Church Cave* located on North side of quarry wall, left intact by quarry workers. Shallow cave entrance shaped like church with spire. According to legend, Indians slept on dry, recessed platforms on each side of cave during stormy weather. Sometime after WW II searchers for Indian relics excavated clay shelves down to rough-edged bedrock. Trees growing from floor of quarry now obscure distant view of cave and shade entrance, and without exposure to sun cave now damp. Pigeons have established roost in steeple and it is no longer a comfortable shelter. "Sun and Moon" limestone spring gushes from quarry wall near where recent housing development established.

104.45 Spectacular views of cliff on opposite side of river thru clearing on riverside. Tremendous sycamores.

104.61 Breakwater.

104.98 Concrete piers of old Nessle bridge crossing river built in 1909 connect with the Williamsport, Nessle, and Martinsburg Railway Bridge destroyed in the 1936 flood. Old grade leads back on berm carring trail, later becoming road. Profuse growth of pawpaws alnong towpath. This line was the Charlton Branch of the Western Maryland Railway.

105.30 Sighted 10-point buck standing in canal bed on Nov. 71 field trip. **Culvert #136, Little Conococheague Creek,** 24'-span, built 1833-1834. Path to right to ruins of Charles (Middlekauffs) Mill.

106.21 Path across canal bed to Dam No. 5 Road paralleling canal to dam. Brick house was *Miller's house of Charles Mill*—2nd we have encountered in this section, one more to go! *Mill also known as Middlekauffs Mill,* it was operating before canal was built. *Beyond house are foundation stones and other evidence of mill, badly damaged by floods. Also known as Colton's Mill.*

106.26 Canal wide here, *apparently old basin.* Charles Bros. (of Charles Mill) mentioned in 1957 *warehouse which went out in 1889 flood.*

106.61 *Cross concrete waste weir* (Lock 44-Dam 5 level); water flows thru from canal. Towpath beyond is on high slanting wall.

FEEDER DAM NO. 5 AND INLET (GUARD) LOCK NO. 5

106.80 *Access: Distance from Williamsport 7.8 m.* Take MD 68 4.5 m. N.W. from Williamsport to MD 56 on which turn left .5 m. to Dam No. 5 Road, where go left 2.8 m. to Dam No. 5 parking lot (10 cars).

Potomac Edison power plant at far side of dam on W. Va. side better maintained by Pot.Ed. then when canal ceased operations in 1924. Dam was constructed 1833-1835 of stone-filled timber cribs. Lock House, 1½ story brick, is on the hill above the lock.

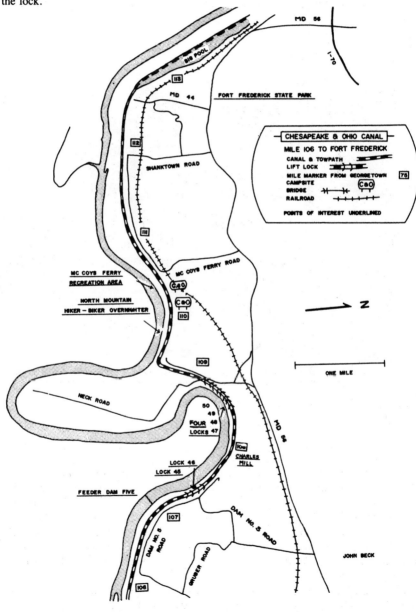

Temporary lock constructed around abutment of dam in 1833 to permit continuation of river trade while dam being built. Stretch between Dams 5 and 6 (27¼ m.) opened to navigation in April 1839. Construction began on 18 foot masonry dam in 1857. On 7 Dec. 1861 Confederates threw shells and shot at Dam No. 5; that and another attempt failed to materially damage the dam. From 17 to 20 Dec. Gen. Stonewall Jackson made concentrated effort to breach dam, which he did. Destruction of dam, however, was not complete and repairs were made in a few days.

Canoeists must portage on either side of the dam. Dam is marked upstream.

Here at Dam 5 loaded boats came down the river outside the narrow strip of land and light boats went up the narrow channel in the river. (National Park Service)

106.82 *Mule crossover bridge was located at upper end of lock to get mules to berm side of canal as slackwater behind Dam 5 used from here to Lock 45, ½ m. upstream.* Bridge washed out in 1936 flood. Towpath follows ledge cut into rock. Area connecting inlet lock with river ill-defined.

106.86 *High water medallion* on rock to right reads, "1942/217.43". Towpath widened to road-like appearance leads along *canal-like ditch to left* separating island from towpath, with steep slope or wall to right. Ditch connects with river in .2 m.

107.13 Previous bare-ledged towpath around rocky point widened considerably and leveled; cliff overhanging it altered.

156

Inlet Lock Number 5, as it looked in the heyday of the C & O. (Courtesy of John Frye)

107.15 Above towpath about 30 feet were entrances to *three small caves, known as Two Locks Caves,* which may have been altered by blasting of cliff. Opening to left is crawlway, floored with river gravel, extending south for 30 feet. Second cave is fissure, apparently connecting with 3rd cave, entrance in small hollow 150 feet to south. Third cave is crawlway extending 100 feet into Beckmantown limestone, with few small side passages at rear. Fine views of river and its environs away from towpath.

107.19 *Part of beautiful rock cliff blasted to widen towpath around rocky points* obliterating some old tow rope marks. Concrete apron laid around rocks replacing former rock ledge for about 285 feet.

LOCK NO. 45

107.27 *Access:* From Lock 46 .15 m. above or Dam No. 5 .47 m. below. *Canal resumes after ½ m. of slackwater navigation thru this inlet (river) lock.* Towpath road remains on berm between Locks 45 and 46. Overgrown path to strip of land opposite, above Lock 45 to Lock 46. Locks known as "Two Locks," as is nearby community of several houses. Lift of lock 7'.

LOCK NO. 46

107.42 *Access: Distance from Williamsport 8.5 m.* See Dam No. 5 106.80. Lock 46 .7 m. from Dam 5 parking lot on continuation of Dam No. 5 Road. Dirt road turns left down steep hill .1 m. to small parking area near lock. Lift of lock 7'.

Upper of "Two Locks" in attractive dark grassy area. Unoccupied, 2½-story brick and stone locktender's house served both locks. Wasteweir filled in. *Towpath formerly crossed back to river side of canal by means of mule crossover bridge called "Roving Bridge" in canal jargon,* at lower end of lock, of which stone piers remain. Tunis ''Bud '' Newkirk's Store and Steel's were located here. Newkirk also rented and sold mules for use on the canal.

107.48 Bluestone widened towpath which began at Dam 5 continues to Four Locks. Impressive rock formations on berm, probably visible from towpath only in winter. Several honey locusts here.

107.62 Stonework to left, semi-formal overflow. Path on berm to old log house in small valley. *Was basin here and Canal Co. boat repair facility associated with old house.*

107.69 Should be *culvert* here according to old records; now a pipe. Work was extremely difficult and expensive between Lock 46 and 47, embankments of canal being made in river, which was 20 feet deep.

107.73 Cliffs on berm side. Wintering ducks seen on January day in river.

107.93 Culvert #137, carries stream from broad ravine, in a 2' pipe.

108.13 *Culvert #138 (Camp Springs Run)* 8'-span. {Benjamin F} Charles Mill and remains of former milling community to right. Mill in ruins, but some walls and millwheel remain; millrace washed out. Apparently basin and landing on canal at this point. Road leads North between mill ruins and houses to Big Spring on MD. 56 (½ m.) and Clear Spring on US 40 (3 m.), but no access to public thru this private property. Cliffs resume on berm beyond culvert. Charles Mill, built 1807, remained in operation until 1924. Mill contained both a plaster mill and a grain mill.

Mule "Cross-over" Bridge at Lock 46, circa 1900. (Courtesy of John Frye)

108.40 Especially fine 75 foot sheer cliff on right. Note drill marks in cliff, especially when sunlight on rocks.

108.49 Could be old basin where present fence and gate are across inlet. Beyond canal bed overgrown and rocky cliffs resume on berm side, after which canal bed cleared and houses appear on cliff.

FOUR LOCKS

Access: From I-70 take Clear Spring exit into center of Clear Spring and go South 2.7 m. on Big Spring Rd. thru Big Spring and' then left on Four Locks Road .7 m. to parking area next to Lock 48. Or from US 40 at Clear Spring take Big Spring Road South as above. Four Locks Recreation area has public boat ramp to 7 m. slackwater lake, extensive picnic area, water, toilets.

Canal leaves river to make ½ m. shortcut across "The Neck" (Prathers Neck), thus bypassing 4 m. bend of river. Locks built at this particular location to avoid otherwise expensive cut. Level to lock 51 is longest on canal. Several houses in community; large stone house on berm is "Hassett House," whose early owner was closely associated with canal affairs. This area was HQ for Union troops defending canal in 1861.

108.64 *LOCK 47 first of Four Locks.* Canal bed between each of 4 locks is grassy and well maintained. Drydock "stocks" for repairing boats may have been built here in 1869s. Lift 8¼'.

108.70 *LOCK 48* with bypass flume "Birm Road," so designated on country road sign. Part of upper gate remains. Potential cave-in of berm lock wall reinforced with timbers. Lock buried for preservation. Lock lift 8¼'.

108.74 *Culvert #139,* 12'-span, carrying stream and Neck Road Junction of Neck and Birm Roads to right. Brick 2½-story house on right was locktender's house for all 4 locks; occupied until 1970 by 4 or 5 generations of Taylor Family. Lock house at Lock 50 was a later addition.

108.80 *LOCK 49* has only bits of upper gate. Footbridge across to road. Note opening in masonry for flume. Towpath partly grassgrown road as canal shortcut across neck begins. Lift lock 8¼'.

108.87 Lock 50, uppermost of "Four Locks," has concrete flume on berm. Part of lower gate intact. Old pictures show grain store, storage and other buildings. Lock house, 1½-story wooden structure is across the road. Barn west of burned house used to house feed and mules over winter, has been tastefully restored by Park Service. 8¼' lift. Note lock tenders "wait" house at upstream end of the lock.

109.32 *Cross concrete waste weir (50-51 level)* and emerge on river bank at upper end of short cut, its two wickets in perfect condition. Fine river views. Three feet-thick elaborate stone wall of waste weir *suggests use other than for drainway,* such as for water power, as lower portion takes route other than natural slope of land.

109.41 Large growth in canal bed. Wintering waterfowl in river on 24 Jan. 1972 included 50 goldeneyes, 20 coots and 2 common mergansers.

The Charles Mill below Four Locks as it appeared about 1915. (National Park Service)

Plenty of wildlife. Red squirrel, an indication of increased altitude. Numerous raccoon tracks.

109.60 Towpath high above river flat. Concrete to left and more in valley below, part of old house belonging to man named Snooks. Broad ravine to right.

109.90 *Culvert #140*, 10'-span. Road culvert. Canal high (48' 9") above river level.

110.10 *Culvert #141*, 4'-span.

110.29 *Stop Gate* may have helped retain water in Big Pool when canal drained, though there was also a stop lock at lower end of Big Pool, presumably for that purpose. Principal reason for use may have been to effect repairs below this point as this was longest level along canal: As there was no lift-lock, stop lock might have been added to reduce the uncontrollable length of the level. Constructed 1838, 17' wide, 20' long.

110.42 Culvert #142, 12'-span. (McCoys Ferry). Constructed 1837, rebuilt in 1839. Western Md. R.R. bridge to north of culvert.

MC COYS FERRY RECREATION AREA

110.42 *Access:* From I-70, take Big Pool exit to reach MD 56; take 2.9 m. to McCoys Ferry Road, from which take .6 m. to McCoys Ferry. From US 40 take MD 56 about 4½ m. to McCoys Ferry Road. Food and lodging on US 40. I-70 has Greyhound Bus Service. Recreation area is open for camping only in summer with toilets, picnic grilles and earthen boat launching ramp to Potomac. McCoys Ferry Road, with Green Spring on berm enters *large culvert* beneath Western

Md. R.R. trestle and goes to campground. Towpath passes over roadway leading to recreation area. Footpath crosses canal to McCoys Ferry Road.

On 23 May 1861 in absence of Clear spring Guards at 2 a.m., some Virginians seized the ferry boat and headed for opposite shore. Home Guards discovered theft when boat was half-way across, called out 3 times and fired. Virginians abandoned the boat and reached Va. shore in a skiff. At dawn Home Guards retrieved the ferry. Here on 10 Oct. 1862 Gen. J. E. B. Stuart crossed Potomac on his 2nd ride around McClellan's Army.

110.45 *Culvert #143 (Green Spring Run)* 6'-span. Road on berm. Canal bed cleared of growth. Long trains frequently appear.

110.80 R.R. ties lashed together lying in shallow water form path across canal to abandoned farm. Squirrels playing in yard.

110.83 *Culvert #144,* 6'-span, wide, open valley. Masses of May apples and honeysuckle. W. Va.'s North Mountains seen, but not river. Chipmunks challenge right to towpath.

110.91 Worn road across canal bed to former pastureland between river and towpath.

111.20 Small farmhouse on berm. This section of. towpath recently used as part of farm. Road on berm may lead to Ft. Frederick area. Begin long straight-away in canal.

111.28 Former boat basin on berm.

111.38 Culvert #145, 6'-span.

111.68 Small stream enters canal on right from large group of evergreens. From this point canal becomes boundary for Ft. Frederick State Park. Packed dirt towpath.

111.98 Towpath becomes rutted dirt road, with cedar trees in field on right. Cleared canal bed with felled trees is dismal sight-point to be considered in development of the Natural Park.

112.05 *Culvert #147,* 4'-span.

112.23 *Culvert #148,* 6'-span.

We have come a way from the hustle and bustle of Georgetown, skirting the Great Falls of the Potomac, hiking through deciduous woods of the Piedmont to the foothills of the Blue Ridge Mountains and beyond, passing historic towns—Harpers Ferry, Shepherdstown, Sharpsburg, Williamsport—and sensing in the distance the larger valley towns of Frederick and Hagerstown, enjoying the slackwaters of the Potomac River, constant companion of the canal, marveling at the natural wonders of the valley and hills and the physical accomplishments of the builders of the canal—dams, lift locks, aqueducts, culverts—to this point, where we enter first a rather placid section, somewhat marred by a paralleling interstate highway ahead, but still a restful prelude to the adventures which await us in the mountainous region ahead.

Restored fort and museum at Fort Frederick State Park.

FORT FREDERICK MARYLAND STATE PARK

112.40 Access: 12 m. E. of Hancock. Reached from I 70 or US 40 via MD 56; about 1½ m. from Big Pool exit of I 70 or 3 m. S. of Indian Springs on US 40; 1 m from park entrance on MD 56 to canal. At edge of canal, road crosses WMd R.R. track on curve with poor visibility. Listen for locomotive whistle. Massive restored fort (7'-thick walls), picnic areas. Two camping areas; large one between canal and river, smaller one near picnic pavilion. Boat ramp, trailer spaces, ball diamond, concession office and souvenir shop, drinking water, toilets. Museum contains Indian and pre-Revolutionary relics. Boat rental for Big Pool and Potomac River. Interpretive programs in season. Bike rental. Tel. 301-842-2155. New interpretive center.

Ft. Frederick was built in 1756 by Prov. Gov. Horatio Sharpe to protect the frontier against the French and Indians after Braddock's defeat. It was part of a chain of colonial forts stretching along entire eastern side of Alleghenies. Fort occupies dominant position on North Mtn 100' above Potomac River. George Washington was here July 1756 and June 1758. Used as a detention camp for British prisoners during the Revolutionary War, garrisoned by Union troops during the Civil War in 1861-62 to protect canal and R.R., and in 1922, deeded to Md. Dept. of Forests and Parks. Civilian Conservation Corps (CCC) restored area to create a visual reminder of colonial days. Reenactments staged in period dress each summer.

Stop gate beside bridge on road from fort to picnic areas along river provides a means of retaining water in Big Pool when canal drained for winter, thus avoiding necessity of filling this large lake when water restored to canal. Stop gate is simple masonry structure of two parallel walls 18' apart, with simple masonry wings 7' in length on upper and lower ends. Base of stone indicates a pivot bridge which rested on lower berm wall and used for both pedestrians and vehicles. Stop gate probably had machinery for lifting a drop gate. Stones in lock wall appear to be rough-cut granite. A dig at this site c1972 revealed the circular pivot mechanism in place. A wooden bridge later replaced the pivot bridge.

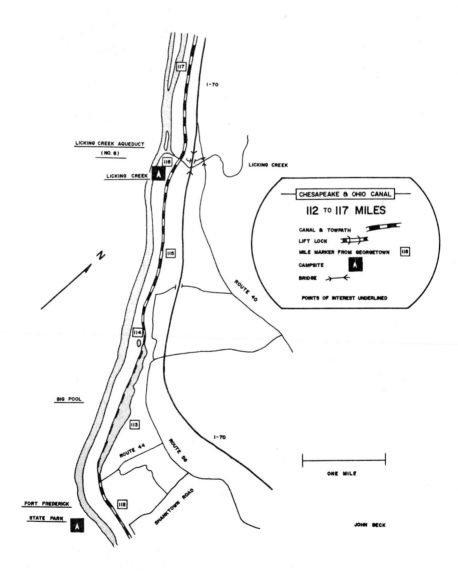

Stop gate at lower end of Big Pool in the early 1900s. Note Pivot Bridge to right.

BIG POOL

112.50 Access: From Ft. Frederick. This fine sheet of water, extending 1½ m. along the canal, was built as result of engineers' decision to utilize natural ridge and create a lake rather than follow contour of land. Great Blue Heron sighted 1983.

113.15 High and deep walls to left mark location of **masonry waste weir** used to control level of Big Pool; now filled with earth. **Elaborate masonry spillway 121'** in length above and adjoining waste weir in need of repair. Mule walked thru shallow water while pedestrians used a plank walkway which rested on stone piers placed 20' apart.

113.48 Houses on far side of lake are village of Big Pool. Lake in winter is abode of many species of wild ducks, especially ruddies, ring-necks, blue-winged teal, buffle-heads and mergansers.

113.89 Marshy pond on left is **excellent bird area.** In April yellow spice-bush and Dutchman's-breeches add color and grackles fuss in thickets. Chisel-marks of pileated woodpeckers on tree trunks and limbs.

113.94 **Big Pool ends** in berm marsh. Notice muskrat channels in mudbanks of swamp.

114.02 Pass under trestle of WMd R.R. liaison track extending along embankment to left and crossing river on steel bridge to connect with B & O R.R. at Cherry Run, WVa. Trestle apparently built after canal closing in 1924 because it provides less than 9' clearance over towpath. WMd R.R. ended across river at Cherry Run until its extension after 1904. In the years around 1904, George Gould was trying to extend his inland R.R. holdings into a thru line to east coast and bought control of WMd R.R. from city of Baltimore. A major gap in his project was Big Pool to Cumberland. Md. approved petition to Cumberland, crossing and re-crossing canal, in 1904. Line to coast was never completed, in spite of WMd extension to Cumberland.

Big Pool above Fort Frederick, circa 1903-1923.

114.15 Stop Gate constructed on concrete over old masonry. Original parallel masonry walls were about 18' apart.

114.21 Historic Culvert #149, 6' span, 4'-high sidewalls, carries stream from fields on berm.

114.43 Historic Culvert #150, 12' span, 7.6'-high sidewalls, carries stream issuing from settled area of Ernstville. Stream has nice lizards tail, pickerel weed and other aquatic plants. **Formerly a rd. culvert** which gave access to river and ferry to Cherry Run. **Provides foot access to canal from US 40** by turning onto Ernstville Rd. 1.15 m., crossing I 70 and R.R. tracks to rd. which leads short distance to culvert; also from I 70 (Big Pool exit) by getting on MD 56 .1 m. and then .75 m. onto rd. to left across R.R. tracks to culvert rd. Previously known as "Dry Run Road Culvert."

114.52 Ernstville. Rd. leads across canal to corner of hard-surfaced rd. To rt. from this corner, village of Big Pool is .7 m.; straight ahead leads 1 m. to US 40 at point 1 m. W. of Indian Springs;

114.83 Historic Culvert #151, of gray limestone, 4'-high-sidewalls, 6' span.

115.02 Historic Culvert #152, 4' span, carrying small stream, is buried to spring line on outflow. Downstream wingwall collapsed.

115.50 Historic Culvert #153, 4' span, nearly completely covered.

LICKING CREEK AQUEDUCT (No. 6)

116.04   **Access:** From Ft. Frederick at 112.40 or from US 40 W of Indian Springs take road on W end of Licking Creek Bridge to near aqueduct. Path leads along creek to river. Trail at far side of aqueduct leads down to creek and affords fine view of arch reflected in quiet, green water. A Jas Johnson built Licking Creek Forge in 1775 at mouth of creek to use pig iron from Green Spring Furnace. Survey of 1795 lists Jacques Forge on Licking Creek near **Potomac River.** Operator probably related to Lancelot and son, Denton Jacques who built Green Springs Furnace near McCoys Ferry about 1768. When the furnace was shut down, the forge was sold to a Mr. Chambers of Chambersburg, Pa., who ran it on pig iron from his Pa. Furnace (Singewald, **Iron Works of Maryland**).

Aqueduct has single arch, 120' span, 15' rise, 180' wing-to-wing—said to be largest built in this country. Located on historical Section 222. Constructed 1835 to 1839 of Tonoloway gray limestone and Conococheague limestone by Enos Childs. Stone from Licking Creek quarry ½ m. N. on Licking Creek and from Prathers Neck quarry. Arch inside parapet, coping and water table are cut stone; rest is rubble masonry. Parapet and coping 7' high, coping 34' above level of creek, waterway 21' wide. Berm parapet replaced with wodden trunk in 1874. Canal co. report for 1870 advises of use of inferior stone during construction which is now cracked in every direction and stones have fallen. The walls, very much bulged, have been secured with iron ties and clamps extending entirely through the aqueduct. Towpath parapet has moved 8" out of line. Arch stones fallen on berm side. Up to 5 ringstones in arch above all skewbacks failing from overload and badly fractured from shear stresses. Wooden trunk rotted out and fallen. To rt. WMd R.R. bridge, steel on concrete piers. One panel of ornamental fence of aqueduct remains in place on downstream, towpath wing wall. Notice single remaining cast iron finial of the posts. **Licking Creek Hiker-Biker Overnighter.**

116.67   Milepost 117 out of position; error continues W. to near Lock 51. Service road parallels canal for next mile or so.

Licking Creek Aqueduct (Aqueduct No. 6), 1975.

116.76 Historic Culvert #160, 6' span. Ringstones of cut limestone. Parapet rises 2½' above keystone. From here to Hancock approach I-70 parrallels canal and roar of traffic is almost constant.

117.17 Park Head Settlement. Area of geological interest by reason of Parkhead sandstone, which takes name from exposure in nearby R.R. cut. This member of Jennings Formation, of Devonian age, consists of shale interbedded with massive sandstone. Sandstone made up mostly of conglomerates, bluish-black when fresh, buff or reddish when weathered. **Lower portions of these conglomerates carry liberal number of fossils.** Parkhead sandstone is 300' thick and especially well exposed in highway cut beyond R.R. to rt. Called "Parkhead Level."

117.30 Spring at edge of towpath.

117.75 Buried Culvert #162?

117.90 High, steep slope on rt. is **end of Orchard Ridge** (formerly Pigskin Ridge); runs N. to Pa. line at crossing of Licking Creek.

118.09 Historic Culvert #163 replaced with corrugated steel (6') pipe in 1865; old culvert is 20' to E. and covered with fill. Access by parallel road.

118.20 Loading dock on berm. V-shaped barrage dam and sluice in river ahead.

118.40 Towpath comes directly onto river bank. Across river, mouth of Sleepy Creek shows beyond end of wooded island. To rt., interesting rock strata exposed in wall of canal and R.R cut. Berm rd. ends.

118.46 Historic Culvert #166 waste weir, 8' span, 4' rise; cut limestone in ringstones, rubble masonry in rest of culvert. Concrete frame, 3 vertical openings, wooden planks for spillway control. 10' square well between berm face of culvert and culvert under WMd R.R., to N. Well-built matched blocks of gray and red sandstone (Parkhead sandstone, Devonian). Culvert in good condition. Historically may have been Waste Weir #20. Wings extend 70 yds. upstream and 180 yds. downstream.

118.90 Site of Village of Millstone (Millstone Point). Approximately 100 people lived here in 1910. Millstone Point was owned by Dr. L. Jacques, a surgeon in the Revolutionary Army. Stagecoach stop on National Road. Notice holly tree which survived the settlement. Former Moffet Station on WMd R.R., presumably named for Wm. Moffet, owner of Millstone Point in 1882. Turn-around basin filled with silt. Old stone wall and stone foundation visible on berm side. Flour mill and tavern served both road and canal. For ½ m. at Millstone Point canal was dug in roadway of National Pike and canal co. had to make a new rd. at considerable expense. An early-day stagecoach with passengers didn't stop in time and landed in canal. During Civil War Millstone Point was HQ for regiment defending canal. Old hotel destroyed by I-70.

Correspondent in Harpers Monthly describes an incident of a journey over an old stage route in 1879 (after stages were gone) thusly:

"At Millstone Point. . .a committee from Hancock. . .came out to meet General Jackson. Some excavations were being made in the neighborhood and several blasts were fired in honor of the occasion as 'Old Hickory' approached. 'Didn't the detonations alarm your horse, general?' inquired a solicitous committeeman. 'No sir', said Jackson emphatically; 'My horse and I have heard a similar sort of music before'." (Scharf, **Hist. of Western Md.**)

119.04 Remains of small canal boat reported in silt to rt. of causeway carrying rough rd. across canal in 1957 no longer visible. American bittern observed April 1979.

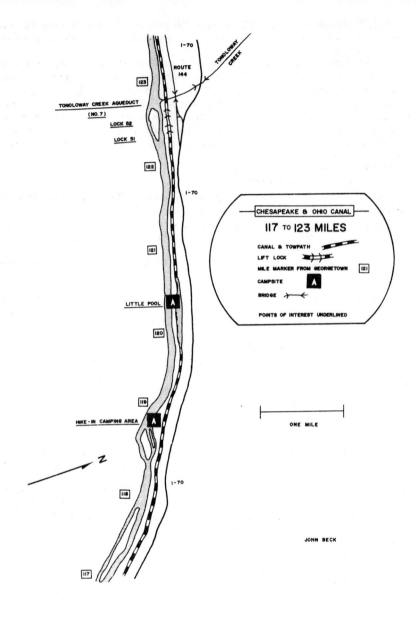

119.51 Historic Culvert #170 and Waste Weir #21 Combination. This is one of five waste weirs on this level. Rebuilt 1975/1976.

119.70 Interesting vertical strata in rock to rt. Large patches of squirrel corn (Dicentra canadensis) bloom here in late April. Also Dutchman's Breeches, spring beauty, trout lily, and wild ginger.

119.71 Stop gate near lower end of Little Pool, used to retain water in this body of water when canal drained for winter. Simple structure consisting of two parallel walls 18' apart with 12' wings. Masonry of well-cut red shale and gray limestone. Date of 'March 26 10' in gate recesses.

168

119.84 Little Pool, lower end. Pretty body of water, nearly 1 m. long, similar in nature to Big Pool. Normal water level 398' above sea level, towpath having risen that much from tidal lock in Georgetown. The pool and adjacent wooden areas are good birding localities. Little Pool was formed by transfering the towpath to an island. Flood 1 Apr. 1886, washed out 50' of towpath. Informal overflow ahead at 119.91. Little Pool is now accessible from I-70 via MD 615. Parking lot at 119.54.

120.39 Little Pool Hiker Biker. Nearest access at 119.54. Next H/B upstream is White Rock at 126.43; downstream is North Mountain at 109.54.

120.75 Upper end of Little Pool, formed by levee leading to rt.

121.19 Historic Culvert #172, 6' span, 3' sidewalls.

121.57 Historic Culvert #173. 8' span. Ditch Run. Rebuilt by NPS.

122.11 Historic Culvert #174, Waste weir #22 . Structure rebuilt 1974-75. Spillway of waste weir and drop inlet of culvert are located on back side of berm dike of canal; 6' span.

122.49 Historic Culvert #175, 4' span. Outflow completely covered.

LOCK No. 51

122.59 Access: From Hancock (1½ m. upstream) or from rd. across from bowling alley on MD 144 at E. end of Hancock; this point (across from bowling alley) also reached from I 70 on Hancock (MD 144) exit—rd. to canal is to left immediately as one comes off exit on to MD 144. Take this rd: .1 m. to canal, cross dry canal bed and walk .34 m. to lock. Lock was completed by William Storey in the fall of 1838. Limestone lock walls in good condition, with some coping stones out of place. Broad bypass flume. Upperberm wing returns parallel to lock walls to from towpath side of bypass flume ditch entrance. Water spilled down on pile of rocks to prevent undercutting. Extra deep recess of 6'' in lower half of lock recess — perhaps to allow gates to be fully opened without shutting wicket gates. One remaining gate strap is of slotted loop type. Lockhouse ruins sit beside towpath at about mid-lock; was 1½ stories of stone over full stone basement. Only first floor plastered inside. Roof and floors gone and rear wall mostly gone. House measured 18' wide x 30' long and was constructed with a mixture of limestone and dark red shale. It had a narrow porch on towpath side and a short porch on downstream side. Inscribed in stone below window sill is "DX Rowland AUG. 1843." Another stone, much more formal, is located near the ground in center of north wall of house. It has a formal XXX border, within which are several stars "*" and words "D. R. 1843." Report of 10 May 1829 advises $800 spent on construction of this lock. Annual reports of Canal Co. list Upton Rowland as locktender for Locks 51 and 52 from 1840 to 1 Apr. 1848, for which he was paid $200 per year. As of latter date he was replaced by J. Miller. First floor had a center chimney with back-to-back fireplaces and walls plastered on the stone. One of few snubbing posts left. In 1957 both posts were visible. Boats were snubbed to these posts while water was being let in or out of locks, else boats would drift down into lower lock gates. A line made fast to the boat clews was tossed up to mule driver who took a turn around nearest snubbing post and paid out or drew in line as boat either sank or rose with water level in lock. Note rope burns on upper section of post. Post is 8'5'' from inner surface of towpath wall and 16' from upper end of lower lock pocket. There were usually two of these posts 6' to 9' from lock walls and lower one seems to have been about one rod (16½') above lower lock pocket and from 16' to 24' below lower end of upper

House at Lock 51, 1972.

lower lock pocket and from 16' to 24' below lower end of upper pocket. Snubbing post is about 12" in diameter by 30" in height. Level of water above this lock seems to have been raised in operating period as was done in several of the locks. Upper lock recesses, upper extensions, turns and upper wings seem to have been raised by bolting 8" thick wooden timbers to these portions to raise the water level above the lock. Most of upper three courses of stone in this lock seem to have been replaced. Lower towpath concrete quoin coping stone shows date which may be "Feb., 1918". Most hardware gone from lock. Entire lock shows much rebuilding. Compass orientation of lock is N. 79° W., pointing straight at Lock 52. Towpath bank lined with battered dry laid stone wall 30' above upper towpath wing, and on canal side by sharply tapered and coped wall extending 28' below lower towpath wing. Below tapered wall, a low dry laid wall extends for some distance. Below lower berm wing, canal side of berm dike also walled with large dry laid stone for 30'. Bypass flume little more than a wide shallow ditch parallel to lock walls and lined with rubble stone. Bypass flume spillway has pile of stones at downstream end to break force of falling water. Face of lower wing walls of lock were whitewashed in days of operation and traces remain. While most of stones in lock are poor grade of limestone, there are four apparently unused quoin stones of excellent quality lying on river side of towpath just above the lock which were probably intended for replacements.

122.85 Rd. across canal prism leads to MD 144 .1 m. away, providing access to Locks 51 and 52 and Tonoloway Aqueduct. Interesting old house on berm.

1972 photograph of Lock 52, by-pass flume to left.

Old view of Lock 52, circa 1903-1923. (National Park Service)

LOCK No. 52

122.89 Access: See Lock 51, but go upstream .04 mi to Lock 52. It gives appearance of being a continuous structure with Aqueduct No. 7 over Tonoloway Creek, as its stone walls are connected with walls of aqueduct. Robert Brown was contractor for Lock 52 and Tonoloway Aqueduct, completing both in summer of 1839. Contract for walls connecting these structures was completed by William Storey by October 1839. Lock walls of limestone in fairly good condition. Towpath lock wall continues to aqueduct and becomes part of riverside portion of that structure. Upper berm wing wall returns to form entrance to lock side of bypass flume. Wide bypass flume has earth bank on lock side, but a 4'-high, battered, well-laid stone wall of dark red shale on back side. Only foundation on the towpath at midlock measuring 18'-11" by 16'-7".

TONOLOWAY CREEK AQUEDUCT (No. 7)

122.96 Access: See Lock 51. Go .15 mi upstream. Given as "Great Tonoloway" on earlier maps. The 110' span appears to be constructed of slaty rock. Both parapet walls gone. Though the general supposition is that the walls collapsed, the physical appearance and condition indicate that the stones were removed to within one course of the top of the barrel stones. The reason probably is that when the flume was leaking badly and the arch so weakened, the stones were removed to help correct the problem. The bed of the canal was then replaced with concrete and heavy timber sills which supported wooden flume as well as a wooden towpath bridge. Modern wooden walkway provides safe crossing. Spillway of aqueduct waste weir located in lower berm parapet wall is built on solid rock; floor of spillway formed of stones set on edge. This waste weir is another three-opening one where concrete was formed, seemingly identical to original timber sizes. Aqueduct was known at one time as "Bowles Aqueduct" on natural rock. Stabilized by NPS 1979-1950. Arches are of unequal length.

123.56 Town line of Hancock, unmarked. **Fragments of hull of canal boat (Canal Towage Co. Barge No. 57) in canal bed;** built about 1909, captained by Ab Davis. Measured and photographed by NPS in 1939.

123.84 Hancock Basin. Old two-story warehouse directly on berm wall, about 150'-long with masonry wall beyond. This warehouse was built about 1878 by Rafe Taney, who grew a long beard which he divided and braided with one braid over each shoulder to hang down his back. In 1902 Hockman family converted second floor to living quarters. Title to property is said to have included agreement with canal co. permitting warehouse to extend to berm of canal itself. In 1936 building was shortened to allow a road between building and canal. Note unique outhouse (privy) overhanging canal from upstream end of the building. **Historic Road Culvert #179,** 12' span at mile 123.95. The warehouse was destroyed by fire in 1979. Warehouse was once owned by R. T. Little. Note basin upstream.

172

Riverside view of Tonoloway Creek Aqueduct (No. 7), 1973.

HANCOCK, MARYLAND

124.10 **Access:** From US 40, I 70 or US 522; Cumberland about 40 m.; Baltimore/Washington about 100 m. Overnight accommodations (Hancock Motel on US 522 near Potomac Bridge), restaurants (National and Weavers among others), bus service. No train service either here on WMd R.R. or at B & O sta. on opposite side of river in W. Va. Most northern point on the Potomac River. Paved back street runs along berm, with backs of buildings facing canal; several perpendicular streets lead to canal. Steel and concrete bridge over canal leads to foot of Church St. NPS Visitor Center on the Main Street, west end of town.

Hancock named for early settler, whom history indicates was famous only for having town named after him. Barton Central Hotel (closed) is probably oldest house. Old name for town was "Hancocktown;" also "The Conolloways" and as the "North Bend" in early colonial days. Stockaded blockhouse, called Fort Tonoloway, was erected on Potomac near here in 1755 (after Braddock's defeat) and was abandoned on completion of Ft. Frederick.

Hancock was an important location on the canal and National Road. In stressing competition between canal and railroad along Potomac River, additional competition from publicly supported roads, which now dominates surface transportation, is sometimes overlooked in the history of transportation. Hancock and Cumberland were important road centers before the construction of canal and B & O R.R., and most freight and passengers passed between these two towns by stagecoach and freight wagon until about 1850 when the railroad gained ascendency and traffic on the national road began slipping. Hancock, before being designated as a route location for the National Rd.

173

late in the Jefferson Administration, was interconnected by wagon roads, and had become a center for taverns, which lasted into canal days. John Donovan opened a tavern in Hancock before 1790. Names of taverns operating before 1810: Sign of the Cross Keys, Sign of the Green Tree, Sign of the Ship (Donovan's), Union Inn and Sign of the Seven Stars. Each displayed an appropriate and sometimes elaborate sign. Gambling and horse racing were reportedly popular during frontier days. A broadside of Sept. 7, 1797 announced three days of horse racing at Hancock during the month of October. "Hack" (charter) stages ran thru from Elizabeth Town (Hagerstown) to Bath in early 1800s. In 1823, mail stage from Baltimore to Wheeling made trip in 3½ days, running 3 times weekly. Increased to 6 times weekly in 1826. Fare Baltimore to Cumberland, $10.50. In 1838, Good Intent and Pilot Stage lines (mail) ran daily, Baltimore to Wheeling and Cincinnati. First churches were not built until

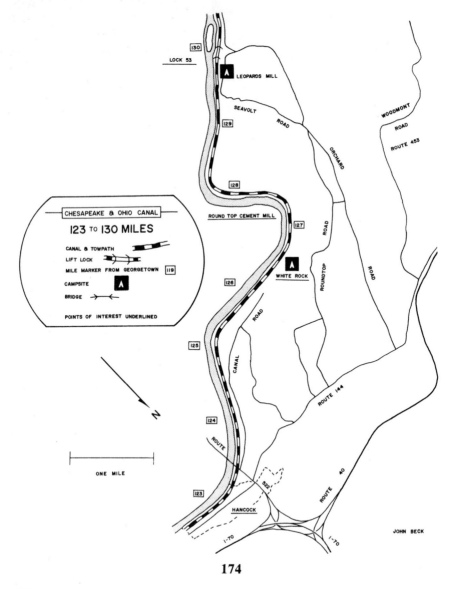

Stern of Canal
Towage Company
Barge No. 57
below Hancock,
1939. (National Park
Service)

1830s, coincidently with construction and opening of canal through Hancock, although the schoolhouse was used for church services prior to that period.

Destruction of the town was threatened in 1862 when a Confederate Army under the command of Stonewall Jackson appeared across the river and began bombardment in retaliation for Union bombardment of Shepherdstown after the Battle of Antietam. Demanding surrender or destruction of the town, the Union commander occupying the town, Gen. F. W. Lander, reportedly sent word to Gen. Jackson that continued shelling of Hancock would kill more friends than enemies ". . . it is a damned secesh place anyhow".

"The Oriole" Pleasure Boat used for trips up and down canal for fishing and picnics from Hancock was built before 1900 by a group of Citizens including Dawsons, Fields, Hendersons and Dr. Staggers, who paid about $25 each. Boat was planned by Dawson and used Dawson's mules. Many boatmen lived here and some boats wintered. The town had several warehouses and boat building facilities.

Since the turn of the present century apple and peach growing have become more important. Business section continues to thrive as merchandise center for orchardists, workers employed in nearby quarries and travelers passing on the intersecting interstate highways. Some of the orchards and packing plants may be seen from the towpath.

Church St. formerly continued left onto bridge across Potomac which completely washed out in 1936; ferry maintained for month or so, then temporary wooden bridge erected on old piers was used until new (present) bridge built. As late as 1882 (and probably much later), a ford and ferry connected town with its R.R. sta. on W. Va. side of the river. Zero on USGS Hancock River Gage is 383.46' above sea level. Record flood here was 18 Mar. 1936 when river was 10' above towpath; towpath elevation is 422'. Fishtraps here and another mile upstream noted in 1960-61. W. Md. R.R. station burned c1982.

124.33 Berm street continues as rd; buildings end. **Parking and picnic area; boat ramp.** Canal watered for recreation and fire protection. Drinking water available in picnic area.

124.38 Little Tonoloway Colvert, #182, 36' span marks western town line of Hancock. Old maps called this Tonoloway Creek, designating larger stream 1 m. below Hancock as "Great Tonoloway." Samuel Rinehart owned a sumac mill located here. Using water purchased from canal co., sumac leaves were processed into a leather tanning extract. (Possible remains about 100' downstream of culvert near towpath.) There was also a bone mill and a saw mill at this location.

175

124.59 Pass under steel and concrete **US 522 Bridge across Potomac** connecting Md. and W. Va. Pa. Turnpike at Breezewood is 26 m. N.; Berkeley Springs is 6 m. S. Curious shape of Md. is emphasized by mileages here: Pa. state line is 1.7 m. to N., W. Va. line is at end of bridge to S. Actually, shore line across river is not W. Va., but Md.; one of many odd points where original river channel changed, leaving state boundary on dry land .1 m. from present shore line. Historic spa of Bath, now Berkeley Springs, well worth side trip. Quarries (not open to public) and works of Pa. Glass Sand Co. 3m. S. are of considerable interest. There fossil-bearing sandstone deposits of Warm Springs Ridge are processed and shipped for variety of uses. **Poor access to canal here but possible via old rd. under bridge to R.R. tracks and across small field.** Continuation of close-by paved berm rd. Cleared, grass-covered canal prism. Field between towpath and river. Eight whistling swans sighted against azure sky in Dec. 1971.

125.10 Spring peepers (in season) start piping at noise of passing train.

125.27 Historic Culvert #183, 4′ span, carries stream beyond R.R. which parallels canal to above Little Orleans. Shalom et Benedictus Wildlife Sanctuary. No Trespassing sign. **R.R. ties provide access to berm road.** Young trees line both sides of towpath from Hancock. Canal watered from this stream.

125.66 Berm rd. swings back from canal to follow R.R. Towpath follows edge of open field beyond, with broad views in all directions. Across river, along B & O R.R., is plant of Pa. Glass Sand Co. Upstream from plant, end of Warm Springs Ridge rises to cliffs of Lovers Leap, with usual Indian legend associated with overworked name. **Prominent mountain ahead directly on canal is Roundtop, with long line of Tonoloway Ridge behind it.**

Old view of Hancock, Maryland.

126.xx NPS milepost 126. Young orchard on rt. with berm rd. ½ m. away on far side. Broad, open field continues on left. Foot of water in canal bed with mallard duck occupants. Muskrat swimming in canal. Beautiful view of W. Va. cliffs across river.

126.32 Locher House on the berm was associated with the Round Top Cement Mill.

126.36 Unused steel and wood bridge over canal with locked gate.

126.42 Historic Culvert #185, 10' span; Loner Siding on WMd R.R. End of open fields continuous for last 2 m. Orchard on berm side. W. Md. RR now abandoned from Hancock to Cumberland.

126.43 White Rock Hiker-Biker Overnighter now abandoned.

126.84 Historic Culvert #186, 4' span, with old waste weir opening at side, carrying stream coming through orchards. Berm beyond becomes natural low rock wall, with hillside fields farther along.

127.10 Flat silted area in canal gives appearance of basin. Towpath on river bank. Pleasant view of river and W. Va. shore with mountain ahead.

127.24 **"Devil's Eyebrow," a large and beautiful fold in the strata on berm.** This anticline in Bloomsburg sandstone frequently photographed from across river. Vegetation here and at cement mill just ahead removed 1974. Upper portion, 25' above canal, forms spacious shelter cave. Canal prism very narrow.

Round Top Cement Company Mill, early 1900s.

ROUND TOP CEMENT MILL

127.40 The persistent ruins of this important old mill, its attendant kilns, the many fine folds in the rock strata, the numerous "caves" and the general appeal of the surrounding area make this one of the towpath's most fascinating sections. Cement plant began operations in 1837, and much of cement and mortar used in masonry of canal structures was produced here. Fine smokestack still standing is a tribute to quality of mortar. First known as Shafer's Cement Mill, brand name survived until 1863, when the Round Top Cement Co. formed by partnership of Robert Bridges and Charles W. Henderson. A report of 1882, describing the operation, survives. Mill employed 75-100 men with another 16-20 working in the cooperage shop where barrels for shipping cement were made. A blacksmith shop with forge was located near Devil's Eyebrow. There were eight cement kilns, each 21' long 10' dia. at base. Kilns fired by coal shipped downstream by canal boat. Material came from four natural cement beds W. of the plant, that is, from Roundtop Hill in side of which were five tunnels, two going all the way thru the hill and all worked constantly. The hydraulic nature of the stone was discovered in 1837 when making cut for canal construction. Strata of cement rock were very twisting, 8-12' thick. Canal water transported by flume to overshot wheel, 16' both in diameter and width, equipped with 13 buckets, each 13" in depth. The four French burr stones used for pulverizing were 5' in diameter. Capacity of the plant was 2,200 bbls. per week. Shipments were made by both canal and B & O R.R. Cable cars shuttled cement across river for loading and storage in the warehouse, the ruins of which can be seen along R.R. tracks across river. Plant burned in 1903, and was rebuilt with capacity of 300 bbls. per day.

Austin Mater of Bolivar, W. Va., recalls working with Round Top cement in 1908, when he started working for B & O building concrete retaining walls to stop rocks from obstructing tracks in areas of rock slides. Cement was packaged in waterproof sacks bearing the name "Setter Brand" with a picture of a setter dog on the sacks. When mixed with water the cement immediately started to set. "One of us would push the wheelbarrow and the other would stir vigorously with a hoe all the way to the retaining wall" Portland processed cement with a slower setting rate came into use later. One of the finest exposures of Wills Creek Formation in Maryland can be seen in the cut of the W. Md. RR behind the cement mill.

Roundtop Hill, rising over 900' above river, affords interesting exploration and number of caves, one on summit of Roundtop, its entrance 15' N. of lane leading to cottage on top. Another, over 400' in length, is in an escarpment 250' above R.R., 500' E. of summit. Four other caves (possibly crawlways to mine shafts) are located in cuts above R.R. at points .1, .2, .5 and .7 m. W. and S.W. from cement mill. Numerous other openings in Tonoloway limestone are former mine passages, dangerous to enter. Details are contained in *Maryland Geological Survey* (1923).

127.4x Stone wall 30' above berm bank of canal. Debris in canal bed, probably from R.R. construction. R.R. directly on berm high above canal. W. Va. side of river unattractive with summer camps, old buses, etc.

127.56 Opening of mine shaft or cave on rt. between canal and R.R.; brick wall inside. Steep curved slope of Roundtop Hill above and ahead.

127.9x High concrete wall supports R.R.

127.95 Concrete tank-like structure at left; used to store and pump water to former sand glass mining operations.

128.18 Wooded flat begins on rt. as river and canal swing away from foot of steep slope. Towpath built-up on repaired section.

128.57 Historic Culvert #188, 4' span; small stone foundation at far side of berm at culvert inflow was a sediment trap. Debris that entered the canal was a problem historically. Canal bed wide and watered ahead with mallard ducks.

128.78 Very large patches of wild ginger (Asarum canadense) and bluebells or cowslips (Mertensia virginica), latter blooming in April. ·

129.xx NPS milepost 129. Wooden bench in pleasant cleared area with backdrop of sycamores. River out of sight 200 yds. away. Alas, bench is gone.

129.44 Berm here 25' rock wall exhibiting attractive horizontal bedding. Roots in towpath make for rough cycling. Mallard ducks in area.

129.77 Rock wall of berm is veritable rock garden of wildflowers.

129.87 Cross concrete and stone waste weir for 52-53 level.

129.88 Leopards Mill Hiker-Biker Overnighter. Next campsite upstream is Cacapon Junction Hiker-Biker at 133.6; downstream is White Rock at 126.43. Nearest access at 130.03. No cememt kilns extant. Little remains of the cememt grinding mill.

LOCK No. 53

129.96 Access: At mileage 130.70. Only foundation remains of lockhouse. On W. Va. side of river is Sir John's Run named after Sir John St. Clair, Quartermaster to Gen. Braddock. **Perhaps here in the stream James Rumsey experimented with a small model of the steamboat which he later demonstrated successfully at Shepherdstown in 1787.** Remains of lock gates in bottom of lock chamber. Lock completed in 1838 by Patrick McGinley.

130.03 Historic Culvert #192, 10' span, carries stream from valley beyond R.R. Rd. leads up valley and thru orchards along foot of Tonoloway Ridge 4 m. via Seavolt and Orchard Rds. to US 40. Berm rd. parallels canal ahead.

130.56 Orchard Planted in 1957 on berm. Also sections of experimental orchard planted by Md. Univ.

130.70 Access: Fm Md. 144 take Roundtop Rd. 3.5 mi. to Orehand Rd, then go 1.65 mi to Deneen Rd. where turn rt. and go .65 mi.

130.72 Historic Culvert #193, 10' span, carries stream from underpass under R.R. on rt. and follows berm ahead. Area appears in early canal data as "Leopard's Mill." Informal overflow at 130.93.

131.24 Historic Culvert #194, 4' span (Swimming Doe Culvert). Large patches of squirrel corn.

131.75 Rd., R.R. and canal pass around point of land. Across river, **Cacapon Mtn. in full view.** View from berm rd. shows layers of R.R., canal and river below. Indian fishtrap in river just below this point. Also at 132.20, 132.9 and 133.5.

131.99 Historic Culvert #195, 4' span (Sick Coon Culvert) carrying stream from large wooded ravine. Deneen Rd. beyond, showing good view of canal, bears away uphill to shortcut across bend of river toward Dam No. 6. Nice river terrace 10 yds. left of towpath.

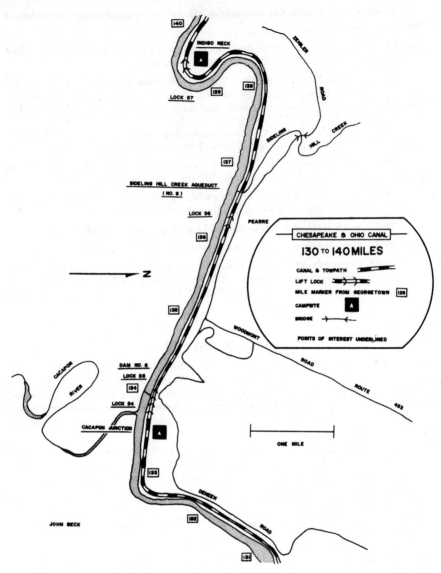

132.10 Canal workers cemetery (unmarked graves) between canal and WMd. R.R. Now cultivated field; nothing visible.

132.40 Historic Culvert #197, 4' span almost silted in; 135' informal overflow. (Rabid Fox Culvert)

132.46 Towpath footway paved with stone for .18 m. River 25 yds. away. Wide canal bed silted in. **"Prospect Point,"** popular viewpoint on WVa. 9 on Cacapon Mtn., above to left.

132.89 Fine folded strata in rock on berm.

132.99 Large anticline exposed in cliff above R.R., 200 yds. above NPS 133 marker. R.R. directly on berm.

133.17 **Concrete waste weir (53-54 level)** nice pool below. Interesting strata in reddish rock continues on. Abundance of squirrel. Many trains passing on WVa. side of river.

133.55 **Beautiful four-arched R.R. bridge over mouth of Cacapon River** on WVa. side; beginning of town of Great Cacapon. Cacapon River, about 75 m. long, originates as Lost River, flows more than 1 m. underground near Wardensville and emerges as Cacapon River. Half mile from its mouth are Fluted Rocks, extremely sharp folds in strata on E. bank, frequently pictured in geology textbooks, best seen when leaves are off trees by following rd. from Great Cacapon up W. side of river toward power plant.

133.6x **Cacapon Junction Hiker-Biker Overnighter.** Next campsite upstream Indigo Neck at 139.2; downstream Leopard Mill at 129.9. Nearest vehicle approach from Deneen Rd. near Lock 54 at 133.96.

133.94 NPS milepost 134. Cross watered feeder canal from Dam No. 6. Towpath previously crossed over mulebridge (abutments of which still stand) but now goes between feeder and canal proper to dam. Occupant of lockhouse in 1962 said bridge over feeder canal washed out in 1924 flood. Apparently no gates in feeder at this end.

LOCK No. 54

133.96 Access: From US 40 or MD 144 W of Hancock take Woodmont Rd S 6.2 mi. to end of unmarked Deneen Rd. where turn rt. 1.4 mi. to overlook of Lock 55 and Dam 6. Walk .10 mi. downstream on towpath to Lock 54. RR Lock walls badly damaged; collapsed on upper berm side. Lock filled with earth to preserve it in 1974. Snubbing post with rope burns extant 1962. Lock was probably completed in 1841. Many boatmen carried lock horns to alert locktenders to open gates by time of arrival of boat. Horns were all sizes and shapes, some straight and a few were twisted like French horns. Avg. length was 2' to 3', and all were old-fashioned fish-horn type with noise made by lips, rather than blowing thru a reed. Lockhouse burned 1981. A real shame.

Boat departing Lock 54 to right, feeder canal from Dam No. 6 to left, and Lock No. 55 ahead, early 1900s. (Smithsonian Institution).

Old view of Dam No. 6 and Guard Lock No. 6.

DAM No. 6, GUARD LOCK No. 6 AND LOCK No. 55

134.06 Access: See Lock 54, mileage 133.96. Lower lock gates of Lock 55 and miscellaneous hardware in lock bed. Lock was completed by Henry Smith by end of 1840. Crumbled lockhouse foundation on berm side between lock and bypass flume. Discrepancy here between NPS mileages and those made by Orville Crowder used in this guide. Dam was completed in April 1839. An interesting area and one which looms large in the history of the canal, for it was at this point that canal construction came to an end in 1842, while the crucial financial struggle for funds to complete the work went on. Eight years were to elapse, with Dam No. 6 as head of navigation, before the difficult section upstream — the notorious "Fifty Miles" — would be ready and the Cumberland goal reached at last.

Dam No. 6 may be the only dam which burned. A wooden structure 475'-long, extending between surviving abutments, was filled with loose rocks. Fisherman started fire during low water on wood-covered structure which blazed out of control. Flood waters have washed rock rubble into a corkscrew rapids with clear channel which is a favorite of canoeists. Guard Lock No. 6 adjoins dam abutment. Extensive masonry work is particularly interesting.

When this was head of navigation for eight years, an agreement was reached with B & O R.R. whereby coal from Cumberland was carried by rail to a point on the opposite shore and there transferred to canal boats for the trip to Georgetown. Boats entered the canal through the guard lock; Locks 54 and 55 were not used until the "Fifty Miles" was opened to navigation. Dam No. 6 represented the upper end of the "Hancock Division" at the height of canal activity; the "Cumberland Division" began above Lock No. 55.

When construction came to a halt here in 1842, $10,000,000 had been spent on contruction plus another two million for interest and losses. Two experienced Erie Canal engineers in 1827 estimated the cost to Cumberland at $4,500,000. And still ahead were the increasingly rugged terrain, a growing scarcity of building stone, 20 locks, 4 aqueducts, 2 dams (1 later omitted) and a daring proposal to tunnel a mountain. Actually, much work upstream was already done; only 18 m. remained to be finished, but it was in scattered small sections and always the most difficult ones. The "Cost to complete" was estimated at $1,500,000 — and the books of the desperate canal company showed liabilities of $1,200,000 in excess of assets. The B & O R.R. reached Cumberland that same year. Little wonder that many thoughtful people doubted "The Fifty Miles" would ever be built.

Floods never failed to leave their mark on Dam No. 6. The 1877 flood (Nov. 24) seriously damaged the abutments; the 1886 freshet (April 1) tore a hole in the center of the dam; the canal-killer of the Johnstown year, 1889, virtually destroyed the structure, completely washing away 100' of the breast. But it was back in service by 1891, and the 1924 washout, which ended operation of the canal, did little damage. The great inundations of 1936 and 1942, however, turned the structure into the pile of rubble one sees today.

During the Civil War, the dam was the objective of several Confederate raids, especially a purported plan to destroy it on 20 Oct. 1861, when the canal management found itself suspected of lukewarmness in its defense measures. The Town of Great Cacapon was the target of another raid, when Confederate cannon, mounted on Cacapon Mtn. directed their fire at the post office, where Union troops were stationed. NPS cleared vegetation from Guard Lock in 1981. Note Bench mark 6 of Transcontinental level of 1878 on downstream end of towpath wall of Lock 55.

134.23 Mouth of Long Hollow. Canal crossing of this stream unusual; retaining wall along towpath backed up "Polly Pond" extending up hollow, and pool became part of canal. Downriver cement boats turned around here. Boats passed under R.R. trestle to reach pond. Piers ahead supported wood spillway. Long 1 m. straight-away of canal. There are the remains of what appears to be two canal boats near the mouth of the pond and to the east. Beyond from about **134.35** exposed strata in hillside and along R.R. cut represent one of best exposed sections of Lower Jennings Formation in Md. NPS installed a double pipe culvert in 1981 to drain the canal. The old stone wall has been replaced.

134.25 Two 22'-long formal masonry spillways flank double shallow waste weirs.

134.62 Fork of berm rd. leads uphill to clubhouse of Woodmont Club of 3,366 ac. founded in 1870. Guest have included Presidents Garfield, Arthur, Benjamin Harrison, Hoover and FDR, and also Babe Ruth and Gene Tunney, all of whom have sat on club's antique, hickory chair adorned with wildcat skins. Stuffed game birds and animals peer at the diners from walls and overhead. Late Henry P. Bridges was the guiding spirit of the club for many years, and hosted members of the Douglas hike in 1954 on the second overnight. Bridges, after expressing disappointment that the Prince of Wales (then the Duke of Windsor), had not been a guest and a silver plate to honor his sitting in the chair, dedicated a name plate to Justice Wm. O. Douglas.

134.94 Paved Long Ridge Rd. (MD 453, probably unmarked) comes downhill on rt. and becomes **Pearre. Rd. becomes Woodmont Rd. farther N.**, leading 6.5 m. to US 40 at point 3.5 m. W. of Hancock, affording approach to towpath at any point in next mile. **Historic culvert #199.** 6' span.

Outflow of Historic Culvert #200, 1961. (Historic American Building Survey) Note the wooden timber foundation and the few wooden planks serving as the flooring.

135.06 Foundation of high pedestrian bridge dated 1914.

135.10 Culvert #200 on Sec. 260 with 10' span carrying stream from two lakes above, rebuilt 1974-75.

135.30 Narrow field on left with fine view ahead to steep end of Sideling Hill Mtn., W. Va. Beyond, houses are part of scattered village of Pearre (pronounced pair-EE).

135.40 Panoramic view of Sideling Hill Mtn. when foliage is off trees.

135.71 Culvert #201 on Sec. 261, 10' span, carries stream from deep ravine. This stretch of canal very beautiful. Prolific birdlife, including wild turkeys.

136.01 Culvert #202 on Sec. 262, 6' span. Note star of Bethlehem.

136.02 Possible all-wood waste weir on berm.

LOCK No. 56 (PEARRE)

136.21 Access: From US 40 3.5 mi. W of Hancock take Woodmont Rd S 6.2 mi. to end of rd. where turn rt. 1.3 mi. on (unmarked) Pearre Rd. Park car along rd. and walk to towpath on park service access rd. Pearre consists of two houses and train sta. Old hotel once here. Unoccupied 2½-story frame lock house on towpath; George Murkey once locktender. Used to be a general store near lock. Lock was probably completed 1848; has 7.7' lift. Stahlmeyer ran the store which sat over the bypass flume. Lock stabilized by NPS in 1985.

View of Sideling Hill Creek Aqueduct (Aqueduct No. 8), 1956. (National Park Service)

SIDELING HILL CREEK AQUEDUCT (No. 8)

136.56 Access: From Lock 56 at 136.21; also from Lillie-Aaron Strauss BSA Wilderness Area. No. 8 of 11 stone aqueducts completed in 1848. Single 110' span. Upstream parapet collapsed, but balance of structure in good condition. Parts of iron railing missing. Limestone used for cut masonry of arch, inside of parapets and coping. Recent repairs made to towpath side of aqueduct. Arch is asymmetrical, downriver end being closest to keystone. On berm past WMd R.R. bridge rises precipitous S. end of Pa.-Md. portion of Sideling Hill, while across river to left towers equally abrupt end of Sideling Hill, W. Va., thus creating a narrow water gap thru which are crowded river, canal, road and two railroads. Beneath aqueduct, slackwater from Dam No. 6 backs up short distance into bed of Sideling Hill Creek to explorer scouts canoe shed and dock. This stream rises far to N. in Bedford Co., Pa. and in its traverse across Md. is marked by many entrenched meanders, producing much rugged and beautiful country well worth exploring on foot. This tortuous water-course is the county boundary; here we leave Washington Co. and enter Allegheny. Canoe and bike rental at Camp Strauss. Tel. 301-678-6912.

Sideling Hill is a syncline, that is, it represents bottom of folded strata rather than top of the fold. Narrow crest both N. and S. of river is capped by Purslane Sandstone, a massive white sandstone and quartz conglomerate more resistant to erosion than surrounding Catskill and Jennings formations. Although Purslane was in trough of fold, it now marks highest point of the mountain. Accordingly, strata on E. side of mountain dip to W. and those

185

on W. side dip E., contrary to what canal observer would expect. Similar structure is found in Town Hill, farther upstream; most of other major ridges are anticlines, with strata roughly paralleling contour of surface.

136.9x Canal prism very narrow. Wood ducks and mallards seen.

137.20 Fine rock exposures in R.R. cut. Pile of rock debris to left of towpath is from R.R. construction and continues for some distance as embankment between towpath and river.

137.7x Sharp left curve in river is Turkey Foot Bend. Canal ahead passes thru strata of Jennings-Catskill formation (Devonian period); flat slabs above R.R. show characteristic alternating layers of red and yellow sandstones off .23 mi.

138.06 **East portal of Indigo Tunnel** to rt.; R.R. cuts thru spur of High Germany Hill for nearly 1 m.. Canal bed completely filled with debris from R.R. cut. Stream just below face of tunnel waters canal above and is home of mallard hen and ducklings May 1972. NPS mile marker off .23 mile.

138.20 Cleared area enhances fine view ahead, across bend of river, of Sideling Hill, W. Va. Berm side a natural rock garden of wildflowers and fern, with steeply dipping strata running into standing water of canal. In these watered patches, wood ducks are common; pairs with 12 to 16 young frequently seen late April and May. Wild turkeys also common. Parkhead formation, which abounds in fossils, begins 150' E. of tunnel portal and continues for 775' where Woodmont Shale begins. Strata at 400' and at 535' W. of tunnel portel are especially fossiliferous.

138.63 **Fine swamp** with dark brown water has developed in canal bed. Many wood ducks and ducklings sighted May 1972. Beaver sighted several years ago. Floodplain lush with spring flowers; spotted turtles slide into the swamp as one approaches; pileated woodpeckers drum in the surrounding forest; and the towering mountain side across the river furnishes a suitable backdrop. This is typical of many wild sections in next 40 m. Opportunities for nature study or for absorbing the refreshment of virtual solitude are many.

139.1x Note **heavy growth of river birch** (Betula nigra) with shaggy strips of yellow bark. Swamp very wide. Pleasant sound of ripples in river.

LOCK No. 57

139.22 **Access:** At Little Orleans at mileage 140.77. In beautiful remote section. Last of original masonry locks for some distance; lock wall has been repaired with concrete on upper half of river side. Thirteen of locks upstream were composite or wood locks, an expedient resorted to for lack of funds and suitability of native building stone. On one approach to lock, four snakes (unidentified) flopped from sill into deep water of lock chamber, also occupied by large snapping turtle. Lower berm gate standing; towpath-side gate in floor of lock chamber. Lock has 8' lift. Stone from river side of lock piled above lockhouse which was 2½-story log cabin; foundation, walls and two fireplaces remain. Canal ahead known as "Five Mile Level." Most of stone-lined bypass flume remains. Lock was probably completed late in 1839 by James Wherry.

139.2x **Indigo Neck Hiker-Biker Overnighter,** adjacent to lock. Usual equipment. Next campsite upstream Fifteenmile Creek Drive-In Camp Area at 140.9; downstream Cacapon Junction Hiker-Biker Overnighter at 133.6x.

139.40 Steep cascade on rt. follows strata on cliff face for interesting effect. Beyond, **berm consists of fine flower-covered cliffs.** Rooster crowing across river in W. Va. between sound of freight trains on same side.

140.03 R.R. comes onto berm from **W. portal of Indigo Tunnel** on E. side of ravine to rt.

140.1x **Swamp.** Fossiliferous Woodmont Shale on face of extremely high cliffs above R.R. Towpath is river bank.

140.66 R.R. crossing to rt., where rd. from Pearre and other points comes down from High Germany Hill and continues ahead between canal and R.R.

140.77 **Fifteenmile Creek Recreation Area.** Room for 16 vehicles with tables, fireplaces, water, toilets. Paved boat ramp and trailer parking on lower level. Supplies, boat and canoe rental, bait, licenses and light meals at Little Orleans General Store. This is the take-out point for canoe and float trips down the 21 river miles thru the Paw Paw Bends. Rock ledges stretching across river in this area were once converted to fishtraps by Indians, according to archeologists. Camp area is open only in the summer.

LITTLE ORLEANS

Early references were to mouth of Fifteenmile Creek where Kings Tavern was operating in 1795, and where Mrs. O'Queen kept a tavern in 1811. Indian camp sites have been located on both sides of mouth of the creek and N. of R.R. track above the aqueduct. On a knoll across the creek from Little Orleans is quaint little St. Patrick's Church, surrounded by a cemetery which predates present church bldg. Earliest burial date noted was 1802. Cemetery contains the graves, many of them unmarked, of Irish canal construction workers and their descendents. Several tombstones show a birthdate and not a date of death, indication possibly that an enterprising peddler of tombstones passed through this community in the late 1800s. Until about 1965 a green shamrock was painted in the circle of the gable facing the river.

Road passing under R.R. to general store formerly extended down to the river and crossed a ¾ m.-long ford diagonally downstream to Orleans Cross Roads, W. Va., which at one time was the post office for both settlements. Rd. W. from store, crossing Fifteenmile Creek, is Oldtown Rd., leading along eastern slope of Town Hill to MD 51 W. of Paw Paw. To reach Paw Paw Tunnel turn left from Oldtown Rd. on Malcolm Rd. See Paw Paw quad map for detailed directions. Village is situated at mouth of Fifteenmile Creek, so named because, on the "new" road of 1760, it was 15 m. from the site of Hancock and 15 m. from Town Creek.

People today seem unaware of the historical interest in this road thru Little Orleans, though it was the main route from Ft. Frederick to Ft. Cumberland for many years. Traffic of all sorts — horseback, supply wagons and stage lines — passed this way until the more direct route across the summits of the mountains was opened.

In December 1758, several years after Braddock's defeat in the French and Indian War, the General Assembly of the Province of Md. was concerned over the difficulty of travel between Fts. Frederick and Cumberland. The original route passed thru Va., crossing the Potomac twice, and many delays were experienced at the fords during periods of high water. A committee was appointed, headed by the ubiquitous Col. Thos. Cresap, to examine a new route which might lie entirely within Md. and avoid river crossings. The committee report recommended the route which was subsequently

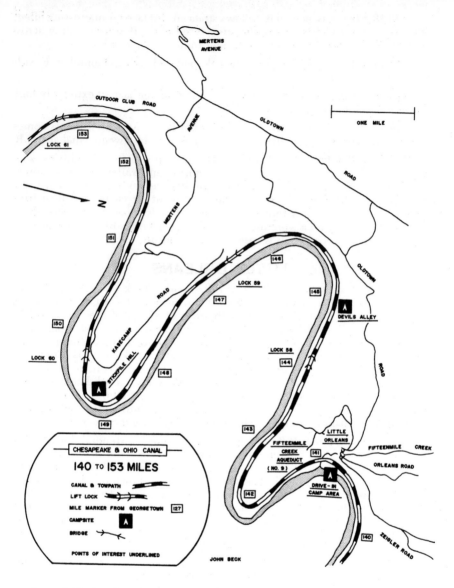

adopted: Ft. Frederick 3½ m. to Licking Creek (where the old route crossed into Va.); 8½ m. to Prakes Creek (probably Great Tonoloway); 12 m. to Fifteen-mile Creek; 15 m. to Town Creek (where the Va. route came back across the Potomac); 4 m. to Col. Cresap's (Oldtown); 15 m. to Ft. Cumberland. This route apparently crossed Fifteenmile Creek at Little Orleans, following approximately the present location of Old Town Rd. and MD 51 to Old Town. The road figured very prominently in the early development of the western part of the province.

A riot of canal construction workers erupted at Little Orleans on 17 May 1838. Following a period of non-payment to workers by the canal contractors and work stoppage, German laborers were hired to replace Irish. A German worker was clubbed to death with swinging shillelaghs, and another German was thrown into a bonfire and burned to death. After reinforcements of 500 duck guns ordered from Baltimore were received and distributed to the Irish from Little Orleans to Paw Paw and a riot near the tunnel in Aug. three companies of state militia from Baltimore confiscated and destroyed guns, burned Irish shanties and confiscated whiskey and suppressed the rebellion. Owners of whiskey sued as non-rioters and court held militia had acted illegally and exceeded authority in confiscating privately-owned whiskey.

The store and garage converted to service station buildings were moved from the banks of the canal by the WMd. R.R. during the construction of the R.R. after the turn of the century. Store has handhewn sills and warehouse later converted to garage had beam extending over canal equipped with large pulley. Rope strung through pulley with portion hanging over canal used to tie cargo on boats. The other end of rope was hitched to mule driven along the berm side of canal, lifting cargo above level of warehouse wharf. Suspended cargo rope was then hooked with a pole and drawn to dock, mule backed short distance and cargo deposited to deck of dock and unfastened. Parts of store building believed to be almost 150 years old by some local people. Little Orleans store is a great place to rest your feet and have a cold brew. Lodging available. Tel. 301-478-2701.

There was also violence here in Aug. and Sept. of 1839 when militia from Allegheny and Washington counties seized firearms, tore down 50-60 canal workers' shacks and arrested 30 persons and took them to Cumberland for trial.

FIFTEENMILE CREEK AQUEDUCT (No. 9)

140.90 Access: Take paved Little Orleans Rd. 6 m. S. from US 40 and turn left at "Little Orleans Grocery Store" sign. This aqueduct, 9th of 11 stone aqueducts, completed 1848-1850, is similar to Sideling Hill Creek Aqueduct. Single span of 110' in comparatively good condition with exception of upstream spandrel. Waste weir at upper end of aqueduct, fed by stream which falls into creek. Fifteenmile Creek rises in Pa. and flows thru wild, mountainous region, cutting deep water gaps directly thru Green Ridge State Forest. US Geological Survey Mark in S.E. corner gives elevation at 459' above sea level. Cement used in the aqueduct was from Lynns Mill at Cumberland and Shafers Mill near Hancock.

141.33 Interesting fold in strata to rt. **Berm fine rock garden** of wildflowers and ferns. Special feature along towpath in April is extensive growth of Dutchman's breeches and squirrel corn. Canal prism very narrow.

141.7x First of many sharp river bends of canal. Here one heads S.E.; in short distance N.W. It takes a keen outdoorsman to retain sense of direction in this area. Stretch from here to lock BF particular beauty. 142.04 Informal overflow.

142.25 Broad river terrace ends as turn completed; **berm again becomes rock wall with nearly vertical strata.** Rocks thruout area are a part of Jennings formation, consisting of slaty gray shales and buff sandy shales, including Parkhead sandstone thru which canal passes periodically. Some terrace gravels, indicating former levels of river bed, some 250' above present river level.

142.75 Across river rocky finger from Purslane Mt. produces one of big bends or loops in river. Beyond river flat is deep ravine, Doe Gully, where the B & O met a grade construction challenge. Highest part of ridge is pierced by Randolph Tunnel which emerges at almost river level 5 m. upstream by towpath. Double track through tunnel shortcut improved later by deep surface cut parallel to N. of tunnel where an additional two tracks are located.

189

Lock No. 58 above Little Orleans, circa 1903-23. (National Park Service)

143.05 Rock folds on berm particularly interesting. Cliff festooned with moss pinks (Phlox subulata) in spring. Also Indian corn, May flower, wild ginger.

143.33 Worn crosspath leads to dirt rd. to rt., providing **access back to Little Orleans.**

143.40 Pass under **WMd. R.R. trestle** (rebuilt 1917), now abandonded RR crosses to continue upstream on opposite side of river. This is first of three crossings of WMd. right-of-way across canal in this section. WMd. R.R. crosses Potomac five times due to meanderings of river. R.R. was constructed 1904-06 as part of Gould interests to obtain thru line from interior to coast. Syndicate was owned by W. Va. Central R.R. with eastern terminus at Cumberland. It bought control of WMd. R.R. from City of Baltimore, western terminus then at Big Pool, Md., W. of Williamsport. Linking these two points involved crossing the canal at various points, a privilege not readily obtained from receivers of canal controlled by B & O R.R. With help of Md. Legislature, rights were obtained, and payment for abutments, such as one at this point, helped B & O recoup a little of its losses — the very losses it was incurring to keep the canal operating so that its rival, the WMd. R.R., might not acquire the route in a forced sale! Back along R.R. track it is ¾ m. to Little Orleans. The Western Md. R.R. is now abandoned between Hancock and North Branch; track removed. A 5'-high beaver dam backs water up to Lock 58. In 1983 there is an active beaver lodge at 143.65.

143.51 Canal widens into attractive birch-bordered pool; many sliders.

143.65 Active beaver lodge right on towpath, 1983.

LOCK No. 58

143.96 Access: From Little Orleans 3 m. downstream. Lock in remote stretch of canal. Lock 58, 1st of 13 upper locks using kyanized (treated) wood fastened to rough-stoned lock walls as substitute for costly finished stones not available in area. Wood created continuous maintenance problems; as this one shows, wood has been largely replaced with concrete. Lockhouse was probably of wood frame over a stone basement; only foundation remains. Green Ridge State Forest circular hiking trail begins at lock and rejoins the canal at Lock 67 for a distance of 21.4 mi. 145.52 Hook shaped Indian fish trap in river.

145.52 Hook-shaped Indian fish trap in the river.

144.54 Canal makes long curve left with another bend of river. **Spectacular rocky cliff.** Towpath is river bank. Nice views of riffles in river. **Devil's Alley Hiker-Biker Overnighter.** Next Hiker-Biker upstream Stickpile Hill at 149.4; downstream Indigo Neck at 139.2. This is quiet, remote area.

146.01 **Concrete waste weir for 58-59 level.** River bend ends and flood-plain widens. Pileated woodpeckers. Good fishing bar in river for carp — sighted several in 10-15 lb. class in spring 1972. Wild turkeys.

LOCK No. 59

146.56 Access: From Kasecamp Rd. 1 m. above, reached from U.S. 40, via Oldtown Rd. and Merten Avenue. Second of 13 composite locks. Little wood planking remains. Lock has a unique wooden quoin (which held gate psot). Lock extended downstream. A large part of the upstream berm wall collapsed in 1983. Stone foundation of lock house on berm.

146.84 Vista clearing.

146.92 Culvert #206 on Sec. 283; 12' span carrying stream from extensive valley known as Devil's Alley. Canal bed swampy. Noted pair of pileated wood-peckers in spring 1972 — one trying to divert attention while other poking head out nest in hole of old tree trunk. Fields on river now mourning dove preserve. Van House ruin on berm downstream was known as "Yellow House" to boatment. Also known as "Pinkney House."

147.18 Pass under **WMd. R.R. trestle** as track comes across river and enters shortcut across neck to rt. Improved Kasecamp Rd. follows R.R. up ravine, leading across neck to old Green Ridge Station. From Green Ridge Sta., Merten Ave. leads uphill to Oldtown Rd., left 8 m. to MD 51 and 10 m. to Paw Paw or rt. 6 m. to Little Orleans. Kasecamp Rd. parallels canal on rt. for 4 m.

"Merten Avenue," applied to a remote country road, is a name with a story. Entire region along Town Hill north of this point — more than 2000 acres — was before the turn of the century the setting for a visionary real estate development of unusual nature and some success. Mertens Orchard Co. laid out along the mountain more than 200 10-acre "orchard plots," like townsite lots, and sold a goodly number of them. Most purchasers were non-residents who arranged with developing company for clearing, planting and picking apples — and sending checks to owners from sale of apples. Plans included a residence area along Merten Avenue overlooking the Potomac Valley. Rine cemetery on Oldtown Rd. near intersection with Merten Ave. may have 100 burials. A trolley line running the length of the valley between Town Hill and Green Ridge was to service the area and help transport apples to market. The scheme petered out. Village and railway never materialized and many of the old 10-acre plots have come into state ownership as part of Green Ridge State Forest. But here and there an old apple tree remains, not yet completely choked out by the pines — and the name of Merten Ave. persists, monument to an all-but-forgotten dream.

147.59 Kasekamp Rd. bears uphill.

147.73 Rough rd. across canal bed to rt. leads to large frame canal house owned by Higgins Brothers (Joseph, Jr. and Raymond), whose father (Joseph L. Higgins) was a division foreman for canal co. who also kept and sold canal mules here. Mrs. Higgins was a cook on her father's work scow.

147.76 Canal house.

148.24 Culvert #207 on Sec. 286; 8' span. Row of rounded hills ahead beyond river bend are shoulders of Purslane Mountain branch of Sideling Hill in W. Va. Deer and raccoon plentiful. Gold finches 1979.

148.88 Begin long 180-degree bend of river. Pileated woodpeckers.

149.36 Stickpile Hill Hiker-Biker Overnighter. Next overnighter upstream Sorrel Ridge at 154.1; downstream Devil's Alley at 144.5.

149.45 Concrete waste weir for 59-60 level.

LOCK No. 60

149.69 Access: From Kasecamp Rd. Lock still shows some of wood construction characteristic of the 13 "economy" locks. Lock was known as the 'Upper Lock in the Seven Mile Bottom.' It was extended on the lower end to accommodate two boats. 8.4' lift. Bit of lockhouse foundation remains, at left; lock houses of upper canal were also economy jobs, less enduring than substantial brick and stone houses downstream. Lock good for study as in nearly original condition.

150.10 Dirt rd. provides access to Kasecamp Rd. and Locks 61 and 62. Many mallards, wood duck, deer. Informal overflow, 180' long at 150.69 ahead. Now called Bond's Landing. Overnight camping with NPS permission.

Old canal boat in what is thought to be Lock 60.

192

150.83 River comes into view on left as long turn completed; towpath now bears W.N.W. Though towpath runs close to river, undergrowth allows only occasional views of river.

151.18 Culvert #208 (described in historical reports "At head of 7-mile Bottom"); 12' span. Carries substantial stream coming from Roby Hollow. Berm is built-up levee. **Access to canal** via this culvert to Kasecamp Rd.

151.20 Busey canal construction cabin up from canal.

151.24 Pass under WMd. R.R. trestle, as line comes from Stickpile Tunnel on rt. and crosses to follow W. Va. side for 3 m. (Tunnel dangerous!)

151.50 Towpath comes onto river bank. Berm becomes rocky hillside with nice cliffs, rocks folds and an occasional shelter cave.

152.xx Lovely view of river at clearing 50 yds. below NPS 152 mile marker. This stretch of river described in **Canoeing White Water** by Randy Carter and **Blue River Voyages** by Corbett and Matacia. Is not white water but makes excellent beginner's trip. Extensive wildflower area; newbane, spring beauty.

153.01 **Concrete waste weir for "Four Mile Level"** between Locks 60 and 61; actual distance 3.4 mi. Beaver working in area in 1983.

LOCK No. 61

153.10 **Access:** From Outdoor Club Rd. (dirt) (off Merten Ave.), which reaches canal just above Lock 61 at 153.28. Merten Ave. reached via Oldtown Rd. from either Paw Paw or Little Orleans. Another wood-lined lock almost entirely faced with concrete. Surprisingly, the composite locks have less tilting in than the masonry ones. The ones covered with concrete, as here, have lost much of their personality. This lock has a lift of 8'. Stone foundation of lockhouse opposite lock just off towpath.

153.28 Stream enters from Twigg Hollow. Footbridge across canal bed to Outdoor Club Rd. slanting back uphill to Merten Ave. Trail from Outdoor Club Rd. to parking area opposite footbridge quite primitive. **Twigg Hollow is a deep ravine of special topographic interest,** best appreciated by map of area. For more than 1 m. it parallels Potomac, but drains in opposite direction. As seen from spectacular viewpoint ½ m. up Outdoor Club Rd., at one point its valley comes within 150 yds. of river gorge then swings away again. This curious arrangement results from fact that the river, cutting away the hill on outside of a sharp bend, has all but captured the Twigg Hollow stream and appropriated its valley. Region is well worth an exploratory side trip. Pathway opposite footbridge leads to good fishing/canoe landing on river.

153.46 Culvert #210 on Sec. 296 with 12' span carries stream from Gross Hollow. Outdoor Club obscured by trees except in winter. Ponds of old Potomac River channel still visible on left opposite culvert.

153.76 **Rock folds and cliffs** Cut exposes an anticlinal fold in shales, interbedded siltstones and conglomeratic sandstones (few seen) of Jennings Formation. Note well-exposed, alternating weak and resistant beds especially near bottom. Small synclinal fold to rt. obscured by vegetation. Cliffs reaching heights of 20-75' from this point to Sorrell Ridge. Entire cut covered with a variety of ferns, lichen, small trees and shrubs.

153.92 **Another cut exposing interesting folds and faults.** Note lock gate in canal bed (probably from Lock No. 62). Towpath comes onto river bank. **This is approximate location for Dam No. 7, building of which was postponed and finally given up entirely.**

154.14 Sorrel Ridge Hiker-Biker Overnighter. Next Hiker-Biker upstream Purslane Run at 157.4; downstream Stickpile Hill at 149.4. Good landing for canoers after coming thru Goosenecks of Potomac.

LIFT LOCK No. 62

154.16 Access: Thru Paw Paw Tunnel, a little over two miles from MD51. This is the 5th of 13 composite locks. Lift 10'. Lock is in an isolated setting in Tunnel Hollow. Some wood lining remains on lock walls. Bypass flume running along rock wall of berm in good condition. Concrete foundation of lockhouse on left under tree near towpath; dimensions about 26x16'. Shale cliffs on berm, covered with variety of ferns, wildflowers, lichen, small trees and vines. Though canal prism heavily cleared of vegetation in 1957, vegetation now heavily re-established well into Tunnel Hollow. Lock tender Joe Davis and his wife were murdered here by shooting in 1934.

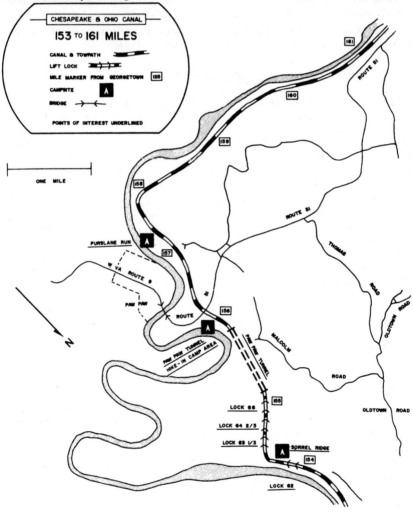

JOHN BECK

154.21 Canal begins turn away from river into **Tunnel Hollow,** originally Athey's Hollow. Old turning basin evident (Sandy Flat Hollow) contains small pond, very swampy. Basin marks foot of Sandy Flat Hollow, with traces of old rd. leading up to Anthony Ridge. Old canal boat remains reported here.

154.28 Masses of wild blue flags bloom in canal bed in May and June from here thru tunnel gorge. Where canal boats once waited their turn to enter tunnel, cattails now grow and redwing blackbirds live where canal bottom is a swamp. Other flowers about are hairy beardtongue (Penstemon hirsutus) growing quite commonly on towpath, on dry banks and in clefts of rocky walls; a wild phlox on towpath banks near Lock 66; yellow mustard; a small blue mint alongside towpath below tunnel; wild cherry; and blackberry. Otter sighted 26 March 1974.

154.29 **Large, elaborate waste weir,** tastefully rebuilt in 1979. Structurally interesting, especially in layout. In plan very much like those used on Erie Canal. Was designed to minimize erosion from flow of water out of canal. Consists of two stone overflow channels curved around to face one another and empty into a common stone central channel which carried water away from canal.

LIFT LOCK No. 63 1/3

154.48 **Access:** Via Paw Paw Tunnel. Extensive concrete replacement bears date 1910. Footbridges cross to each of three locks here. Lock recesses concrete lined. Only bolts remain from wooden sheathing. This is an excellent place to study the mitre sill and upper gate recess floor construction as it is all in place and in excellent condition. Snubbing post on upper towpath side of lock. Some stones of lock chamber shifted or missing. No sign of lockhouse. Peculiar numbering of Locks 63 1/3 and 64 2/3 was way canal co. compensated for omission of Lock 65 as economy measure and yet retained general system of lock numbering. In keeping with that numbering system, they added 4/3 to Lock 62 and next two locks, coming up with 62 1/3; 63 2/3; and 66. All three locks in poor condition. Seldom seen nocturnal marbled salamander, hibernating in rotted stump, identified here during Dec. 1966.

154.5x **Flora and fauna.** Forest around Paw Paw tunnel is mostly deciduous, some lovely long-needle pines grow along towpath below tunnel. Mixture of oaks seems to dominate but in fall reds of maples, sumach, dogwood and even orangey sassafras stand out. Oaks suffered blight in 1965 but seem to have recovered. In May one sees lovely wild blue flags growing in wet bottom of canal prism, spider wort, mustard, small mints, blackberry, blueberry, cherry, saxifrage, dogwood, giant chickweed, bluettes or Quaker ladies, laurel, azalea, Jack-in-the-pulpit, wild pink, columbine, rue anemone, cinquefoil, dewberry, yellow and purple sorrel, rattlesnake weed and a hawthorne-like tree, with a rather rotten flower growing along the canal. In July there are strawflower, blueweed (Echium vulgare), daisies, wild rose in profusion, Queen Anne's lace, butter-and-eggs (Linaria linaria) and what may be leatherflower (Clematis viorna), also known as vase vine. In September cardinal flowers grow in the canal bed and a good deal of jewelweed grows on the banks of canal and downstream from North Portal. Michaelmas daisy also very common.

The canal bed, being very marshy in area below tunnel, harbors red-wing blackbirds in profusion. Most of species common to area seen there at one time or another. In evenings the woodthrush sings his lovely song through all the woods, and from the hills one hears the haunting voice of the whip-poor-wills in the valleys below. From time-to-time a wild turkey can be seen near the tunnel.

Deer, squirrels, chipmunks, woodchucks and an occasional field mouse seem to comprise the visible mammal population, though in 1965 the woods were full of flying squirrels at night. Copperheads and black snakes and other species of both land and water snakes are present as are salamanders and colorful skinks which live in and near the canal.

LOCK 64 2/3

154.60 Access: Via Paw Paw Tunnel. Lock once sheathed in wood, some of which remains on each side. Upstream lock gates gone; downstream gates leaning drunkenly in place. Butt of snubbing post on towpath side of lock. Rather rough bypass flume. Lower berm wing wall crumbling badly. Pile of more-or-less finished sandstones piled on bank across from towpath at upstream end of this lock and at Lock 63 1/3 suggests stones may have been removed when locks repaired with concrete in 1919. Level Walkers Franklin think they have found the spot where lockhouse stood — if so, this is the first lockhouse site to have been identified in this section. Site is on a small plateau or bench (probably composed of tailings from construction of tunnel) about 10' above towpath grade up a ravine at upper part of lock on towpath side. Foundations to house about right size to be a lockhouse remain.

LOCK No. 66

154.70 Access: Via Paw Paw Tunnel. Ruined upstream gates still more-or-less in place. Lock walls have bolts to hold sheathing in place but no wood remains. Old lock gate on berm bank above bypass flume under trees. Charred remains of large frame carpenter shop which burned in early 1960s. Lock gate being worked on when shop abandoned remains inside the rubble. Creosote tank into which lumber was dipped also survives at rear of downstream side of building foundation. Lock house was back on berm ahead.

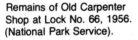
Remains of Old Carpenter Shop at Lock No. 66, 1956. (National Park Service).

154.85 Diagonal trail to left is route of old tunnel construction rd. leading to and over Tunnel Hill and down to upstream portal of Paw Paw Tunnel; used to carry away tailings from tunnel construction. This not only reduced tailings but reduced runoff of surface water back down into gorge, thus helping prevent landslides induced by water. Massive fills of broken rock clearly visible along this rd. give impressive evidence of quantity of material moved. Canal co's telephone line (in 1879 the 100 m.-long telephone system with 43 stations was the longest in the U.S.) ran over Tunnel Hill.

154.95 Cliff over towpath, now only about 10' high is mossy and green, with good deal of water running and dripping down it. Just overhead is spring once used as source of water by passing boats. Spring is covered with little wood-roofed stone house. Used to be double stairs from towpath to spring. In winter flow creates massive and beautiful ice sheaths on cliff. Ahead ravine steepens into deep, "V" cut, making spectacular approach to Paw Paw Tunnel portel via historically-rendered towpath boardwalk. On left, cut follows rock strata, exposing very interesting examples of "slickenslide" — slipjointing between strata causing frequent slides. Iron pins evident in attempt to stabilize rock. Note horizontal rope burns at first bend below tunnel.

155.xx Canal cleared thru this steep part of gorge. Clearing brought to life remnants wooden sheets piling on berm.

PAW PAW TUNNEL

155.20 North (Downstream) Portal. Massive slides continue on cliffs over berm side of canal at portal. New material, piled upon that already there, fills canal bed with massive blocks of rock to level well over head of person standing on towpath. Several overhanging large slabs of rock on west wall are cracking away and it appears there is more rock to come down. Gorge at this end is considerably steeper than that at other end — this entrance to tunnel is really quite spectacular. There is a mighty fold in the rock just overhead, and if you back off a bit, you can see that the rocks form almost a natural arch over the tunnel. In fact, this was counted upon by canal co. engineers to help prevent falls inside the tunnel during and after construction. Rock is mainly a stratified shale. Volume in cut at lower end was 120,000 cubic yds. Slides removed 1977-1978.

A good deal of water falls down cliffs over the portal, possibly including genuine springs as well as runoff. In wintertime cliffs are covered with great frozen waterfalls of ice. This has induced rock falls and slides from time to time; a massive slide that occurred in 1968 or 1969 engulfed canal prism to towpath level just at the portal. It did only minor damage to the towpath, but it did obscure somewhat the view of the portal. Portal has keystone bearing legend "J.M. Coale, President, 1850." On berm was a swinging boom used to drop timbers into slots in masonry of portal so as to form a stop gate sealing off canal, making it possible to drain canal downstream for repairs and maintenance. Platform of raised stones on berm to store timbers is covered by rock slide and may have been damaged.

Tunnel. The Paw Paw Tunnel is one of the major features of the canal, built as a bypass to some very difficult terrain along the Potomac River in Paw Paw Bends. Here the river makes a series of gargantuan loops, the tunnel route cutting across one large double loop takes 1 m. where river takes 6. While tunnel route involved cutting thru 3118' of solid rock, the Md. shore of river route contains some impressive cliffs coming right down to the river.

View of Tunnel Gorge looking down the canal from the North Portal of the Paw Paw Tunnel, early 1900s. (Smithsonian Institution).

To have followed river would have required either crossing to W. Va. shore and back, hacking out canal along those cliffs or damming river at lower end of bend to form a slackwater and cutting a towpath along cliffs or putting towpath on W. Va. side. The alternatives were thoroughly debated within the canal co. and, due largely to enthusiastic advocacy of newly-appointed engineer, Charles B. Fisk, the tunnel plan won out. Even when work was well advanced the board of directors seriously contemplated abandonment of the partially-completed tunnel in favor of a dam. Decision was made to proceed with the tunnel in Feb. 1836, with completion date set for July 1838. In actual fact, tunnel was not completed until 1850, though holed thru in 1840. Two other men responsible for building of the tunnel were Fisk's assistant, Elwood Morris and the contractor, Lee Montgomery.

Morris played a significant part as principal liaison between canal co. and contractor. Montgomery was not around at the finish and emerges finally as a tragic figure. Against all sorts of odds, some of his own making, Montgomery succeeded in driving the tunnel thru, though not in finishing the entire job. In so doing, he apparently sank his own resources and himself. Grossly overextending his credit, he was finally caught in one of the periodic financial crises of the canal co. and went under. The tunnel he had built was acclaimed "A Wonder of the World," while he was tossed aside, a sacrifice to creditors to whom he had indebted himself trying to fulfill his contract. He disappears from sight in a welter of litigation. No wonder a local legend among the superstitious for many years had it that the tunnel was haunted by a headless man!

Bitter arguments would go on when two boats would meet in the middle. A boy was sent ahead to post a lantern at the other end, so that an oncoming boat would know that the tunnel was already occupied and would wait turn. This didn't always work, however, and from time to time canal boats, with their stubborn captains, would meet in the middle. On one memorable occasion, neither side would back down for days. Boats piled up for miles, bets laid and company accountants tore their hair. Finally the section superin-

Excursion Boat Oak Spring at the North Portal of the Paw Paw Tunnel, early 1900s.
(National Park Service)

tendent could stand it no longer. He went out to nearby farms and bought all the green corn he could find and then at the upwind end of the tunnel he built a roaring fire and threw on green cornstalks. With remarkable speed the dispute was settled and the tunnel cleared.

During 1836 there were riots among Irish laborers working on other portions of the canal, but Montgomery managed to keep his work force going without interruption. In early 1837, however, unrest among his own men over the pay situation and rivalries among the various national groups finally exploded into violence. The Irish terrorized work camps and drove off British workers for a time. More riots occured in 1838, Irish vs. English and "Dutch." The tavern at Oldtown was destroyed and workmens' shanties were burned. A general strike occured in May, 1838, along the whole line of the canal, based on failure of contractors to meet payrolls. Local militia, who by this time strongly sympathized with workers, turned out reluctantly to restore order. Montgomery fired and blacklisted 130 men and work was resumed. More rioting broke out in 1839, this time at Little Orleans and once again militia called in.

Somehow, despite failing finances and violent unrest, work continued thru 1840 and 1841, but in 1842 the canal co. collapsed and work on the entire canal ceased. The canal was completed and operating up to Dam No. 6 (134.1), about 20 m. below the tunnel. In addition, much of the stretch above the tunnel to Cumberland had been finished. Montgomery, who now disappears in a maze of lawsuits, his personal fortune sunk in abortive attempt to finish the tunnel, had actually driven it thru, but a great deal of work remained. North of the tunnel the deep cut, plagued by slide was not fully cleared, and of course the canal in this cut had to be completed. The tunnel itself was not yet completed and still had to have brick lining installed. Morris by this time found Montgomery and his patented machine made poor brick. Fortunately for the canal, state and federal interests were involved and ways were found to raise enough money to resume work under a new contractor in 1847. The tunnel and canal were finished and opened to traffic in 1850.

One should take a flashlight, or preferably an electric lantern, in going thru the tunnel. Not that the towpath isn't in perfect shape — it is — and there is no danger, but there are things to see inside, such as rope burns on the railing, locations of the vertical shafts, and at times the evaporation of ground water thru the walls creates a snowlike mineral deposit that is very pretty to see. On a later trip (perhaps the return), it is also interesting to go thru without using a light and feel one's way by touching the railing.

At the tunnel entrance the tunnel lining is dressed stone and from then on to 26' below south portal it is brick four courses thick except under the vertical shafts where it is six. Tunnel has 12' radius set on 11' vertical walls. Towpath runs on a ledge about 4' wide and equipped with a stout railing a little better than waist high. Top rail is a square stout beam, in many places showing deep ruts burned into it by tow ropes of muledrawn barges. There are wooden railings or bumpers on both inner sides of tunnel to keep barges from scraping brick walls. Height of tunnel 24½'; 17½' above water. Volume of rock cut out in tunnel 82,000 cubic yds. Greatest depth 44'. Canal 17' wide.

"Weep" holes are occasionally placed at spring line of arch to prevent seepage water from building up and coming directly thru brick, an admirable precaution, but one sees that it does not seem entirely effective as a great many patches are visible in the lining. Park Service did a thorough renovation of interior of tunnel in 1966; it now remains in excellent shape. The two sets of vertical shafts from surface of hill overhead are fairly easy to locate by extensive seepage of water coming thru brick lining from them.

Montgomery, a Methodist minister with previous tunnel-building experience (600' tunnel on Union Canal near Lebanon, Pa.), contracted to build the tunnel in the spring of 1836. He appears to have been a rough, tough customer, but energetic and not unimaginative. Bricks were scarce in the area, so he brought in a patented brickmaking machine from Baltimore and set up his own brick works, unsuccessfully as it turned out. Much of the tunneling work involved cutting thru rock and the construction of sophisticated brickwork and masonry. The Irish laborers who built much of the canal were not particularly skilled in some of the things to be done, so Montgomery brought in English masons and English and Welsh miners and local Pa. and Md. "Dutch" masons and laborers. Those moves, rational as they seemed, were later to contribute to his downfall. Montgomery accepted the contract at much too low a cost. On all sides the optimism was great as to the ease and speed with which the job could be done. The rock formation thru which tunnel was to be dug was a natural arch of shale, thus protecting from cave-ins. The same formations easily slid and drastically slowed the work. It was estimated early that "a single hand can bore from seven to eight feet per day. . ." whereas in actual fact the rate of progress for entire crew at each tunnel face was 10 to 12' **per week.** The tunnel was a large undertaking, employing up to 44 men at a time. Rising costs and unexpected expenses bedeviled Montgomery from the beginning; by the end of the first year he was already trying to renegotiate his contract. Overruns have a long history! Because of lack of funds he fell behind in payments to his men, further unrest and discontentment further reducing his efficiency. The canal co. paid off in monthly installments, according to how far work had progressed. However, as an earnest of contractor's intention to fulfill contract in entirety, a certain percentage was retained by the co. to be paid at completion of work. While co. from time to time relinquished portions of retained money to help keep Montgomery going, he was forced to invest more and more of his own resources.

Construction was an impressive feat. It involved not only 3118' of tunnel, but also 200' of deep cut at the southern end and 890' at the northern. In order to speed work, two sets of vertical shafts (one at 122' and one at 188') were dug down from the hill overhead (two shafts per set to provide ventilation) until tunnel level was reached, and then digging was carried out along tunnel line in each direction from there. With faces moving in from each end, there were six active digging faces; because of slides in the deep cut, the face at north portal was not as active as others. Vertical shafts were 8' in diameter, with 23' between centers of each in a pair. Each pair was located in a ravine overhead to shorten vertical distance. One pair was about 370' in from the north portal and the other about 900'. They can be located inside tunnel by dripping of water flowing down them and thru the brick lining and also where weep holes in brick walls at towpath level are closer together; and on hill above by the still-visible digging scars. Digging of the tunnel was done by blasting out big pieces with black powder and reducing with sledges and picks. Spoil was hauled up shafts by winches and carted to spoil heaps in ravines by (probably horse-drawn) rail cars, or else hauled out of portals by rail cars to spoil heaps mostly on river side of canal. Those heaps are still clearly visible, particularly above the towpath, downstream of the tunnel.

There are many tales and legends about the tunnel. One involves an Irishman who operated a sort of elevator at one of the vertical shafts as tunnel was being dug, bringing loads of rock to the surface and lowering men and supplies, and his mule. The Irishman and mule shared one characteristic — a very short temper. They quarreled more and more as work went on, until one day the mule kicked the Irishman where it hurt. Incensed, the Irishman kicked back, only unfortunately the mule was standing at the edge of the shaft. Down he went, to land angry but unhurt at the bottom (this is the hard part to swallow — the shafts were 400' deep). Only now there was no way to get him to the top again, so the Irishman, in addition to his other duties, had to lower bales of hay and buckets of water down the shaft to the mule until workers could link up the tunnel coming in from a portal to get him out.

South Portal
of Paw Paw
Tunnel, 1974.
(National Park Service).

155.78 South (upstream) Portal. Canal exits tunnel. Portal has stone steps on each side, by which one can climb to top. Some of exposed strata, mostly shales, at top and running down berm side, contain fossil shells. Engraved keystone marked "C. B. Fisk, Engineer: for Charles B. Fisk, without whose enthusiasm (some say "shortsighted"), tunnel would most probably have never been built!" He was the canal co. engineer who pushed thru the tunnel project from the beginning, and who, in spite of fact the expense of the tunnel undoubtedly helped bring the canal co. to ruin, and was Chief Engineer when it was finished in 1850. Volume in cut at upper end was 10,000 cubic yds. In wintertime there is sometimes a great wooden wall blocking the entire portal to protect brick lining of tunnel from alternating freezing and thawing. One can, however, pass thru a small door in the wall.

Trail leaves towpath at entrance to tunnel and climbs hill to rt., over Tunnel Hill and rejoins towpath on other side. It is well-marked and makes a pleasant 20-30 minute walk. At top of hill, trail crosses Tunnel Hill Rd. A turning to left on this rd. for several hundred yds. brings one to point directly over tunnel. From there, with survey map in one hand and compass in other, one can trace route directly over tunnel. There is no trail, but woods are open and going easy—watch out for copperheads! On top of each small ridge crossed is an old stone marker (first of which is on portal side of Tunnel Hill Rd. on one's left a few ft. from edge of rd. as one arrives at intersection of rd. with line of tunnel), though some of five (were originally six) markers are leaning or fallen. Each marker has grooves on top once set transverse to line of tunnel; used to establish a tunnel line and to assist in measuring progress. Various white and gaily-colored ribbons in trees show where other surveyors have already found them. In small ravines between markers three and four and between four and five are heads of shafts used in digging tunnel. Each shaft is 8' in diameter but tapers at top to 2' in diameter in last 12' of shaft. Hole of each is capped with a split capstone of 5' diameter buried under several ft. of watertight clay fill. Depression between markers four and five indicates NPS effort to dig into shaft to capstone to reduce leakage of ground water into tunnel. Ravines also contain piles of spoil—rock brought up and dumped as tunnel was dug—forming very impressive banks giving appearance of glacial morraines. (Much of the material on the Paw Paw was provided by the Level Walkers, Alan and Kit Franklin.)

156.0x Paw Paw Tunnel Canoe Camp. Access at MD 51 .3 m. upstream. Next upstream Town Creek at 162.1, downstream Sorrel Ridge at 154.14. Whistling swans sighted 3/27/74.

156.2x Canal section superintendent's house recently repaired with brick foundation, wood siding and metal roof. Doors and windows securely boarded. In 1970 thousands of brick were turned up in field between section house and MD 51. Bricks probably were those made by Lee Montgomery using the portable brick-making machine from Baltimore using local material. That there were so many brick left over fits report from Asst. Engineer Elwood Morris on 16 Mar. 1838 to Eng. Charles B. Fisk stating Montgomery's bricks were of poor quality—they were probably never used. Montgomery's kiln may have been at upstream end of field where large quantity of cinders and coal were revealed by recent bulldozing.

Indian occupation. In common with most of Potomac Valley, area was probably site of Indian occupation over many thousands of years, but very little known about it. At least three areas in existence where spear points and worked flakes are on surface. Finds suggest a fairly extensive use of area by Indians who go back more than 3000 yrs. Remember—artifacts are not to be removed from National Park property without permission.

Stretch of river here is fine for semi-skilled canoeist. There are several small but definite ledges to pass over, but in normal summertime conditions water is slow enough so that with mild back paddling one can pick his way. Around the first bend (across which tunnel cuts) are a number of spectacular cliffs overlooking the river, where severe folding of rocks that formed Appalachians can be seen. It is also clear why canal co. chose to go thru rather than around this bend. One can put in at little campground at 156.2 (Paw Paw Tunnel Carry-In Camp Area) just off towpath after short portage down from car at MD 51 bridge, or near rd. bridge over Potomac in Paw Paw. One can also take out below Green Ridge Station, but the first really convenient take-out below Paw Paw is Little Orleans. At end of first bend (from campground at 156.2) one comes to upstream end of long island separated from left bank of river by a narrow channel. This channel forms a delightful little woodland stream, heavily shaded and with several small rapids, negotiable but fun for the novice. **Sorrel Ridge Hiker-Biker** at 154.1 lies on left river bank just after this channel, making a convenient landing.

156.24 Pass under MD 51 bridge near Paw Paw, W. Va., built after abandonment of canal. Prior to creation of this route, Paw Paw was reached by ferry and ford 1 m. upstream. To left on MD 51, Potomac River bridge is ½ m. to left; Oldtown 10 m.; Cumberland 25 m. W. Va. 9 leads S. from Paw Paw to Berkeley Springs and thence Hancock via US 522. Shoulder of MD 51 at S. end of bridge over canal is wide enough to accomodate several cars. Towpath is short distance down dirt rd.

Paw Paw was once a stopping point on B & O and a minor industrial center. Tannery was located there because of abundance of oak bark in vicinity. Also an important concentration point for Union troops during Civil War, quartering as many as 16,000 at one time. Paw Paw Gaging Station at highway bridge of interest to students of flood history of river. Zero on gauge equals 483' above sea level. Only flood to reach above towpath level here was that of 1936 reaching 54'. Low water is 2', annual high-water probability is 24'. Flood stage is 40'. Crests of both 1877 and 1889 (Johnstown year) floods were 45'. Towpath level is 45'.

156.51 Pass under Western Md. R.R. bridge; R.R. follows berm side for several miles. Scenery between here and mouth of Little Cacapon River pleasant. Groceries, restaurant in Paw Paw, W. Va.

156.66 Canal reaches river bank. Towpath crosses deep **masonry waste weir;** adjacent is a buried masonry spillway. Upstream end of Mitchell's Neck Deep Cut. Berm is cliff here. Abundance of wood ducks.

156.94 Flood plain and overgrown field were sites of shanty construction camp where approximately 200 men lived during construction of canal.

157.22 Keifers. RR Sta., grassy rd. descends around end of field toward river. This deeply-entrenched route is old main rd. to Paw Paw ferry and ford. Ferry was approximately in line with rd.; ford was somewhat upstream. canal worker's cemetery ahead on berm at 157.27. Pileated woodpeckers and ruby-crowned kinglets.

157.40 Purslane Run Culvert; #211 with 14' span, known as "Road culvert on Davis' farm." Referred to in 1851 as "road culvert at Greenwell's Hollow." Valley of Purslane Run of special interest geologically, for it represents a former channel of Potomac River, reaching 2 m. inland from its present bed. Referring to topographic map, old route becomes obvious. It diverges from present valley at mouth of Little Cacapon 1½ m. upstream, goes N.W. for 1½ m. to present location of MD 51, swings in a 180-degree bend to follow Purslane Run Valley, crosses present course of river at right angle at this point, then curves completely around far side of Paw Paw before returning to its modern river bed. Terrace gravels deposited along way at levels far above present channel attest to this dramatic change of course. **Purslane Run Hiker-Biker Overnighter.** Next hiker-biker upstream is Town Creek at 162.1; downstream Paw Paw Tunnel at 156.0. Nearest access from MD 51 .9 m. downstream. Note: camping above Paw Paw Tunnel is for canoeists only.

157.4x In spring extensive patches of stone crop (Sedum ternatum) border towpath and surrounding fields are yellow with ding devil or hawk-weed (Hieracium pratense). Canal bed contains large stands of blue flag (Iris versicolor).

158.00 Canal swings away from river, leaving wide wooded floodplain. On far side of river is steep end of Devils Nose with interesting ravines and waterfalls.

158.79 Culvert #212, 8' span, Fairplay Station. Stream comes from Reckley Flat, valley on rt. which is former route of Potomac. Rechanneling of river is amazing and merits study of topographic map. Berm cliff ahead is festooned with cactus and ferns.

159.06 Towpath comes onto river bank, with islands on left. Border of sugar maple trees, rare along canal farther east.

159.41 R.R. follows close to canal, with concrete retaining wall; cliffs above. R.R. construction constricts canal in a place or two along here.

159.60 Opposite mouth of Little Cacapon River. Good view of R.R. arches in winter. Here was important crossing of Potomac in 18th C., before building of fort-to-fort rd. in 1759. Braddock's orders of the day for 7 May 1755 called for a march W. "to Mr. Cox's at mouth of Little Cacapon, 12 miles," and add this interesting note: "If the· water in the Little Cacapon is high the Troops must encamp opposite to Cox's. At the mouth of the Little Cacapon the Potomack is to be crossed in a Float. Four miles beyond this they cross Town Creek. If the float should not be finished Canoes will be provided." Braddock's two armies, one marching thru Md. and other via Va. joined near here on Md. side on their march against the French and Indians. Later, route sometimes now referred to as "Old Braddock Rd." continued up Va. side of Potomac to Okonoko Ford, 2 m. upstream. Abels Tavern was operating Md. side near this ford in 1795. Flat near river called Terry Fields.

159.72 Culvert leading into #313 or #314 carries stream from ravine beyond R.R. Poison ivy profuse and late summer finds dense stands of sunflower-like wingstem (Verbesine occidentalis) and Jerusalem artichoke (Helianthus tuberosus). Wood duck with young are frequent sight in May, wild turkeys occasionally seen and cerulean warblers are regular summer residents at mouths of watered ravines.

160.26 Double masonry spillway/weir combination.

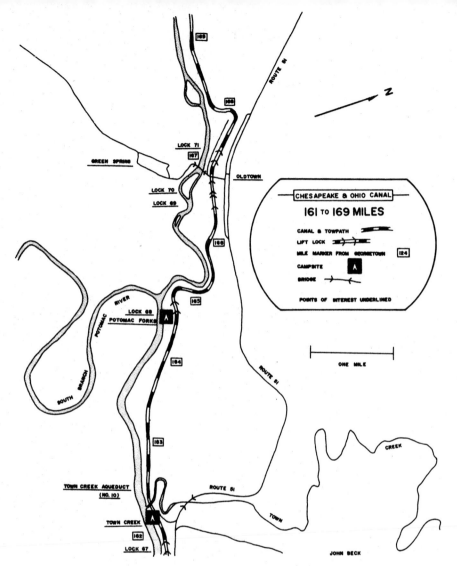

160.60 Most complete section of upper part of Jennings formation seen in Md. (Middle and Upper Devonian)

160.66 Spirifer disjunctus (Cytospirifer disjunctus) a brachiopod typical of Chemung member--an interesting double-wing shaped shell--common here. Plenty of muskrats and sliders in canal bed.

161.30 Prominent knobs and steep slopes across river are end of Town Hill. This mtn. rises again in Md. to N. Like Sideling Hill farther E., it is a syncline, rather than more common anticline. Strata here reach bottom of one of their folds, but harder formations in trough of fold have become top of mtn., while softer rocks of lower strata have eroded into side valleys. Virtually all other ridges from this point to Cumberland are anticlines. Many fossils in Parkhead member from here to 161.37 Pileated woodpeckers in abundance 1984. Ruby-crowned Kinglets.

LOCK No. 67

161.76 Access: From MD 51. Parking along rd. above towpath, to reach which walk down path across R.R. tracks. At head of "Tunnel Level," another economy lock originally built of kyanized (treated) wood and now largely replaced with concrete. Only foundation of frame lockhouse at left. According to Isaac Long, long-time recent occupant of Lock 68, this was once known as "[Hughey] Darkey's Lock" and boasted a saloon by Gene Stumph, whose 5-7 red-headed daughters were a landmark of the upper canal. Lower lock gates missing. Above lock worn wheelway crosses to MD 51, which has descended slope to parallel far side of R.R. Nearby upstream was a well with two oaken buckets on opposite ends of a rope which slid thru a pulley. Favorite stop of boaters on canal.

161.82 Culvert #215, 16' span, brick-lined with barrel exposed carrying Big Run which drains eastern slope of Green Ridge. To left, old rd. formerly ran diagonally back to Okonoko Ford, connecting with rd. up Miller Hollow on W. Va. side. In area are numerous exposures of Parkhead member of Jennings formation (Devonian) which are extremely interesting. Best examples are along R.R. cuts. The many fossils include Cytospirifer disjunctus, a brachiopod with an interesting double-wing-shaped shell. Tree roots in towpath must be watched for by cyclists.

162.1x Town Creek Hiker-Biker Overnighter. Nearest access is at Lock 67, .3 m. downstream. Next hiker-biker upstream is Potomac Forks at 164.8; downstream is Purslane Run at 157.4.

Surviving canal workers report a high mortality rate for mules working on canal. Mule burying crews were kept busy. Hole dug beside dead mule slightly larger than animal and dead mule rolled over by grasping hoofs and into hole. Dirt from hole used to refill hole and cover animal with mound. Some of skeletons were later uncovered and shipped to bone grinding mills which sold bone meal for fertilizer.

Lockhouse at Lock No. 68 (Crabtrees Lock), 1961. (Historic American Building Survey)

TOWN CREEK AQUEDUCT (No. 10)

162.34 Access: From Lock 67. .58 m. below. This, 10th of 11 stone aqueducts, carries canal over Town Creek on a single 100' span. Much of the aqueduct was rebuilt in 1977 and is now in a stabilized condition, though the appearance is lacking in authenticity and somewhat in sensitivity. Town Creek, one of the larger streams of Allegany Co., exhibits number of interesting geologic features, particularly its entrenched meanders, one of which may be observed just beyond R.R. track to rt. From vantage point on one of nearby mtns., it is readily seen that flat tops of lower ridges were once the floor of a broad, nearly-level valley, in which Town Creek swung back and forth in its changing meanders. As valley floor was uplifted, the stream cut faster, its bends became restricted by the rock structure and the entrenched meanders of today resulted. Fine view of this condition 3½ m. N. on Green Ridge Rd., which starts from MD 51 just E. of this point. Topographic map reveals other interesting features, such as surprising course of Sawpit Run, an erratic tributary of Town Creek. Craigs Mill operated here in late 1700s, followed by successor water-powered mills. Some foundation ruins may be seen above R.R. trestle. Park lands include flat W. of Town Creek R.R. embankment where canal workers were buried in unmarked graves.

162.38 Low concrete dam in canal backs water up to form fishing pond. This is first of several levels of fishing pools extending to Lock 71 beyond Oldtown which were constructed in 1945 by volunteer groups of Western Md. sportsmen in cooperation with state. Sometimes called "Battie Mixon's Fishing Hole" after Allegany Co. Game Warden who conceived idea and directed work of volunteers. Levels stocked with fish, one of which is reserved for children and is scene of annual fishing "rodeo." Oldtown Sportsmen Club, using dock with railings, sponsors an annual fishing day for crippled children. Aside from fishing, pools tend to give canal much of its original appearance. For next 2 m. floodplain consists of broad fields while berm becomes steep wooded hillside with frequent cliffs. Six bluebirds sighted together 11/25/72 in this pleasant hiking area. Frequent trains passing by.

163.81 Pond in edge of meadow. Prolific birdlife. Patch of adder tongue. Pond gone 1985, but marshy area remains

164.7x Causeway across canal provides NPS access.

LOCK No. 68

164.82 Access: Best from MD 51 at Lock 67 (161.76); dirt rd. to rt. of lock leading 1.2 m. back to MD 51 is thru private property. Lock is opposite mouth of South Branch of Potomac in a nice setting. Old name was "Crabtree's Lock." Lock extended upward and downstream. Purpose of downstream extensions was to permit passage of two boats thru lock at one time. Purpose of the upward extension above coping was to allow greater depth of water, possibly necessitated by siltation problems. Parts of lock gate lie on towpath side of canal about 30 yds. below lock and again on river side of towpath just before one reaches the lock. Old steel and wood bridge across lower end of lock, 12'-high piers of which give appearance of being tied into lock itself. Bridge carries rd. which once led from Uhl Highway (MD 51) ½ m. to river ford and ferry to settlement of South Branch Depot, later French Station, on B&O R.R. All but quoins of lock replaced with concrete. Lower lock gates missing. Stop gate and earthen dam used as expedient to prevent downstream flow of water. Concrete wall at upper end of lock used to keep 68 level watered. Poorly-defined, unlined bypass flume. Footbridge across lower end of lock leads to fine well and picnic area and

Remains of canal boat at Lock No. 69.

part of **Potomac Forks Hiker-Biker Overnighter.** Next hiker-biker upstream Pigmans Ferry at 169.1; downstream Town Creek at 162.1. Beyond well on berm, trails lead up interesting rocky hillside, affording picturesque alternate route with rewarding view. Since canal is normally watered, one must return here to recross. Unoccupied lockhouse of wood frame in good condition. Behind lockhouse is camping area for hiker-biker. Numerous lock stones located on riverside of towpath upstream of lockhouse.

Two generation of Crabtrees tended this lock. Last locktender, Dennis Crabtree, was living in Oldtown in 1964 at age 90. His memory reached back to happenings in the 1870s. He related how some boatmen stole vegetables from his garden and others traded coal for food. Large tract opposite mouth of South Branch was patented by Thomas Cresap under name of Indian Fields. Much of the flat lands along the river had been used to plant corn. Former occupant of many yrs. is Isaac Long of Paw Paw, WVa. From setting of house, bridge, outbuildings and beautiful trees, living at this lockhouse must have been a satisfying experience to the Longs.

Division of Potomac here into North and South Branches marks an important point in both the geography and history of the river. North Branch carries more water, but South Branch is longer. For many years a dispute continued as to which was the true river, and therefore stipulated the boundary between Md. and Va. (now W. Va.). Canal follows North Branch, commonly referred to simply as the Potomac. Had not the Fairfax Stone, at the head of North Branch, been accepted ultimately as the Potomac River's source, present day Md. would have a significantly different shape.

South Branch was long considered a potential source of water for the canal; **early plans called for construction of Dam No. 7 here** to utilize its flow. **Later, a stream pump was installed** and finally put into operation in 1858 and used whenever low water required it. Twenty years later pump was relocated 10 m. upstream, near Lock 72, where oil-driven pumps were eventually used.

208

165.08 Stumps appear in canal bed when water level down. Towpath comes onto river bank as canal and river make sharp curve known as Yorker Bend. **Top of fine rhododendron-covered cliffs on berm locally called Falling Rocks, a very scenic area not duplicated elsewhere on the canal.** Favored spot for mallards in canal and river. Known as 'Yorkers Bend.' Fragrant water lily.

165.33 River and canal make sharp turn. Cliffs on rt. give way to broad valley where earlier course of river swung ½ m. farther N. Canal becomes wide basin, retained by berm levee. Field begins here and continues almost into Oldtown. Lack of trees on canal side of towpath gives drained canal an almost barren appearance—a factor to be considered on unwatered stretches, such as above Middlekaufs Basin and below Ft. Frederick, where barren aspects are unattractive. Landscaping much improved 1978.

165.45 Culvert #216 on Sec. #330, 6' span. Uhl Highway (MD 51) visible beyond WMd. R.R. to rt.

165.5x Birds noted in area.

Blackbird, red-winged
Bluebird, eastern
Bufflehead
Bunting, indigo
Cardinal
Chickadee, black-capped
Crow, common
Cuckoo, yellow-billed
Dove, mourning
Duck, wood
Flicker, yellow-shafted
Goldfinch, American
Grackle, common
Grosbeak, evening
Hawk, red-tailed
Hawk, sparrow
Heron, great blue
Heron, green
Kingfisher, belted
Nuthatch, white-breasted
Phoebe, eastern
Redwing
Robin
Sparrow, chipping
Sparrow, house
Sparrow, song
Sparrow, white-throated
Starling
Swallow, rough-winged
Thrasher, brown
Thrush, wood
Titmouse, tufted
Vulture, turkey
Warbler, blue-winged
Warbler, yellow
Woodpecker, downey
Woodpecker, hairy
Woodpecker, pileated
Woodpecker, red-bellied
Wren, Carolina
Yellowthroat

Other wildlife: Rabbit, muskrat, groundhog, squirrel, leopard frog, cricket frog, bull frog, painted turtle, chipmunk and tree frog.

Trees: Dogwood, elm, black oak, red oak, black (sugar) maple, birch, locust, black gum, black walnut, wild cherry, willow, sycamore, yellow pine, apple, ball wood, red cedar, box elder, holly, red bud, white pine and Virginia pine.

Other plant life: Tree of heaven, wild grape, elderberry, raspberry, dew berry, wild strawberry, black alder, sumac, sassafrass, honeysuckle, purple water iris, columbine, pink milkweed, wild rose, bracken, cattail, service berry, thorn apple, cinnamon fern, rock fern, May apple, tall Solomon seal, poison oak, poison ivy, forsythia, spice bush, shadbush, rhododendron, aborted buttercup, bluebell, Dutchmans-breeches, henbit, mustard, false Solomon's seal, spring beauty, toothwart, violet (purple and white) and Christmas fern.

165.70 Canal swings away from river to follow valley of Mill Run, formerly Big Spring Run. Valley of this stream is curious as it drains W. side of Warrior Mtn. and flows to within 1 m. of Potomac, then suddenly swings E. to parallel Potomac for nearly 4 m. before joining it. Canal route utilizes this side valley, passing thru Oldtown and returning to Potomac thru interesting cut which may have been an early channel of Big Spring Run.

166.10 Culvert #217, 20' span, extra large, with inscription "1920 I. C. Wilson" in good condition carries Cresap Mill and Seven Springs Runs. Iris abounds along edges of canal

166.24 Concrete **waste weir** with inscription "1920 W. M. Burgoyne." Beaver at work on berm in 1985.

LOCK No. 69 (TWIGGS LOCK)

166.44 Access: See Lock 70. First of three Oldtown locks, all of which were originally of Kyanized wood, largely replaced with concrete. Lock extended upwards and may have been extended downstream. Bypass flume runs from basin above lock and discharges thru slope wall. Stop gate maintains water level above, forming another pool of Battie Mixon fishing area. Locks 68, 69, 70 and 71 were completed in the latter part of 1849 or in the early part of 1850. Parallel path runs along berm separating canal from bed of Mill Run. To left of towpath is a marsh, beyond which is where Ft. Lininger, a Union fort, once stood. Fort was located opposite South Branch Cliff or "Walnut Bottom." Marsh area was probably created by construction workers taking earth to build towpath.

Twigg family members were active along the canal during its period of operation from Little Orleans to Cumberland, leaving a legacy of locations bearing the name Twigg. Twigg family was one of first settlers in the upper Potomac. John and Rebecca Twigg built a cabin in the mid-1700s in Sink Hill Bottom, a lime stone sink which could be the source of Blue Spring, NE of Spring Gap. Their two sons, Robert and Fleetwood John, are credited with starting the family feud between the "blue-eyed Twiggs" and the "black-eyed Twiggs," Young John spent much of his time on hunting and fishing expeditions. After an absence of several weeks he returned to the family homestead with an Indian maiden trailing behind him. His father and family refused their admittance into the household. Fleetwood John and his new wife built a cabin at the edge of the meadow on the opposite side of the natural pond in the middle of the sink hole, and started raising "black-eyed Twiggs." His brother Robert married and raised "blue-eyed Twiggs" on his

Lock No. 69 (Twiggs Lock) and lockhouse, in 1940s.

side of the pond. "Blue-eyed Twigg" children were never permitted to play with "black-eyed Twigg" children. This continued for a couple of more generations until a "blue-eyed Twigg" fell in love with a "black-eyed Twigg," and that ended the Twigg family feud.

LOCK No. 70 (OLDTOWN)

166.70 Access: From MD 51 at either end of Oldtown. Oldtown, at rd. crossing, foot of Lock 70. Rd. to left leads to only private toll bridge across Potomac to Green Spring, W. Va. The original Thomas Cresap Mill was located near the present toll house for the bridge across the Potomac River. A canal store was once located behind the lockhouse. A 1906 photo shows a large barn-like structure across the canal. Lockhouse to left of towpath is two-story frame building. Above lock is broad basin of canal, former dock area for Oldtown. Paralleling canal to rt. is stream bed of Mill Run, formerly Big Spring Run, whose valley canal is following at this point, separated from Potomac River (North Branch) by hills at left. Towpath here heavily cleared in 1957, leaving none of the shade trees which had developed since shutdown of canal in 1924. Hillside near lock is covered with Dutchman's breeches. Canoe ramp at the river bridge.

Canal bridge built here in 1850 was a high covered structure, leading to a ford in the river. It was in Aug. 1864 the scene of a dramatic Civil War encounter when Confederate troops, returning to Va. after the raid on Chambersburg, were overtaken by Confederate cavalry. Federals, from the ridge (Alum Hill) between the canal and river, blocked Gen. Johnson's attempt to cross the canal bridge, but were themselves driven across the Potomac ford by McCauslan's cavalry, which had crossed the canal farther up. The Federals took refuge in an armored train on the B & O tracks. A battery was brought across the canal to shell the train, exploded the locomotive boiler with its first shot (which is said to have gone right down the smokestack) and stampeded the Union troops. The Confederate cavalry then crossed the river and completed the capture, opening the way for their forces to retire to Va. Three yrs. earlier, in Aug. 1861, three men of a Md. company of Union troops were wounded at the same point on a march to Springfield, Va., the first blood shed by Union troops.

The first wooden canal bridge (along with the lockhouse and store) burned in 1906; it was replaced with a high wood and steel bridge similar to the one at Lock 68. Since the canal went out of operation in 1924, the present bridge replaced the high bridges of the past.

Oldtown has a long and entrancing history. Here some claim the famed Warriors Path — Athiamiowee, Path of the Armed ones — forded the Potomac. Others claim this was a branch. Horace Hobbs, recognized authority on Indians in the Potomac area, along with others, claims it crossed Potomac at mouth of Conocoheague (Williamsport). John Luzader, former NPS historian assigned to canal, made a case for its crossing at McCoys Ferry. Long before the coming of white men, widely separated Indian tribes met and transacted business. Several mtn. ridges come to center in Oldtown and there were five Indian trails leading thereto: Warriors Trail, Bear Hill Trail, Creek Road Trail, Dry Run Trail and Mill or Big Spring Trail. In 1692 a group of Shawnees settled here and the village later became known as King Opessa's Town, after the local Shawnee chief. When the first white settler, the celebrated Col. Thomas Cresap arrived, the place was referred to as Shawnee Old Town, the Indians having moved on. "Col. Cresap's House" was a true landmark of the 18th century, visited by Washington, Braddock and hundreds of westbound pioneers. The main street of the village is the old rd. to Ft. Cumberland

Possible Lock 70
(Oldtown) before it
burned, 1906.
(National Park Service)

and until the shorter route across the mountain ridges was built, this was a busy stopping place for the westbound stagecoach lines.

Col. Thomas Cresap, the first white settler here in 1741 or 1742, bought the King's Patent of 200 acres (Oldtown), built a stockade fort and called it Fort Skipton after his birthplace in England, where he was born in probably 1703. He, too, laid out the plans for the town, the first in Allegany Co. as a trading post. Cresap came to America in 1718 and settled at the mouth of the Susquehanna River and married a girl from Spesutia Island in 1727. He later rented a farm on the lower Potomac and then ran the Lapidum Ferry. He was involved in many situations such as a border conflict, the Blue Rock Ferry affair and then went to Philadelphia in 1736. He later acquired a house on Antietam Creek near the Potomac River and went bankrupt for the third time. He died in 1790, leaving five children (three boys, Michael youngest).

During the following years the town prospered on westbound pioneer trade. More business was brought in later with the building of the canal. Oldtown was given its present name in 1744. It provided aid for troops who fought in the French and Indian War after Braddock's defeat. When George Washington was 16, he worked as a surveyor at Fort Skipton. Later, when he called for troops in 1775, they met in the "House of History" and marched to Frederick and on to Boston.

To the west of Lock 70, in a field overlooking the river, are the ruins of a stone chimney where Thomas Cresap built his fortified house in 1740. Here the 16-year-old George Washington on a surveying mission for Lord Fairfax, spent five nights in Mar. 1748, delayed by high water on the Potomac. Cresap was active in exploration and trail building for the Ohio Co., and acted as commissary for Braddock's troops, who camped here before and after their fateful venture to the west. After Braddock's defeat, the early settlers took refuge in Cresap's "fort," but later even Cresap had to abandon it and retire to Conococheague (Williamsport). He was back in 1767 with his son Michael and soon was advertising building lots in the **Maryland Gazette.** Michael Cresap's house, a worn structure with a later brick addition, still stands on Main St., called the "House of History." The house has been partially restored and is undoubtedly one of the historical treasures of Western Maryland. Open on weekends in season.

212

LOCK No. 71 (OLDTOWN)

167.04 Access: From Lock 70 .34 m. below. Third of Oldtown locks, another example of "economy" locks of upper canal, originally lined with kyanized (treated) wood, now largely replaced with concrete. Lock 71 still shows some of the bolts used to hold wooden sheathing in place. Vertical grooves in crude stone work to hold stop planks plainly visible. For those interested 6"x6" openings in upper lock pockets were used to hold wooden posts so gates wouldn't bang into lock. New footbridge crosses upper part of lock to path on berm levee. Above lock, stretch of fishing pools ends and canal bed becomes a running stream. Lockhouse, 2½-story frame bldg. at left, is now storage space for National Park Service. Oldtown Sportsmen Club did much of the canal improvement in this area in 1957. Flowers at North Branch include bellwort, hairy rock cress, Johnny-Jump-Up, moss pinks and a variety of violets.

167.11 Masonry Spillway/waste weir formerly discharged into Mill Run. Ahead, stream comes into canal thru hole in berm levee made to provide water supply for fishing pools. Houses of Oldtown to rt., beyond Mill Run.

167.51 Rd. crosses canal on timber bridge, joining parallel rd. on left with MD 51 at W. end of Oldtown. This, according to canal mileages of 1851, is site of "Cresap's Mill," built by James Cresap, grandson of Thomas, son of Daniel, who had 11 children. Canal turns sharply left into deep cut beyond. When canal was built, water 'or the raceway of the mill was carried over the top of the canal in a flume, which burned about 1910-11. Sheer walls of shale rise on both sides and towpath is ledge cut into crumbly rock; this is "Alum Hill Deep Cut." Abutments for flume of Cresap's Mill over the canal.

167.99 Deep cut ends as canal reaches river and turns sharp rt. Paralleling dirt rd. returns to towpath, with side rd. leading down left to river. Canal here heavily cleared in 1957 remains rather bare and sunny. Oak Ridge Hunting Club grounds parallel canal on left for mile or so.

168.42 Pool on rt. fills mouth of ravine, continuing beyond R.R. fill. WMd. R.R. returns to berm side and parallels canal for next 7 m. Orville Crowder's notes of 1957 state that a freight car was under water here, but it is not apparent at present. Over-cleared section ends at 168.46 and beyond is pleasant, shaded towpath. Rds. to fields cross towpath from time to time.

168.95 Foundation of bank barn was probably associated with the canal.

169.17 Historic Culvert #221 carries Pigmans Run from beyond R.R. embankment. Pigmans Ferry Hiker-Biker Overnighter.; usual facilities. Next camping upstream Spring Gap Drive-In Camping Area at 173.3; downstream Potomac Forks Hiker-Biker at 164.8 Nearest access at Kelly's Rd. Culvert at 170.84.

170.0x Approximate location for Shelhorn Tavern operating in 1795.

170.37 Historic Culvert #222, 6' span, brick-lined; ringstones are 18" in depth of face.

170.84 Historic Culvert #223, 10' span, known as "Kelly's Road Culvert" of earliest canal days. Thru culvert, at former Sloan Station, dirt rd. leads up hill to left of ravine, reaching MD 51 in 1.5 m. Note stone masons' marks.

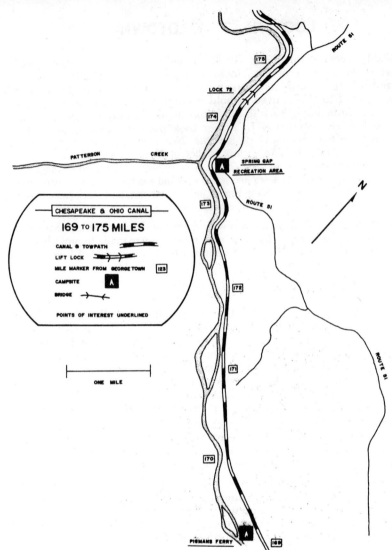

171.35 Stream runs directly into canal. Rocks help prevent erosion.

171.45 Masonry Spillway 250' long. Note concrete piers which allowed mule tenders to walk across on wooden planks.

172.10 Historic Culvert #228, drains a large area, including Brice and Frog Hollows and slopes of Collier and Martin Mtns.

172.50 Canal widens into dry basin, referred to in 1851 canal data as "Basin at Alkyre's House," said to be an 'asylum' in the 1800s. Great house ruin on berm. Gill-over-the-ground, spring beauty.

172.81 Location of earlier washout, beyond which towpath follows river bank for 250 yds. as canal curves around hill with cliffs and interesting rock folds. Rhododendron, lichens beautiful.

173.16 Remains of canal boat, bow and stern sections of which showed in 1957. Now gone.

173.37 Spring Gap Recreation Area (no water) at culvert #230 (not original). Good road access from MD 51. Camping and picnic spaces and boat ramp. MD 51 comes onto berm and parallels canal for next 2 m. The area is open to camping only during the summer. Spring Gap PO and store ½ m. E. back along MD 51 beyond R.R. overpass. End of Collier Mtn. ahead to rt.

173.47 Path leads left thru woods to river, where view of W. Va. side of river includes sheer cliffs at end of Patterson Creek Ridge and adjacent broad valley of Patterson Creek. Extensive patch of Virginia blue bells.

173.64 Large stone bridge abutment on left carried on old covered rd. bridge across canal; a small portion of abutment remains riverside. The stone work is especially interesting, the individual stones having been cut out to fit jig-saw fashion rather than laid in straight-line courses. Patterson's Creek Bridge, as bridge was known, burned night of 30 May 1861 by mob on authority of Va. troops. B&O bridge on opposite side also burned. This rd. led to river ford to village of Patterson Creek. The bridge is also known as Frankforts Ford Bridge built 1846-1848. **173.72** boat basin.

173.78 Culvert #231, 12' span carries Collier Run.

174.18 Site of canal water supply pumps. Unusual concrete trough and pump emplacements are interesting, but little of original structures remain. Steam pump was installed here to maintain water level in canal. Following description of the steam pump as newly installed was made by William R. Hutton, consulting engineer, in the 47th Annual Stockholders Report, June 7th, 1875. This pump replaced the one at Lock 68

A centrifugal pump guaranteed to raise 24 cubic feet of water per second to a height of 25 feet. Pump turns on vertical shaft in well of brick work 6 feet in diameter. Water rises in well, flowing over top into circular channel and then to canal by way of flume. Engine house, wood 23 feet by 23 feet and boiler room of brick 18½ x 32 feet - floors of concrete. Water from river admitted by culvert 6 feet wide, 6½ feet high. Cost $20,504.40

174.32 Concrete waste weir. MD 51 is berm bank.

174.40 Path to left leads to **Blue Spring, one of the largest springs in the Eastern United States** with average temperature of 54 degrees in summer. Also known as "Blue Hole."

LOCK No. 72 (THE NARROWS)

174.44 Access: From MD 51; best approach is from E.; parking near lock. This and remaining locks, finished around 1840, were constructed of stone from a nearby quarry, making use of kyanized wood (as used in Locks 58-71) unnecessary. This lock of design using a "slope wall" **across lower end of wing wall and bypass flume. One upper lock gate in place; lower lock gate** in canal bed. Lock was probably completed in latter part of 1849 or early part of 1850. Lockhouse on left is two story frame building in fairly good condition; porch affords emergency shelter. Footbridge leads to MD 51 past filled-in concrete emplacements which supported oil tanks to supply pump at 174.18. Cumberland is 7 m. by MD 51, Oldtown 8 m. Ahead canal, highway and R.R. are squeezed into the tight place between river and ends of Nicholas Ridge and Irons Mtn., an area famous in canal days as "The Narrows." Canal prism cleared here in 1957. Lock was known in operating days as "Ten Mile Lock." Lock has a 9' lift.

Lock-keeper's shanty and drop-gate of Lock 74, early 1900s.

175.02 Historic Culvert #233 (Moores Hollow), 4' span.

175.30 Head of "The Narrows." River and canal swing sharply left. **Culvert;** path on near side leads to MD 51. Long S-bend of river and canal **begins. By towpath it is 9 mi. to center of Cumberland.**

175.35 Historic Culvert #234, 6' span.

LOCK NO. 73—(North Branch)

175.36 Access: From MD 51. 1st of three locks at North Branch. Foundation of lockhouse to left. **Irons Mtn. Hiker-Biker Overnighter.** Backward view of mtn. wall along the Narrows impressive. Stone for Locks 73, 74 and 75 came from Evitts Creek Quarry. Locks 73 thru 75 were probably completed before the end of 1840. Lockhouse foundation on towpath. Lock has 9' lift. Lock is built of limestone from Evitts Quarry.

175.43 B & O R.R., which comes across river from left, crosses canal on steel bridge, coming back into Md. after its long crossing thru W. Va. chosen as a result of fight with canal at Point of Rocks to Harpers Ferry. Bridge #65 was built in 1923. First bridge at this site was built 1842.

LOCK NO. 74—(North Branch)

175.47 Access: From MD 51. Ample parking; picnic area: toilets. Paved rd. crosses center of lock and forks rt. along R.R. Lock was rebuilt 1869. Lock has 10' lift.

To left fork along embankment, rd. leads to Pittsburgh Plate Glass Plant and to MD 51. Past lockhouse burned in 1974, rd. parallels canal. All three locks of North Branch had drop gates; this at first had mitre gates. Part of the lock gate mechanism remains. Road indications are that there was a pivot bridge here. 117.58 late period waste weir. Lock may have been extended downstream. Some hardware from these locks (and perhaps even others along the canal) was used in WWII scrap iron drive. While in the area be sure to visit THE CUMBERLAND, a canal boat replica, at Lock 75 above. Open sporadically in season. C&O Canal Boat Festival is held here the last full weekend in August.

Lock No. 75 in early 1900s. Note the log lockhouse to the left.

LOCK NO. 75—(North Branch)

175.60 Access: From MD 51. Last numbered lock of canal. The 9 m. level beginning here extends to guard lock at head of canal in Cumberland. Part of drop gate mechanism remains. This lock is constructed of well-cut, laid and mortared gray limestone built in accordance with the 1836 specifications. Both lock walls were elevated 6" with wood. The lockhouse is log, two stories over a full stone basement, measuring 17' x 29'3". Stabilized 1978. Lock has a 10' lift and was rebuilt in 1869.

176.00 Large sediment basins part of PPG complex. Plant property line follows canal berm for considerable distance. Basins are being phased out and filled by PPG. New plant recently opened at Carlisle, Pa. incorporates latest glassmaking technology, resulting in reduced operations here. Canoeists should avoid the Pittsburgh Plate Glass Dam. Instead of using the river at this point, put in at Spring Gap at mile 173.

176.51 Small iron-fenced cemetery in field to left. Somewhere in vicinity was "Van Metre's Ferry" of early canal. Note service-berry trees on berm.

176.87 Former basin in canal, now a marsh, has attraction for marsh birds (bitterns are seen here) and other wildlife.

177.67 Historic Culvert #235, 4' span.

177.69 Rd. on left leads to paved rd. Farther left is Mexico Farm's small aircraft landing field and beyond, on W. Va. side of river, atop hill, is Cumberland Municipal Airport. Indian village once located on Mexico Farm subdivision, which was converted to a training airport for Army Air Corps during WW I. Somewhere in this area was the "Ferry on the Mexico Tract" mentioned in 1851 canal data. Canal here now watered after cleaning of canal banks in 1979.

178.50 WMd. R.R. track crosses river ½ m. to left and short cut across neck of river to Cumberland. Good access to MD 51. Bridge number of 1610 indicates it was 161 miles to Baltimore.

178.84 Paved rd. crosses canal leading rt. .8 m. to MD 51 providing access To left was **location of Kirkendall Ferry of early canal days.** Cut-leaf, toothwort, gill-over-the-ground, trout lily.

179.10 Historic Culvert #236, 4' span.

179.31 Historic Culvert (4' span) **waste weir combination.** Culvert #231 from height of several feet rather than near ground level as was customary. Across canal berm bank conceals large wall to left of waste weir. Worth viewing. **Be careful. Berm bank of canal crops abruptly. Rebuilt 1978.**

179.99 Evitts Creek Hiker-Biker Overnighter; last hiker-biker; next downstream Irons Mtn. at 175.36. Good view of river valley.

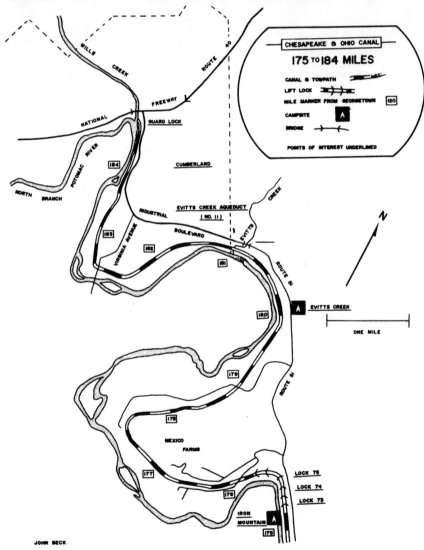

JOHN BECK

218

Lock No. 75, circa 1903 (National Park Service)
The canal has been re-watered to Evitts Creek Aqueduct.

180.01 Historic Culvert #239, 7' span. Originally a 10' high rd. culvert, now blocked on berm side by debris dumped as fill by R.R. (Up and down canal from this point several culverts on berm side drain waste water into canal.) Canal route here is thru fine mature oak woods and affords a pleasant walk despite narrowness of this wild strip amid the increasing scars of civilization.

180.35 Berm here is cattail marsh with aquatic plants and much bird life. Nearest bicycle repair shop is Cycles & Things in Cumberland, 165 N. Centre Street, Tel. 301-722-5496.

EVITTS CREEK AQUEDUCT (No. 11)

180.66 Access: From MD 51. Last of the canal aqueducts, it is also the smallest, with single 70' span. Completed around 1840, it has partially collapsed at both ends on upper side. To rt. is culvert carrying Evitts Creek under B&O R.R. yards. MD 51 bridge completed in 1958 is on far side of culvert. Stabilization work by NPS in 1979 and 1983.

180.75 Cross **Cumberland city line.**

180.86 Low cliffs exhibit interesting rock strata.

181.20 Historic culvert #240, 10' span.

181.26 Canal emerges from woods and bears away from R.R. **Former basin area in canal** now marshy area filled with cattails and stagnant water.

181.30 Culvert. (modern, 4' span).

181.76 Cumberland Sewage Disposal Plant. To left, behind plant, is site of **Civil War river crossing named "Thistles Ferry."** Flat top of cliff across river is Cumberland Municiapl Airport. Attractive Riverside Recreation complex. Canal cleared.

181.83 Candoc Recreation Area, flooded for winter **ice skating.** Accessible by road (Candoc Lane) which parallels canal, Candoc is acronym for C and O Canal

182.22 WMd. R.R. crosses canal, having come from Welton Tunnel across river. Bridge #1628, built 1904.

182.62 Wiley Ford Bridge to left as paved rd. crosses canal. Earlier ford was somewhat downstream. Daring raid by Confederates, taking two major-generals from their beds while 6-8,000 Union troops occupied town. Beyond is small **culvert,** after which canal bears rt. into Cumberland industrial district. Zero mark at bridge is 585' above sea level. Flood stage is 18' on gage; towpath level is 27'. 1889, 1924 and 1936 floods were above towpath level.

182.63 Historic Culvert #241, 4' span.

182.97 Pass under WMd. R.R. bridge, which crosses river. Canal bed cleared to stop gate upstream. Bridge #1631, built 1904.

183.39 Masonry piers of old stop gate in canal to rt., designed to retain water in Cumberland basins when canal below drained for winter repairs. Built 1849.
Across canal is old quarry.

183.55 Long concrete spillway. Note concrete was built around an earlier stone waste weir at upper end, the drainage gate for Cumberland Basin. Beyond, towpath runs along high embankment which slopes left to river. Berm is a cliff, with B & O R.R. yards above. Ahead is splendid view of Cumberland, with Wills Creek Narrows prominent behind city to left. **Flood control project completed in the 1950's has altered, often beyond recognition, the canal and river from here to guard lock terminus.**

Twin Guard Locks at the terminus of the C & O Canal at Cumberland, Maryland, 1940s.

Consolidation Coal Company Boatyard in Cumberland,
early 1900s (Smithsonian Institution)

184.1x The scene here has been vastly altered since canal days, for the **entire area ahead. was the busy Cumberland Basin:** Two arms of the basin stretched ahead, one leading straight to the guard lock and inlet behind Dam No. 8, the other forming a large pool reaching to rt. and extending well into the business area of Cumberland across what is now highway. Close by, at rt., a long peninsula jutted N. into the basin, carrying R.R. tracks (long since disappeared) to boat-loading stations on both sides which facilitated the dropping of coal into boats with hatch covers removed (it's much less messy that way). Beyond the basin, were streets with stores and saloons catering to the canallers, many of whom spent the winter here, living in their boats. Several firms built canal boats in this area. The canal company steam dredge, one of two on the canal, and the repair scows were moored here. The scene is difficult to visualize today, when industrial land fills and the extensive reclamation work along the river front have totally altered the picture.

An interesting account of the WMd. R.R.'s use of the canal is contained in Scharf's *History of Western Maryland*, II, p. 1431, published 1882:

"The Western Maryland Railway has an office in Cumberland where freight and cars are shipped over the C & O Canal to Williamsport, a distance of 100 miles, and thence by this railway to tidewater in Baltimore, the eastern terminus of the road. The first shipment from Baltimore to Cumberland over this road in connection with the canal was made August 5, 1876, when it reduced the tariff rates carried by the B & O Railway. The road has a regular line of boats to carry its freight on the Canal from Cumberland to Williamsport, where it is transferred to the cars. The railway has a warehouse at the head of the basin in Cumberland, where it receives freight from or for boats."

Before WMd. R.R. station was built within canal basin, towpath extended up Wills Creek where R.R. tracks to station are now located. Basin extended beyond Baltimore St. to include site of Algonquian Hotel, parking area in rear and flat beyond. Canal co. boatyard was originally located on upper basin. It was a two-story building with steps leading to towpath and loading yard. Bldg. included blacksmith shop, tool and parts shop and a large fireplace was used to heat pitch for oakum for calking boat seams. It also included a carpentry shop and offices. Man named Dodd built only lock gates and lived in house adjacent. There was also a second bldg. for processing oakum and calking. Planing mill nearby was operated by Louis Young for exclusive use of canal co. Boats were hauled from basin for repair by capstan with mule providing pulling power. At the reduced, lower basin, encircled by area known as "Shanty Town," canal co. HQ was located in section of now abandoned Mid-City Ball Park. Here boats were hauled from basin for repair by electric motor power using marine railway. Canal co. operation was located on a prong of the basin then called Shriver Basin which extended to dye plant building which is still standing. Merten's Sons lumber and boatyard was located on downstream section of lower basin. W. Wallace McKaig operated McKaig Foundries where six steam-propelled canal boats were constructed. First boat placed in service was called "You Know," and second, "I Know." Mrs. Anna Ella McGreevey was born aboard "You Know" in 1885. Her father, William Elkins, who died in 1930, was captain of the boat. Elkins also constructed Presidents' chair for Henry Bridges and Woodmont Club.

184.37 Alteration of surface is so great that original canal route is obscure. Proceeding along towpath (following the paralleling R.R. tracks) to confluence of Wills Creek and North Branch one sees all that remains of Dam No. 8, a stone abutment on side of bank to left. Dam No. 8, last of canal supply dams, was obliterated by flood control work. **Canal route passes end of dam and continues to point where guard locks and inlet mark end of canal. The 400' long, 17' high dam was destroyed in 1958.**

OPENING OF THE CANAL IN CUMBERLAND

(From the Daily National Intelligencer, Washington, D.C. Tuesday, 15 October, 1850 prefacing an article from a Cumberland newspaper covering the opening of the C & O Canal on 10 October)

In another column will be found an account, from one of the Cumberland papers, of the brief ceremony of the opening, on Thursday last of the navigation of the Chesapeake and Ohio Canal from Cumberland to Georgetown, Washington, and Alexandria; an event long anxiously looked for, and the consequence of which is out of all proportion to the little stir that has been made about it. Already the Coal of the Mountains has reached the tidewater, in boats averaging probably each one hundred tons burden; one of which at least was constructed, as we learn, of timber from trees which were in full vigor of growth on the top of the Mountain not more than five weeks before the boat was under way in the canal, laden with coal.

These facts announce the spring of enterprise at the entrepot of the Coal region, and the arrival there of practical builders and boatmen, who have been taught their vocation on the New York Canals; through whose labors we may expect to see our Canal alive with boats this Fall for a period of navigation prolonged for weeks beyond the time when the canals of the North are closed by the earlier winter in that region.

(From a Cumberland newspaper) This great work, commencing nearly a quarter of a century ago, is at length so far completed as to be in a navigable condition from Cumberland to tide water. The opening was celebrated at Cumberland on Thursday last. The Alleghanian days:

Cumberland Basin, early 1900s (Smithsonian Institution)

On Wednesday evening the President and Directors of the Canal Company, the State's agents, and a number of guests from several counties of Maryland, Virginia, and the District cities, accompanied by the Independent Blues' Band of Baltimore, arrived in our city, via the railroad, to participate in the opening ceremonies.

On Thursday morning, at 8 o'clock, Col. Davidson's company of light artillerists, from the Eckhart mines, arrived and about one hour after a procession, made up of the military, the canal board, and guests, the corporate authorities and citizens, was formed in Baltimore Street, under the direction of Col. Pickell, of Baltimore, and marched to the head of the canal. On arriving at this point, and after the firing of a salute by the artillerists, Wm. Price, Esq., on behalf of the corporate authorities and citizens, in a neat speech, welcomed the canal board and their guests and congratulated them upon the occurrence of the event so long looked for—the opening of the canal to Cumberland. Gen. James M. Coale, President of the Canal Company, responded in appropriate terms, and embraced the occasion to briefly review the history of the progress of the work.

About 11 o'clock the several boats fitted up for the occasion, pretty well crowded, proceeded down the canal in the following order: Way's excursion boat *Jenny Lind,* having on board the Canal Board and their guests from abroad; the *Charles B. Fisk,* with the Baltimore band and a large number of citizens; Mr. Clarke's boat, with the Eckhart artillerists and the Mechanics' Band of Cumberland. These were followed by the Southampton, Delaware, and *Ohio*, of Mssrs. McCaig & Agnew's merchant line, and the *Freemen Rawdon,* of the Cumberland line, all bound for Alexandria, laden with coal and Mr. Mong's *Elizabeth,* with coal, for Harper's Ferry.

The Canal Board and their guests landed about nine miles below Cumberland, where they partook of an abundant collation, prepared for the occasion, on board the Charles B. Fisk. The company returned to Cumberland in the evening delighted with the excursion.

The proceedings of the day closed with a Supper and Ball in the evening, given by citizens at Heflefinger's hotel.

There were plans and talk of extending the canal to Pittsburgh for a number of years after the opening of the canal to Cumberland in 1850. In an 1874 convention an 8.4 m. tunnel was proposed thru the mountains. This was the last major drive to push the canal to the Ohio River. Sanderlin states on p. 297

of **The Great National Project:** "Of the projected western section, the best indication of its proposed course is the main line of the Baltimore and Ohio Railroad from Cumberland to Pittsburgh. According to the army engineers in 1874-1875, the railroad occupies the identical route surveyed for the canal, with the exception of the ambitious tunnel on the summit level."

Though the decline of the canal had been in the making for some years prior to its closing in 1924, the decline in coal transported after supplying most of the Navy's coal by canal during WW I and swift decline in the postwar period, the George's Creek strike of 1922-23 and the shift to supply of coal from sources outside the Potomac Basin with transport by rail, left little impetus for repair of the canal after final blow of 1924 flood.

184.50 Guard Locks and Inlet. Lock had 6' lift. Traces of the guard locks and inlet remain under the railroad trestle, which used the filled-in locks as solid building foundations. The lockkeeper's house sat between inlet and guard locks and was removed at time of flood control work. Until 1957, Skat Eaton ("Little Skat" when his father was alive) lived in the family's long-time dwelling on the bit of land between the Guard Locks and the Inlet. At that very recent date, the flood control construction completely wiped out the canal's terminal, filled in the locks, ousted the Eatons and tore down the house. Skat Eaton, senior, born in 1875, had 10 children born on the canal. After the shut-down in 1924, the family lived on their canal boat tied up in the basin here until 1928. Dam No. 8, finished sometime in 1849 or 1850, measured 400' and was anchored onto solid rock at bottom of river. **Access:** From Western MD R.R. Sta. Walk .10 m. downriver, with caution. There is a parking lot near the station at Canal and Baltimore Streets. Western MD R.R. Sta. now restored and open to visitors. For information call 301-739-4200 or 301-678-5463.

CUMBERLAND

Each boat averaged about 25 round trips between Cumberland, Md., and Washington, D. C., each season and some of men on the crews had to have a place to "blow off steam" at the terminals.

Cumberland's Shantytown was the ideal spot for such diversion and even when the number of boats working the Canal dwindled to less than 100, Shantytown remained the popular hangout.

Shantytown was the "Casbah" of Cumberland in the old days. Approximately twenty-five buildings comprised this area that started at the B & O underpass at the lower end of Wineow Street and ended near the old Footers Dye Works. Just about all of the houses were made of wood and looked not unlike those of the early Western type in that they were almost all two stories high with flat roofs and some even had the famous false fronts. The only brick house was at the lower end and near the underpass. This was Murphys' Grocery Store. Most of the other houses were saloons, pool halls, lunch rooms, gaming rooms, brothels, and houses of ill fame where anything could happen and usually did.

All of the buildings were on one side of the narrow street facing the Canal loading wharf and the boat-building yard which was only a few hundred feet away. The B & O railroad went right through the back yards of these houses.

Segregation was no problem here. Whites, colored and foreigners all lived, ate, drank and slept together in Shantytown, and very often the one who wakened first "rolled" the others. On one of my frequent visits there, I had my pants stolen right from my body while I slept."

George "Hooper" Wolfe

Cumberland was laid out as a town in 1787, and for many years prior to the coming of railroad and canal was an important town on the famous National Road. The Braddock Road went out what is now Greene Street, and crossed

the gap in Haystack Mountain visible from the canal. The new National Road in 1821 followed this general route, but when the macadamizing of the road was undertaken in 1834, the newer route up the valley of Wills Creek and thru the Narrows was adopted. From 1834 to 1845 this road from Baltimore to St. Louis was widely regarded as the finest road in the world for its length. Competing stagecoach lines operated on frequent schedules and Cumberland became a bustling metropolis of the route. The discovery of the rich coal veins in the Georges Creek region gave impetus to the construction of both the railroad and the canal. The railroad reached Cumberland in 1842 and the canal in 1850, and use of the National Pike began to decline. The last through stage lines ceased operation in 1853.

Today, Cumberland is a busy industrial city of nearly 50,000. Accommodations of all classes are available, and there are numerous good restaurants. Frequent bus service offers connection with Washington, Baltimore, and other points for towpath hikers who may reach the final mile of the canal without automobile support. Daily, but infrequent train service.

Skyline view of Cumberland, Maryland.

Cumberland is known as the Queen City of the Alleghenies and the Gateway to the West because of its strategic location in the gap of the Appalachian mountain range. Cumberland has a great potential as the logical terminus for the C & O Canal National Historical Park and a major center of historical features. A concurrent thought is the canal terminus as the hub of a trail system branching from the canal terminus like the spokes of a wheel: local walks thru history in the town, trails along the nearby ridges with overlooks, a trail up the South Branch terminating at Spruce Knob, trail thru Narrows, over Dans Rock, Dans Mtn., length of Big Savage Mtn. which would make connection with Laurel Ridge Trail connecting to west with Pittsburgh via Ohio Pile on Yock and connecting with trails in Midwest and Pacific Coast, eastward on Laurel Ridge connecting with Horseshoe Trail and Appalachian Trail north of Harrisburg, and thence to New England, northward to Baker Trail in N.E. Pa. to Finger Lakes Trail and Bruce Trail extending into Canada. Potential path connections boggle the imagination. (Justice Wm. O. Douglas).

Other Canal Publications Offered by the American Canal and Transportation Center

Towpath Guide to the C&O Canal—228 pages, 123 illustrations, 27 maps.

Ferry Hill Plantation Journal—1975 reprint of Life on the Potomac River and C&O Canal, Jan. 4, 1838 to Jan. 15, 1839.—170 pages, with illustrations.

Ellet and Roebling—by Donald Sayenga. The interaction between two of America's greatest engineers and bridge builders. Illustrated, 60 pages. Paper.

The Amazing Pennsylvania Canals—Special Three-Hundredth Anniversary Edition of Pennsylvania's historic 1200-mile canal system, by Engineer-Historian William Shank. 126 pages, 118 illustrations, includes a new appendix of locks, distances, etc.

Chesapeake and Ohio Canal Old Picture Album—A pictorial history of the C&O Canal through 100 historic photos and captions by Industrial Archaeologist/Canal Historian Tom Hahn. About 100 pages. Soft and hard covers available.

Map of the Canals and Rivers of the United States—(1905)

Three Hundred Years with the Pennsylvania Traveler—1976 First Edition of this 8½x11 in., 200 page, two-color picture history of all forms of travel in the Keystone State since the time of the Indians. Text by William H. Shank, P.E.

Chesapeake and Ohio Canal Medallion—with canal boat and lock scene at Great Falls and the old company seal. Bronze, 1½ inches, in rigid plastic case.

The Best From "American Canals" #1—Articles from the publication of The American Canal Society from 1972 to 1980. 92 pages, 8½ x 11. Edited by Hahn, Shank, & Trout.

The C&O Canal Boatmen, 1892-1924—1980 Edition. Personal experiences of the operators of the canal boats on the C&O Canal in later years.

The C&O Canal: An Illustrated History—Over 100 drawings of canal landscape, canal features, and historic buildings by artist Diana Suttenfield-Abshire, text by Dr. Tom Hahn. 84 pages.

Journey Through Pennsylvania (1835): By Canal, Rail, and Stage Coach. (Nicklin)—Illustrated with Hoffman drawings plus historical photos. Reprint, 92 pages.

When Horses Pulled Boats—Reprint of the 1936 by Alvin F. Harlow with Hoffman illustrations added. Bibliography, paper, 72 pages.

Towpaths to Tugboats: A History of American Canal Engineering—Eds. Shank, Hahn, Hobbs, Mayo. Paper, 130 illustrations, 76 pages, 8½ x 11.

Home on the Canal—By Elizabeth Kytle. C&O Canal history and stories of eleven men and women "canal people." Hard-cover, illustrated, annotated, glossary, bibliography, index, 304 pages.

The Best from "American Canals" #2—Articles from the publication of the American Canal Society from 1980 to 1983. 88 pages, over 140 illustrations, Edited by Hahn, Shank, & Trout.

The Canallers Song Book—Words, music and chords for 30 canal songs by William Hullfish. 88 pages, 8½x11, illustrated.

The Chesapeake and Ohio Canal: Pathway to the Nation's Capital—By Capt. Tom Hahn. Hard cover, 269 pages, illustrated, index. Combines several canal publications plus a guide to major sights to visit on the canal.

The Columbia-Philadelphia Railroad and Its Successor—Reprint of an 1896 publication by the railroad's civil engineer, William Hasell Wilson. 72 pages, 40 illustrations.

(Publications are soft covers unless noted otherwise. Orders may be addressed to American Canal and Transportation Center (WV), Box 310 Shepherdstown, WV 25443. In West Virginia add 5% to cover State Sales Tax. Send a self-addressed, stamped envelope for a price listing of our publications. Trade discount schedules are also available.)